D0467395

LOSING
BIN
LADEN

LOSING BIN LADEN

How Bill Clinton's Failures Unleashed Global Terror

RICHARD MINITER

Since 1947
REGNERY PUBLISHING, INC.
An Eagle Publishing Company • Washington, DC

Copyright © 2003 by Richard Miniter

All rights reserved. No part of this publication may be reproduced or transmitted in any form or by any means electronic or mechanical, including photocopy, recording, or any information storage and retrieval system now known or to be invented, without permission in writing from the publisher, except by a reviewer who wishes to quote brief passages in connection with a review written for inclusion in a magazine, newspaper, or broadcast.

Cataloging-in-Publication Data on file with the Library of Congress.

ISBN 0-89526-074-3

Published in the United States by
Regnery Publishing, Inc.
An Eagle Publishing Company
One Massachusetts Avenue, NW
Washington, DC 20001

Visit us at www.regnery.com

Distributed to the trade by
National Book Network
4720-A Boston Way
Lanham, MD 20706
Printed on acid-free paper
Manufactured in the United States of America

10 9 8 7 6 5 4 3 2 1

Books are available in quantity for promotional or premium use. Write to Director of Special Sales, Regnery Publishing, Inc., One Massachusetts Avenue, NW, Washington, DC 20001, for information on discounts and terms, or call (202) 216-0600.

To all the victims of Osama bin Laden from 1989 to today, may their families find peace and their deaths be avenged.

ACKNOWLEDGMENTS

To the many sources in the intelligence services and foreign services of America and other nations whom I cannot publicly name, especially those who supplied me with documents and eyewitness accounts, thank you.

There are also many sources who were able to go "on the record," whom I'd like to thank here: Tony Lake, Clinton's first National Security Advisor; Sandy Berger, Clinton's second National Security Advisor; Madeleine Albright, Secretary of State; Richard Clarke, Clinton's counterterrorism coordinator; Dick Morris, Clinton's pollster and confidant (who supplied an early prepublication chapter of his book *Off with Their Heads*); James Woolsey, Clinton's first director of Central Intelligence, who spent a lot of time (that he didn't really have to spare) talking to me; Milt Bearden and Bill Piekney, two former CIA station chiefs who had the guts to go on the record; director of Central Intelligence George Tenet and the agency press spokesman Bill Harlow (who was magnificently patient with last-minute requests); Frank Anderson, a former director of operations for the CIA; Steve Schwartz, State Department; David Shinn, former director of East Africa Affairs at the State Department; Tim Carney, a former U.S. ambassador to Sudan and to Haiti, and his wife, Vicky Butler; Congressman Bill McCollum;

Susan Rice, Assistant Secretary of State; Ottilie English, onetime lobbyist for the Northern Alliance; Janet McElligott, onetime lobbyist for Sudan, who gave me an endless stream of phone numbers in Sudan and Egypt and even cooked lunch; Mansoor Ijaz, international man of mystery; Reuel Marc Gerecht, a former CIA officer who supplied a great lead; Senator Dennis DeConcini; Michael Sheehan, ambassador for counterterrorism at the State Department; Joe Wilson, National Security Council expert on African affairs, special assistant to the president, and ambassador to the Gabonese Republic; Fatih Erwa, Sudan's ambassador to the United Nations; Richard Perle, former chairman of the Defense Advisory Board, whose advice and leads were invaluable; Kenneth Adelman, who graciously read the manuscript several times and introduced me to several high-level sources, and his wife, Carol, who was always encouraging; Senator Richard Shelby; Bill Duhnke, Senate Intelligence Committee staff director; Jay Winik, former Defense Department official and author of *April 1865*, and his wife, Lyric; Congressman Dana Rohrbacher; Congressman Porter Goss, chairman of the House Intelligence Committee; Haroun Amin, former Washington representative of the Northern Alliance; Michael Ledeen, author of *The War Against the Terror Masters*, who provided a lot of good advice and leads; Laurie Mylroie, author of *The War Against America*, who provided many leads and comments; Bryan Sierra, Department of Justice; Steve Berry, FBI; Buck Revell, former assistant director of operations at the FBI; Gutbi el-Mahdi, Sudan's former intelligence chief, who spent hours with me in Khartoum; Mahdi Ibrahim, Sudan's former ambassador to the United State, who met with me several times; Sudan's Peace and Development Minister Ghazi and El-Mahdi Habib-Alla, who described to me his meeting with Abdullah Azzam in Jordan; also, Abdul Ali Hodari and Abdel Mahmoud al Koronky, at Sudan's embassy in London; Jon Randal, a former *Washington Post* reporter who is writing a book on bin Laden and who went out of his way to help me; the managing editor of the *New Republic*, Sarah Blustain, who was willing to take on the CIA; David Bass, for introducing me to Saudi sources and always staying for one more at the Palm; and Fox News' Geraldo Rivera, a prince of a guy and a diehard reporter.

And I really want to thank Christian de Fouloy for organizing a lunch in Paris to introduce me to French intelligence.

I'd also like to thank some of the "gatekeepers" who made sure that I would get some interview time with key sources: Cris Myers, Meridith Webster, Bev Roundtree, and Jared Kaplan. They were often called at the eleventh hour and never lost their good humor.

I'd also like to thank several authors and reporters whom I've never met, but whose work was vital to my understanding al Qaeda, intelligence, or military operations: Peter Bergen, Yossef Bodansky, and Rohan Gunaratna, Mark Bowden, Simon Reeve, Robert Baer, Bruce Hoffman, Colonel Lawrence E. Kasper, Colonel David Hackworth, the *Washington Times'* Bill Gertz, the *Washington Post's* Barton Gellman, Rick Atkinson and Matthew Brzezinski, *Newsweek's* Evan Thomas, the *New Yorker's* Elizabeth Drew and Sy Hersh, the BBC's Jane Corbin, and CNN's Phil Hirschkorn. And the *Financial Times'* Mark Huband, whose long articles and long phone call to me were invaluable.

I'd also like to thank my researcher, the indefatigable Martin Morse Wooster, my typist, Lina Jarl, my transcribers, Elizabeth and Courtenay, and one of my two Arabic-language translators, Dr. Ahmed Sayed Ahmed. The other I cannot name. And James Rogers, who designed the map you'll find in the book and on my personal website.

I'd like to thank the owners and staff of Portner's in Alexandria, Virginia, and L'Entrée Des Artistes and Habana Corner in Brussels. They let me work for hours in their fine establishments while ordering only coffee and water and they never complained about the cigars or the dog, Boxer.

I'd also like to thank my friend Stephen Grey, who ran the investigative team (Insight) at the *Sunday Times* of London. Looking at Clinton's record on bin Laden was his idea in November 2001. Together, with a large team, we wrote a great four-part award-winning series and had fun doing it. I'd also like to thank the *Sunday Times* as a whole—its editors and writers are world class.

And I'd like to thank my brother Brendan Miniter, the only member of the *Wall Street Journal* editorial page staff to hunt wild turkeys and run 10ks. He survived the September 11 attacks through a quirk of fate and, months later when he was allowed to return to his *Journal* office overlooking Ground Zero, he could look into the saddest hole in the world. On good days, I call him three times a day to argue and listen. On bad days, I call more often.

Hats off to Harry Crocker, a great book editor, my friend Bill Schulz (who gives me good advice that I don't always take), law professor Eugene Kontorovich (any man who wears a hat as well as Seth Lipsky and smokes cigars like H.L. Mencken should junk the law and return to journalism), journalist Sam Dealey (why is *your* land mine better?), James Taranto (thanks for that phone number), editorial writer Brett Decker (a great soul who actually read my first book), Pulitzer finalist Robert Pollock (who demonstrated the proper way to run a debate in 1992, impersonated a prince in 1993, and introduced me to Brussels in 1999), British journalist Stephen Pollard (who was right about Iraq and everything else and whose enthusiasm was contagious), Dr. Tim Evans (who when he visited never seemed surprised to find me on the phone at 7 a.m. shouting through a bad connection to the Middle East), the always ebullient Horace Cooper (who should learn someday to swing from chandeliers like a proper libertarian), Doug Heye (who will get into the London papers one of these days), and Kevin Washington, a true friend and gentleman who doesn't really need to practice his short putt.

Several people were just plain encouraging, which counts for a lot when writing a book. Cathy and Paul Windels, Adam Bellow,

Bill Dal Col, Joel Rosenberg, Daniel Casse, John Fund, Dennis Fisher with Ziff Davis, Heidi Kingstone, Teresa Harnett, Cecilia Kindstand and Karl Isaakson, Per Heister, Alberto Mingardi, Gawain Towler, Jeremy Slater, Ulrike Dennerborg, Bill Echikson at Dow Jones Newswires, Reagan's National Security Advisor Dick Allen, Deborah Amos and Chris Isham at ABC News, Nigel Ashford, and Eric Spinotto at Fox News. And also Bob Lowe, the *Reader's Digest* editor in charge of Europe who always understood how the book kept me from writing the article I kept promising to write.

Most important, I'd like to thank an extraordinary person who put up with—on two continents—an obsessive, sleep-skipping, coffee-drinking, cigar-smoking grouch who was trying to write a book. Sometimes people ask me if it is hard being a writer and I always say, "No, but it is hard being with one." To Janie Kong, for her truly remarkable and unending support, without whom this book would not have been possible.

CONTENTS

ALL ENEMIES, FOREIGN AND DOMESTIC

"The U.S. knows that I have attacked it, by the grace of God, for more than ten years."
—Osama bin Laden, 1998[1]

Osama bin Laden is the unfinished business of the Clinton Administration. Bin Laden's first strike against Americans occurred in two towering hotels housing American troops in Yemen in December 1992—in the midst of Clinton's presidential transition. Less than a month after Clinton was sworn in as president, bin Laden struck again by bombing the World Trade Center in February 1993. Seven Americans were killed (counting the unborn child of one of the victims) and more than one thousand were injured in the first-ever foreign terrorist attack on U.S. soil. Clinton never even visited the site to assess the damage, nor did he order swift retaliation. It was the start of a pattern.

Bin Laden's attacks gradually escalated throughout the Clinton years: the battles in the streets of Mogadishu, Somalia, in September and October 1993; the Riyadh bombing in November 1995; the near-simultaneous attacks on U.S. embassies in Nairobi and Dar es Salaam, which killed hundreds and injured thousands. Bin Laden's attacks in the Clinton years climaxed with a deadly assault on the

USS *Cole* in Aden harbor, the most deadly attack on a U.S. warship since World War II.

Many of bin Laden's near-misses, which are not widely known, might have added to the terrorist death toll during the Clinton years. The thwarted "Project Bojinka" in the Philippines could have killed upwards of three thousand Americans. A second wave of attacks on U.S. embassies in Africa and Central Asia could have murdered hundreds more. The "Millennium plots" in 1999 might have killed thousands of Americans. The failed midnight assault on an American naval vessel, the USS *The Sullivans*, might have killed hundreds in January 2000. If anything, America should be grateful that bin Laden did not kill more people during Clinton's two terms.

If President Clinton had been more engaged in the fight against bin Laden, history might have been very different. Early in the Clinton Administration, it would have been comparatively easy to smash bin Laden's emerging network. Instead the arch-terrorist's strength, reach, and lethality were allowed to relentlessly build over the course of the eight Clinton years. In 1993, bin Laden was a small-time funder of militant Muslim terrorists in Sudan, Yemen, and Afghanistan. By the end of 2000, Clinton's last year in office, bin Laden's terror network was operating in more than fifty-five countries and already responsible for the deaths of thousands (including fifty-nine Americans).[2]

Yet Clinton responded only with brave words, empty gestures, meaningless cruise-missile strikes, and halfhearted covert operations. Sometimes America's special forces, allied forces, or foreign governments came heartbreakingly close to killing or capturing the terrorist mastermind. Yet every time, Clinton officials failed to give the final orders for such covert operations or even castigated allies for trying to kill bin Laden. After the president learned that bin Laden was planning to assassinate him, Clinton still could not bring himself to take the kind of strong measures that seem second nature to the current Bush Administration.

It took more than five years for Clinton to sign the first of three confidential executive orders to kill bin Laden. But the legal and political restrictions imposed on these secret orders made success all but impossible.

That is not to say that the Clinton Administration did nothing to stop bin Laden in the 1990s. The federal government, especially at the street level, was active. Indeed, given the bureaucratic and political obstacles erected by the president's political appointees, it is surprising that these dedicated civil servants won even small victories against bin Laden.

The higher up the chain of command one climbed, the more bureaucratic delay and political paralysis seemed to take over. Clinton's senior political appointees at the Departments of State, Defense, and Justice, as well as the heads of the FBI and the CIA, often hid behind legalisms or were distracted by feuds. When they looked to the White House, they saw a pattern of dithering and delay—not leadership. Inside the White House, in the wood-paneled Situation Room or in the rabbit warren of offices packed into the West Wing, senior Clinton officials usually fretted that there just was not enough "actionable intelligence" to do anything decisive. They wanted to act, really they did, but something almost always seemed to get in the way.

Clinton himself, especially in the early years of his first administration, was largely missing in action. With a single phone call he could have settled feuds among agencies and demanded immediate action, but he did not. He let anti-terror efforts drift on autopilot; he devoted his attention to bin Laden only when reporters or lawmakers made it impossible for him to do otherwise.

Why? There is a confluence of causes behind Clinton's unwillingness to confront bin Laden. Clinton feared that a publicly declared war on America's terrorist enemies would hurt his standing in the polls or undercut his image as a peacemaker. He was deeply ambivalent about the use of American power—stemming from his formative, youthful opposition to the Vietnam War. He knew that he needed the liberal wing of the Democratic Party in order to govern and to protect himself from the political consequences of personal scandal; if he took tough-minded action against terrorists, his liberal allies might have deserted him. An antiwar movement might have emerged that would have cost Clinton dearly. Whatever the reasons, political calculation seemed to triumph over the president's constitutional oath to protect America from "all enemies, foreign and domestic."

■ ■ ■

The full story of Clinton and bin Laden has not yet been told. To do that, one must clear away the misperceptions of the Clinton record, held by partisans on both sides.

Before September 11, no one knew about Osama bin Laden. This is a favorite chestnut of Clinton defenders. In fact, bin Laden was tracked by the CIA as early as December 1992. Starting in 1995, the State Department reports described bin Laden as one of the most dangerous terrorists in the world. During the Clinton years, Congressional Research Service reports described bin Laden and his reign of terror extensively. Both sets of these reports were available to the public at the time.

What's more, major news outlets, including *Time*, *Reader's Digest*, CNN, and ABC News, devoted a lot of space to bin Laden. Indeed, the headline on a 1998 *Reader's Digest* cover story on bin Laden could not be more clear: "This man wants you dead."

Clinton didn't do anything. This is one of the most persistent myths about President Clinton. This view has some appeal. President Clinton's attention to foreign affairs, especially in the early days of his administration, was episodic at best. But the legacy of a president is not simply the sum of actions that he personally undertakes; it is the sum of the many actions taken in his name by the far-flung departments of the executive branch. The hardworking street-level agents of the FBI, the CIA, and other counterterrorism agencies deserve credit for their work during the Clinton years. Generally, presidents get the credit or the blame for what happens in the bureaucracy on their watch. With this understanding, it has to be admitted that the Clinton Administration did do something about bin Laden—just not enough.

Fair-minded critics of the president accept this. Senator Richard Shelby, the former vice chairman of the Senate Intelligence Committee, told me: "The Clinton Administration did give more than lip service to the fight against terrorism, specifically dealing with the Osama bin Laden group, but the effort was never sustained in any way. I don't think that effort was ever, ever in any way considered bold action, such as the [Bush] Administration is now employing."

Did Clinton launch a determined, sustained effort to defeat bin Laden? Could he have done more? After reading the evidence in these pages, the reader can be the judge of that.

Unlike Bush, Clinton never had a chance to show his mettle by being tested by momentous events.[3] This view, voiced privately by many liberals and former Clinton officials, seems to be that Bush is lucky to have been at the helm when nearly three thousand Americans died on September 11, 2001. The atrocity gave him the scope and stature to be a truly great president. Clinton, they say, never had this "opportunity." This is their gnawing worry about Clinton's legacy.

They are wrong. Clinton was tested by a historic, global conflict, the first phase of America's war on terror. He was president when bin Laden declared war on America. He had many chances to defeat bin Laden; he simply did not take them. If, in the wake of the 1998 embassy bombings, Clinton had rallied the public and the Congress to fight bin Laden and smash terrorism, he might have become the Winston Churchill of his generation. But, instead, he chose the role of Neville Chamberlain.

Clinton only used force against bin Laden to distract the nation from his scandals. When President Clinton ordered cruise-missile strikes on a pharmaceutical factory in Sudan and on bin Laden's mountain strongholds in Afghanistan in August 1998, the press was quick to point out the "suspicious" timing. After all, the Monica Lewinsky scandal was dominating the national conversation. "Wag the Dog" and all that.

But think the "suspicious timing" issue through to its logical conclusion. President Clinton didn't delay the retaliatory missile strikes, as he knew that the House of Representatives might vote on impeachment. That would have been suspicious timing. Instead, he ordered retaliation on bin Laden almost immediately.

Clinton's motives were not entirely pure, of course. The missile strike may have had some fleeting political benefits for the scandal-plagued president. But the national-security case for retaliating against bin Laden was sound. Not responding with military force when American diplomats were murdered in their own embassies would have been a *real* scandal.

In fact, this "Wag the Dog" cynicism puts things exactly backwards. The president wasn't doing too much because of a sex scandal, but too little. Clinton should have ordered many more strikes on bin Laden.

The Republican-led Congress stopped Clinton from doing more on terrorism. This is provably false. Republicans, especially after the 1998 embassy bombings, strongly supported the president's efforts to defeat bin Laden. Indeed, some Republicans, including Senator Richard Shelby and Senator Orrin Hatch, called for even bolder action against terrorism. In the dark days of the Lewinsky scandal, every senior congressional Republican who appeared on television publicly supported Clinton's missile attacks on bin Laden. The story of the Clinton years, beginning with Republican congressman Bill McCollum in 1993, is of Republicans pleading with the president to take a harder line on terrorism.

The polls were against a war on terror. This argument is frequently made inside the beltway that encircles Washington, D.C., but it is essentially a fallacy followed by a false fact. The premise is that presidents are necessarily poll-driven or that polls set the scope of allowable presidential action. This may be cynical and clever, but it is not true.[4] Presidents can shape public opinion. They can oppose it when it is wrong—this is what truly great leaders do.

Now we come to the false fact. In truth, the American public strongly supported sterner action against terrorists. Public opinion surveys as early as 1996 showed that American voters strongly supported military action against terrorists. A major speech given by a gifted communicator like President Clinton would have only solidified and strengthened the view of the majority. The popular president even had a perfect moment to call for a war on terror: August 7, 1998, the day that two U.S. embassies were simultaneously attacked and a dozen Americans lost their lives. He could have made it a date that would live in infamy. But he was too consumed by scandal to do what President Bush is doing now.

■ ■ ■

To uncover the real record of Clinton and bin Laden, I traveled to Khartoum, Cairo, Paris, London, Frankfurt, New York, and Washington, D.C., surveyed tens of thousands of pages of court documents and government reports, studied the growing academic literature on bin Laden and terrorism, and examined unpublished private papers.

I have interviewed and re-interviewed dozens of participants and experts, including almost two dozen working and retired members of the intelligence services of the United States, Western Europe, East Africa, and the Middle East who were helpful in providing documents, recollections, and insights. Much of what they told me has never been reported and I am grateful for their time and trust.

Perhaps the most valuable sources of information—outside of the intelligence community—were the many high-ranking Clinton Administration officials who agreed to be interviewed, either on or off the record. They had a profound desire to set the record straight and this book would not have been possible without them.

An alert reader will notice that there is one major terrorist incident that is not covered in this book: the June 1996 attack on the U.S. Air Force barracks in Dhahran, Saudi Arabia. Bin Laden is popularly credited with the 1996 attack, and many intelligence analysts and law-enforcement professionals believe that bin Laden's organization was behind the attack. They may well be right. On balance, I decided to take the view held by several well-informed, high-ranking sources that the attack was really the work of Iran, not al Qaeda.

The reader will also find that there are many unnamed sources in this book. This is unavoidable when interviewing intelligence sources, both foreign and domestic, as well as military officers and current and retired government officials. I have tried to tell the reader as much as possible about each anonymous source, revealing his function, nationality, or region in many cases. I have granted anonymity to sources only when it was an absolute requirement for the interview. Most authors, working with similar material or sources, have made the same hard bargains.

In cases where documents or sources differ, I have tried to point out the discrepancy and indicate which accounts seem most reliable. When quoting from foreign news outlets (especially Arabic-language publications), which might be unfamiliar to the reader, I have described their editorial line. When citing *Al-Quds al-Arabi*, for example, I've reminded the reader of that newspaper's pro-bin Laden stance. When I have relied on translations that might be subject to multiple interpretations, I have told the reader the source of those translations. In cases where I have received Arabic-language documents from foreign governments, I have indicated which governments supplied them and I had the documents independently translated.

Many of the details and descriptions are based on things that I have seen or that have been described to me by reliable eyewitnesses. Others were culled from court records, government reports, and similar authoritative documents. Still others were carefully assembled from reams of congressional reports, news accounts, and other sources. While such reconstructions have become a staple of journalism, they are unavoidably limited by the recollections and biases of witnesses, the thoroughness of secondary sources, and the author's interpretations.

Journalists like to say that deadline reporting is the first draft of history. And that is true. But the second draft of history is narrative; a fully rounded account of the particular personalities and specific scenes that makes the recent past understandable. That is what I have attempted to write. The third and final drafts belong to the historians.

Osama bin Laden's Area of Operations
During the Clinton Years

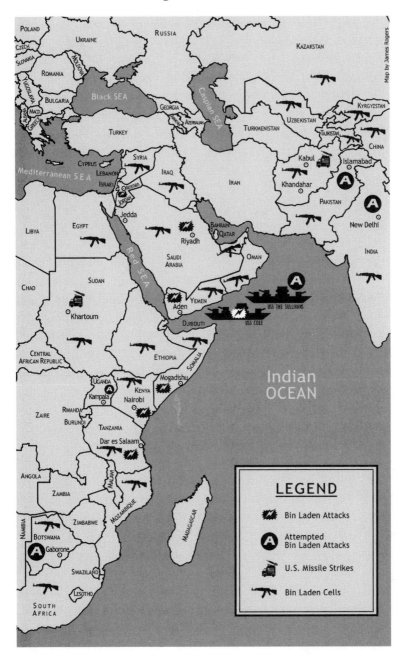

CHAPTER ONE

BIN LADEN STEPS OUT OF THE SHADOWS

ADEN, YEMEN—Osama bin Laden's first attack on Americans began as the sky darkened over the windy port city of Aden, in an unstable desert republic called Yemen, located on the southwestern tip of the Arabian Peninsula.

This largely unknown attack was the start of a deadly pattern. It was President-elect William Jefferson Clinton's first face-off with bin Laden. It was December 29, 1992.

Bin Laden's men looked forward to a night of murder and glory. They had trained and fought together in Afghanistan.[1] They had patiently studied their targets and built their bombs. In less than an hour, they would start a new jihad.

Their targets were two skyscrapers at opposite ends of the harbor, the Goldmore and Aden Hotels. These hotels were islands of Western culture, with alcohol, rock music, and even Christmas lights.[2] And, as the only international five-star hotels in the city, they were also beacons of luxury that offered swimming pools and a disco, places where casually dressed men and women could flirt, drink, and dance. There was much in these targets that would displease a fundamentalist Muslim.

But, most importantly, these hotels were temporary homes to almost one hundred U.S. Marines.

For the Marines, it was not supposed to be a combat posting, just a standard supply operation hundreds of miles from battle. The Marine Corps' Aerial Refueler/Transport Squadron 352, part of the Third Marine Aircraft wing, were there to fly giant KC-130 Hercules transports out of Aden to Somalia. For the other Marine units, Aden was a way station, a comfortable bed in a luxury hotel before shipping out to the dusty, dangerous outskirts of Mogadishu, Somalia.

There was no compelling military reason to station Marines in Yemen, where they handled only one major cargo flight per day— out of the eighteen per day bound for Somalia from other, more active bases. This was political make-work. At the time, Yemen was a terrorist haven that famously abstained from a UN vote condemning Iraq's invasion of Kuwait. Still, both the U.S. State Department and Yemen were eager to improve relations, provided by stationing a few Marines in Aden.

Yet, it was the symbolic presence of the U.S. Marines on the Arabian Peninsula that enraged Osama bin Laden. Days before Clinton was to be sworn in as president, bin Laden was all but unknown to American intelligence. But they were about to find out.

It was after nine in the evening when a security guard spotted two men[3] squatting near a parked car in front of the Aden Hotel.[4] Were they trying to place something under the car? Car bombs were common enough in Yemen to make the guard suspicious. As the guard walked over to investigate, one of the men ran toward him, toting a suitcase.[5] The man had a grim look on his face. Before the guard could speak to him, the bomb-rigged suitcase exploded.[6] The terrorist howled in pain; his right arm had vanished in the blast. His clothes were singed and coated in his own blood. Hot debris from the bomb slammed into both the guard and the bomber's accomplice, a shaking eighteen-year-old. All three lay wounded and stunned.

Police arrived quickly. The wounded guard gave a hurried report. One team took the guard and the two injured terrorists to a hospital. Another police unit set to work to disarm the bomb placed under a parked car.[7] The Aden police were experienced with bombs and worked quickly. They were fortunate. The bomb was meant to explode in minutes.

Meanwhile, a timer on a massive TNT charge was ticking to zero in a hall closet on the fourth floor of the Goldmore Hotel.[8] Investigators still don't know if bin Laden's men bribed a hotel desk clerk or brazenly walked past the front desk carrying a mysterious suitcase. But there is little doubt about the bomb they left behind.

At about 9:15 P.M. local time, a janitor was walking down the hall of the Goldmore Hotel.[9] The timer triggered the blast, spraying a lethal wave of shrapnel. The janitor was killed instantly.

Inside the hotel restaurant, Herbert Denes, a seventy-year-old Austrian man on vacation, was having dinner with his wife. A giant wall of blast-driven glass shards rushed toward him. In seconds, he was bleeding to death. His wife, her face slashed by glass, was critically injured. Five other hotel guests were cut and bleeding.[10] Around them sharp glass glittered on the floor and blood coated the walls.

In the hall and in five rooms beyond, a fire raged. The bloodied victims were temporarily cut off from rescuers.

Back at the Aden Hotel, the bomb planted beneath the car was disarmed and police searched a vehicle that had been driven by the terrorists. Police Major Kassem Mohammed later told reporters that his officers had found twenty-five bombs, two anti-tank mines, and two detonators in the truck.[11] Yemen's state-run television later added to this deadly inventory: two sticks of dynamite, two machine guns, and a pistol. Clearly, a larger attack had been planned.

Yemeni intelligence was quick to connect bin Laden to the Aden bombings. The two terrorists who were wounded in the blast in the Aden hotel parking lot admitted they had trained in camps in Afghanistan funded by bin Laden. Four more men were arrested in the following days; each had a connection to bin Laden. (All four later escaped in a jailbreak. Eight years later, one of the four escapees was detained in a police sweep after the attack by bin Laden's organization on the USS *Cole* in Aden harbor in October 2000.) As the investigation widened, still more links to bin Laden appeared. Police searched the apartment of one of the terrorists and found a large amount of cash, "twenty-one explosive devices, TNT, detonators," and documents written in code.[12] Those documents also connected the attackers to bin Laden.

The hunt for bin Laden was on, at least on the Yemeni side. Within days, Yemen's Ministry of Interior publicly blamed "hirelings of foreign elements."[13] But, in private, they were not so vague about the perpetrator. The Ministry of Interior, which supervises Yemen's police and intelligence services, contacted Interpol, an international body that coordinates efforts to capture transnational criminals and terrorists. Yemen wanted help tracking down Osama bin Laden.

But no help ever came, over the next few weeks and months, from the Clinton Administration. If Clinton had energetically swung behind Yemen's efforts to arrest a terrorist who plotted to kill Americans, bin Laden might have been stopped years before September 11, 2001—and thousands of lives would have been saved.

The Aden bombings are believed to have been Osama bin Laden's first attack on Americans,[14] the beginning in a long series that would culminate in the September 11 attacks on New York and Washington. But it was a misfire.

Unbeknownst to the terrorists, the American soldiers staying at the Goldmore had checked out two days earlier. While there were some one hundred U.S. Marines still at the Aden Hotel, a sharp-eyed security guard had foiled that attack. The terrorists had failed to kill or wound a single American. It was not a miscalculation that bin Laden would make again.

But bin Laden won anyway.

Within hours of the blasts, all American military personnel were immediately evacuated from Aden. By midnight, most Americans had been airlifted out. A spokesman for the U.S. Naval Forces Central Command dryly told the Associated Press that the evacuation was ordered "because of concern about the security situation."[15] A quick victory for bin Laden.

Quick victories, the Clinton Administration would soon painfully learn, only emboldened bin Laden. The rapid evacuation allowed bin Laden to turn a misfire into triumph.

Bin Laden's war on America had begun.

LANGLEY, VIRGINIA—The headquarters of the Central Intelligence Agency are perched on a high ridge west of the Potomac River, obscured by a wall of maples and pines, ringed by a chain-link fence, patrolled by armed guards, and surveyed by a battery of exposed and hidden cameras. Behind its various gates is a sprawling campus of concrete parking garages, grassy terraces, and a pile of nondescript office buildings.

About an hour after the explosion in Yemen, the CIA's station chief there telephoned the CIA's Counter-Terrorism Center.[16]

The Center was established under President Reagan, on February 1, 1986, to combat a wave of terror attacks backed by Iran and Syria. It was supposed to break down the bureaucratic barriers among CIA operations, which were divided into Near East, Middle East, and Africa stations. Properly run, the CTC—as it was known internally—could help the agency prevent attacks. In the late 1980s, it was an exciting place to be an analyst; by all accounts, it helped the operations division win some important clandestine victories over terrorists.

But by the end of the first Bush Administration, morale was plunging. The CTC was still resented by many operations officers as an invasion of their turf. The number of interesting assignments was shrinking. The Center's principal enemies, the Abu Nidal Operation and Hezbollah, seemed to be reducing their attacks. Some of the best analysts were retiring or seeking transfers.

Even the CTC's mission seemed obsolete. Some intelligence

analysts believed that terrorism would wither away with the demise of the Soviet Union, which had been a major source of terrorist funding.

With two bomb blasts in faraway Aden, all of that was about to change.

The agents at the CTC got the news just after lunch. The CIA's station chief in Yemen said that Yemen's intelligence service suspected a mastermind named Osama bin Laden.

The supervisor paused for a moment. To whom could he assign the case?

The CTC is a large room with a low ceiling, sliced into rows of cubicles.[17] Each row is devoted to studying, tracking, and stopping particular terrorists. Signs point the way to "Abu Nidal Boulevard" and "Tamil Tiger Terrace," but in December 1992, there was no "Bin Laden Boulevard."[18] The CIA would not set up a bin Laden "station" until January 1996,[19] after a meeting of National Security Advisor Tony Lake and the National Security Council.[20]

Bin Laden was not well known to the CIA's Middle East specialists. "It was only after this bomb in Aden that first word came through of bin Laden's connections and how he might target America," said one former senior official at the CIA's directorate of operations.[21]

At the time, bin Laden was well known to Middle Eastern and East African intelligence services. Saudi Arabia, Yemen, and Egypt had, for different reasons, developed dossiers on bin Laden. If the incoming Clinton Administration had asked its Arab allies for information or even asked the CIA, which was rapidly developing information, it might have learned a good deal about the Arab arch-terrorist. But no one on Clinton's transition team was curious about their new nemesis. Clinton himself was absorbed with picking political appointees and the details of inauguration parties.

JEDDAH, SAUDI ARABIA—The only son of Mohammed bin Awaz bin Laden, a Saudi construction magnate from Yemen, and his least-favored wife, a Jordanian named Alia, Osama bin Laden grew up mocked and isolated. As his older half-brothers basked in their father's attention and were rewarded with well-paying jobs in the family construction firm, Osama retreated into books and religion. He soon gravitated to a severe form of Islam, which, in addition to traditional Islam's strictures against drinking and unveiled women, forbids all music, movies, television, smoking, dancing, and singing. By all accounts, his father approved, but did not share, Osama's zealous form of Islam.

Osama had only two consistent ways of winning his father's attention: speaking knowledgeably with his father and older relatives about the Koran after Friday night prayer services and gleefully forgoing all creature comforts during the family's annual two-week excursion into the Saudi desert. There they would camp in tents, without electricity or running water, in 110-degree heat. In time, these two traits—extreme religiosity and survivalism—would fuse to make the bin Laden we know today.

Radical ideology was the catalyst. While studying at King Abdul Aziz University in Jeddah, Saudi Arabia, in the late 1970s, he joined the Muslim Brotherhood, a radical Islamic group founded in Egypt in 1928. The group, which was banned by many Arab governments, is believed to have cells across the Middle East. The Brotherhood specializes in recruiting university students and young professionals, many of whom later move on to even more radical and violent Islamist organizations. The Brotherhood believes that all Arab dictatorships should fall because they are insufficiently "Islamic" and that a return to the seventh-century values of Mohammed will raise the Arab world to global preeminence. These soon became the views of Osama bin Laden.

While still at the university, bin Laden graduated to a more violent brand of Islamism. Sometime in 1978, he met a Palestinian firebrand named Abdullah Azzam. Azzam, a tall, charismatic man with arresting eyes, spoke with conviction and passion. His theme was holy war, *jihad*. He did not mean a spiritual struggle, as some

American jihad apologists say, but violence. Azzam was quite clear that jihad meant war. Ten years later, a videotape of Azzam's fiery set speech on jihad surfaced at an Islamist conference in Oklahoma City. "The jihad, the fighting, is obligatory on you wherever you can perform it. And just as when you are in America you must fast—unless you are ill or on a voyage—so, too, must you wage jihad. The word jihad means fighting only, fighting with the sword."[22]

Such was his power as a speaker that a videotape of a single speech would lead young men to abandon their studies, their families, and their jobs, to train for war. Even Azzam's enemies came to respect his ability to recruit and inspire thousands of terrorists. Israel's former ambassador to the United Nations, Dore Gold, recently wrote: "It is difficult to overstate the impact that this Islamic radical [Azzam] had."[23]

Young bin Laden saw Azzam in person in 1978. It changed his life. Without Azzam, bin Laden might have become a Saudi executive with a soft spot for radical ideas. With Azzam, he started on a path to become the most feared and hated terrorist of our time.

Less than a year later, two cataclysmic events at the frontiers of the Muslim world completed bin Laden's transformation from a radical to a jihadi. In November 1979, Islamic extremists led a coup in Tehran, the capital of Iran. The Iranian revolution showed to bin Laden and his generation of Islamists that their dream of a Koranic theocracy was actually possible. They could change the world. Just as the 1917 Soviet revolution in Russia electrified communists across Europe, the Iranian revolution energized radicals across the Muslim world.

The Iranian revolution taught bin Laden and his comrades-in-arms a second deadly lesson: not to fear the United States. Iranian militants took fifty-two American diplomats hostage in the U.S. embassy in Teheran. America did nothing. As the months ticked by, President Carter seemed increasingly weak and ineffectual. Carter's feeble response surprised the Islamic radicals. According to their speeches and printed propaganda, militants became convinced that Allah was protecting the fundamentalist revolution in Iran and holding America at bay. They were elated and emboldened. No one could stop them now.

Then, in December 1979, the Soviet Union toppled its own puppet regime in Afghanistan with a massive invasion of airborne special forces, paratroopers, tanks, and self-propelled artillery. Saudi Arabia saw a potential threat to its oil fields and to the Arab world. On its eastern flank, Iran saw a threat to its revolution from its ancient enemy—the Russians—and was alarmed that its allies in Afghanistan were among the first gunned down by Soviet troops. The word went out: Islam is in danger. Azzam repeated the call to arms in his spellbinding speeches.

Bin Laden heard the call. "When the invasion of Afghanistan started, I was enraged and went there at once," he told British journalist Robert Fisk, the only Westerner to interview the archterrorist three times. "I arrived within days, before the end of 1979."[24] For what it is worth, bin Laden is probably lying. The Soviet invasion began on December 25, 1979, and the Islamist effort took weeks and months to organize. But the lie illustrates bin Laden's reaction nonetheless; he was provoked and he took action.

In neighboring Pakistan, bin Laden soon linked up with Azzam. There were thousands of other recruits—many drawn by Azzam's speeches—from around the Arab world. They became known as the Arab Afghans. They lacked guns, training, and organization. Azzam busied himself trying to negotiate alliances among the various factions—it would take unity to defeat the largest army in the world. But the unity rarely held and the Arab Afghans spent much of their energy fighting among themselves. As a result, the Arab Afghans failed to play a decisive role against the Soviets. Meanwhile, bin Laden searched for a role for himself. Azzam told him an army also needs a quartermaster.

With Azzam's help, bin Laden opened the "bureau of services," the Maktab Khadamat al-Mujihideen, in Peshawar, Pakistan. (In 1989, this organization was renamed al Qaeda, Arabic for "the base.") Bin Laden returned to Saudi Arabia to raise money and buy supplies. He returned with his family's construction vehicles to cut roads and build bomb-proof bunkers. He bought strings of houses to quarter the holy warriors, the mujihideen. And, critically, he set up a central office to track recruits. Once registered with bin Laden's "bureau of services,"[25] a recruit was assured food, medical care, and, if he died in combat, a letter to his parents lionizing his martyrdom. Since the recruits came from as far away as Morocco and the Philippines, bin Laden ended up with a vast database of Islamic militants from around the world. That roster would enable him to set up cells of trusted terrorists in more than fifty-five countries in the 1990s.

As the Afghan jihad wore on, the Reagan Administration decided to join the Saudis and various Gulf state sheikhs (who had been financing the Afghan war since 1980) in financing the anti-Soviet revolt. As a rule, America financed Afghan natives while Saudi Arabia funded Islamic extremists from outside Afghanistan. Many Muslim nations—from Morocco to Indonesia—opened their jails and bought one-way tickets for their local Islamic militants. The American and Saudi-led Muslim efforts were separate; only a common Communist enemy united them. The Saudis saw the effort as a way of protecting their kingdom, spreading their severe version of Islam, and extending their influence to the non-Arab Muslim world. The Reagan Administration officials saw the war as a way of weakening and demoralizing the Soviet Union. A joke, popular in conservative circles at the time, captured the essence of the strategy: "How do you say Vietnam in Russian? Afghanistan." The Reagan Administration was no more responsible for the anti-Soviet Arab Afghans than bin Laden and his fellow jihadis were responsible for Reagan's principled anti-communism stance.

Ultimately, the Reagan Administration pumped in more than $3 billion between 1985 and 1989.[26] The author talked to two former CIA Chiefs of Station in Pakistan—who, at different times, supervised funding for anti-communist rebels in Afghanistan in the 1980s. Both flatly and firmly denied that any CIA funds ever went to bin Laden. Bill Peikney, who was CIA station chief in Islamabad, Pakistan, from 1984 to 1986, and Milt Bearden, who was CIA station chief from 1986 to 1989, oversaw the intelligence operations during the entire period of American financial support for the anti-Soviet guerrillas. Funding the Afghan resistance began in earnest under Bearden, who was in charge of disbursing almost $1 billion per year at its height. (The Saudis agreed to match U.S. expenditures dollar-for-dollar, but the Saudi funds went to the Arab Afghans, possibly including bin Laden.) In an interview with the author, Bearden scorned the idea that any U.S. government funds ever went to bin Laden: "I challenge anyone to give any proof that we gave one dollar to any Afghan Arabs, let alone bin Laden."[27]

There are many reasons to believe the senior CIA officials. Bearden was in charge of all CIA funds at the time and knew where the money went. He retired from the CIA in 1995 to write books[28] and to become an international consultant—he has no motive to mouth an agency line. The other CIA official, Bill Peikney, strongly supports Bearden's account. He adds in an e-mail to the author: "I don't even recall UBL [bin Laden] coming across my screen when I was there."[29] The CIA simply did not even know who bin Laden was in the mid-1980s. It is hard to fund someone you don't know exists.

In addition, bin Laden simply did not need the CIA's money. He was awash in money from Saudi and Persian Gulf sources. Besides, the CIA financed Afghans fighting for their country, not extremist Arabs like bin Laden. And the Arab Afghans rarely ventured up to the front. Indeed, many of these so-called holy warriors were killed by rival Islamist factions in Pakistan. Why invest in people who were not actively fighting Soviet troops?

And even if the CIA wanted to pay Arab Afghans—which top agency officials insist they did not—bin Laden would be a far from obvious choice. Bin Laden himself rarely left the safety of Pakistan's northwestern cities and commanded no troops of his own. There was simply no reason for the CIA to give bin Laden a dime.

Moreover, the handful of Americans who had heard of bin Laden in the 1980s knew him mainly for his violent anti-American views. Dana Rohrbacher, now a Republican congressman from Orange County, California, told the author about a trip he took with the mujihideen in 1987. At the time, Rohrbacher was a Reagan aide who delighted in taking long overland trips inside Afghanistan with anti-communist forces. On one such trek, his guide told him not to speak English for the next few hours because they were passing by bin Laden's encampment. Rohrbacher was told: "If he hears an American, he will kill you."[30] If a CIA operative had tried to recruit bin Laden, he probably would not have lived through the experience. Just why and how could the CIA fund someone who hated America and would most likely kill the courier?

Finally, there is no evidence that the CIA ever paid bin Laden. No canceled checks. No contemporary news accounts published in English in any newspaper in the world. Indeed, the earliest article to mention bin Laden (or any variant spelling of his names) appears in a February 1992 edition of *The Guardian*—and it does not mention CIA funding. Subsequent congressional and media investigations have turned up nothing.[31] The charges of CIA funding came later—and with no evidence attached.

The claim that the CIA somehow supported bin Laden is mostly made by those who opposed President Reagan's support of guerrilla movements to roll back Soviet communism. They had warned that Reagan's strategy would inevitably cause "blowback," which they now claim is embodied by bin Laden. Perhaps they hope to use bin Laden to win an argument they lost long ago.

By February 1989, the Soviets had retreated and bin Laden had joined the civil war to turn once-tolerant Afghanistan into a model Islamic state. He financed the construction of vast training camps and bankrolled militant factions. His activities seemed to increase as the Soviets shrank back.

Bin Laden now thought his former mentor Azzam was too moderate—and too much in his way. Bin Laden and Azzam quarreled over tactics. On November 24, 1989, Azzam put his two sons into his car to go to Friday prayers. He turned the key. The car exploded. There were no survivors. Pakistani investigators were never able to prove that bin Laden was behind the blast,[32] but he was surely its direct beneficiary. He was now the undisputed master of a global network of terror with no one to overrule or question him. He began looking for another jihad.

In Saudi Arabia, bin Laden was widely admired for his battle against the Soviets. Wild stories circulated of bin Laden's derring-do in the face of Russian machine guns and his "miraculous" survival when a 105-mm shell landed at his feet but did not explode.[33] These stories are almost certainly false, but Saudi Arabia was so short of heroes that any doubts were put aside. Bin Laden was their hero.

At first, bin Laden went to work in the Jeddah office of his family's construction business. He seemed to be making a transition to civilian life and resuming his position among the kingdom's wealthiest citizens. He was hardworking and his family members were impressed with his energy and focus. But soon Saudi intelligence tracked terrorists—Yemenis, Saudis, and, ominously from the Saudi point of view, Egyptians, the presumed experts in terrorism in the Arab world—to bin Laden's office. Under the cover of his family's business, bin Laden was deepening his ties with Islamic extremists from his Afghan days.

Then on August 2, 1990, Iraqi tanks rolled across the Kuwait border. The government of Saudi Arabia was nervous. Its military was considerably smaller than Iraq's, then the fourth-largest in the world. What would stop Saddam Hussein from seizing their oil fields? Saudi officials called on America for help.

Bin Laden had different ideas. He sought out Prince Sultan, Saudi Arabia's Minister of Defense. The Saudi jihadi made an unusual offer in a ten-page plan: he would use his family's construction business to ring the border of Iraq with new fortifications and would supply thousands of Muslim veterans from the Afghan war to defend the oil kingdom. In return, Saudi Arabia had to forgo an American military presence.[34] Bin Laden strongly argued against allowing American airmen and soldiers onto the holy sands of Saudi Arabia, even en route to another country. He claimed that allowing non-Muslims into the kingdom violated a well-known passage in the Koran that says that "there shall be no two religions in Arabia." He repeated his offer to the director of the Saudi General Intelligence Department, Prince Turki al-Faisal.[35] He presented a detailed alternative plan: an army of thousands of Arab Afghans fighting a guerrilla/terrorist war against Iraq's massive army.[36] When his plan was rejected, his hatred of America and the Saudi royal family deepened.

By February 1991, American and Allied forces were victorious in liberating Kuwait. But American forces stayed on in Saudi Arabia to patrol the no-fly zones in northern and southern Iraq and to preserve the peace. To bin Laden, the continued American presence on Saudi soil felt like betrayal and he became increasingly vocal and hostile in his opposition to the Saudi royal family as 1991 wore on.

Bin Laden began to give Friday speeches in mosques across Arabia accusing the royal family of corruption and of violating the tenets of Islam. The Saudi government responded by limiting his movements, what the New York–based Council on Foreign Relations later called "virtual house arrest."[37]

Bin Laden fled Saudi Arabia in April 1991. He arrived in Khartoum, Sudan, where the new Islamic regime welcomed him with a small reception at the separate VIP terminal at the Khartoum airport, according to a Sudanese official interviewed by the author. He was greeted by Hassan al-Turabi, the speaker of Sudan's assembly and a leader in the growing Islamist movement. Within days, bin Laden was sipping tea at the world's largest convention of international terrorists, formally known as the Popular Arab and Islamic Conference.[38] U.S. officials later called the annual gatherings "terrorist conventions." It is easy to see why. Everyone was there, from Hamas and Fatah to Egyptian Islamic Jihad and Yasser Arafat, representing the PLO. It gave the arch-terrorist another web of deadly contacts: bomb makers, passport forgers, and safe houses across the Muslim world.

Although officially an investor and businessman in Sudan, bin Laden had never really ceased running his terrorist network. Now he would be able to operate freely and openly—as long as he kept building roads for one of the world's poorest nations. And his anti-American fervor had grown. He considered the stationing of non-Muslim troops in Saudi Arabia to be tantamount to defiling a mosque. Now he would bring the jihad to them, in Yemen, in the first days of the Clinton presidency.

In time, the Aden bombings would be seen as part of a classic bin Laden pattern: the use of Arab Afghans,[39] hidden bombs, simultaneous explosions, a willingness to kill civilians (even Muslims) to annihilate his enemies, and the use of Yemen as a staging area.[40] But it was too soon for analysts to detect such patterns; they would have to learn from many more blasts.

Worse, the CIA was blinded by its own obsolete doctrines. For the next few years, intelligence analysts and counterterrorism specialists continued to believe that bin Laden, like most terrorists, would stick to military or symbolic targets and try to avoid hurting fellow Muslims. They underestimated bin Laden. He set his own rules of engagement.

Still, the CIA was learning to pay attention to bin Laden by January 1993, the month that Clinton was sworn into office. It would take three years for the Clinton White House to learn the same lesson.

THE WHITE HOUSE—Outside the Oval Office in the west wing of the White House is a narrow corridor lined with blue carpet. In a few short steps, President Clinton could walk left, past the curved white wall of the cabinet room, with its double doors, to the offices of his top advisors: his Chief of Staff, Mack McLarty, and his National Security Advisor, Tony Lake. And those trusted aides could make the same trip in reverse to advise the president about emerging threats to the United States.

But in the first few weeks of the new administration, it seems that no one walked down the narrow corridor, momentarily crowded with open boxes and antique furniture, to brief Clinton about the emerging threat of Osama bin Laden or the Aden bombings. It was deemed too trivial for the president. Besides, it happened a month before Clinton took office; not his responsibility they could argue.

But an attack on American troops—even a failed one—is serious. Some would counter that the attacks had occurred in the last days of the Bush Administration and that the "lame-duck" president should have done something about them. However, outgoing administrations typically brief incoming ones extensively and defer to incoming administrations before taking action. It is a tradition of presidential courtesy. In practical terms, the decision was not Bush's prerogative, but Clinton's.

Reconstructing the decisions inside the Clinton White House concerning the Aden bombing is very difficult. Clinton's first National Security Advisor, Tony Lake, said he simply did not remember, when the author asked him about it. His memory loss is plausible—in his position one has to deal with a constant barrage of crises—but it also suggests what little importance Clinton and his senior officials initially put on responding to terrorist attacks on American troops. Clinton could have worked with Yemen and Saudi Arabia to track bin Laden and his deadly lieutenants. He could have put the U.S. military in the region on high alert. He could have ordered an interagency task force to assess the bin Laden threat. But he did none of these things. And this neglect blinded the Clinton Administration to the hidden pattern in the next attack, which would come just thirty-eight days later.

CAPITOL HILL—The Clinton White House was repeatedly warned about bin Laden in 1993 from a surprising source. Congressman Bill McCollum, a Florida Republican whose district included Disney World, repeatedly wrote the president, the National Security Advisor, and the Director of Central Intelligence, beginning in 1993. He was hoping to persuade the Clinton Administration to focus on global terrorism, including Osama bin Laden. It wasn't easy.

Congressman McCollum was the founder and chairman of the House Taskforce on Terrorism and Unconventional Warfare.[41] Until September 11, 2001, there was no House subcommittee solely devoted to terrorism. During the 1990s, McCollum's task force became a valuable repository of information on terrorism, at a time when few in Washington were paying attention. Today, the taskforce reports seem eerily prescient. And Congressman McCollum had valuable human intelligence. He developed a wealth of contacts among the mujihideen in Afghanistan. The CIA essentially lost interest in Afghanistan after the Soviets retreated north of the Oxus River. But Congressman McCollum, a minority-party congressman with a safe seat, and a well-connected staffer, Yossef Bodansky, a former consultant to the Defense Department, had stayed engaged.[42] Bodansky speaks Arabic and Farsi and learned a lot about terrorism from "open sources:" Arab newspapers, magazines, and state-run broadcasts across the Middle East. Bodansky would go on to write two books on the growing terrorist threat to America, including an authoritative biography of bin Laden. Congressman McCollum was doomed to be Clinton's Cassandra, a prophet whose warnings were ignored.

McCollum's sources among the former mujihideen, who visited Washington several times a year, provided the kind of information that the CIA could get only from its human intelligence sources, if it had any left in Afghanistan. Not everything the mujihideen said was accurate, but some of their street-level observations were dead on.

They warned that bin Laden wanted to impose an Iranian-style, Islamic republic on their country. They emphasized that he wanted to murder Americans. His men were connected to a chain of bombings, assassination plots, and other terrorist acts in Afghanistan, Pakistan, and now Yemen. "Sheikh Osama," as the former freedom fighters called him, was becoming more and more powerful. They mentioned the growing number of terrorist training camps in Pakistan and Afghanistan, which graduated a new class of terrorists every six months. McCollum told the author, "We knew that it was just a matter of time before we saw a major terrorist attack on America."[43]

Frustrated, McCollum couldn't believe that the Clinton Administration would ignore such serious intelligence that he had developed about a real and present threat. But that is what happened.

It would be years before the Clinton Administration would take McCollum's warnings seriously—after dozens of Americans had died.

CHAPTER TWO

BIN LADEN AND
THE TWIN TOWERS

NEW YORK—Before daybreak on February 26, 1993, a yellow Ford 350 Econoline van threaded its way through the Holland Tunnel toward lower Manhattan. At the wheel was Mohammed Salameh, an illegal immigrant with eyesight so poor that he had failed his New Jersey driver's license exam four times.[1]

Salameh would have to be careful. He was transporting dangerous cargo. Behind his seat, packed into unmarked cardboard boxes, was fifteen hundred pounds of ammonium nitrate, three tanks of hydrogen gas, four cylinders of nitroglycerin, blasting caps, and four twenty-foot long fuses.[2] The first foreign terrorist attack on American soil was under way.

Beside Salameh was a man he knew little about. He knew that the man in the passenger seat was the leader of their cell and a master bomb maker. Salameh also knew that the man had traveled the world killing the enemies of Islam. That meant that he deserved respect and that he got it. Finally, he knew that on that morning the man hoped to murder as many as 250,000 people. For this attempted atrocity, he would later boast, "Yes, I am a terrorist and I am proud of it."[3]

Most of all, the man in the passenger seat was a professional. Though he was most likely born in the wild tribal lands of western

Pakistan, members of his terror cell believed that he was an Iraqi. He did carry an Iraqi passport, as well as a British passport under the name of Azan Mohammed, a (forged) Pakistani passport under the name Abdul Basit, and at least ten other passports under ten other aliases.[4]

They knew the man as Rashid the Iraqi. Investigators later called him Ramzi Yousef.

What Salameh and his cell didn't know was that each of them, except for their leader, was what intelligence experts call "classic expendables." They were supposed to be caught. In fact, Yousef had ensured it.

"Expendables" are a common feature of sophisticated terrorist operations; they serve as cannon fodder to fool the target nation into believing that they have caught all of the perpetrators and thereby cloak the wider conspiracy. The "expendables" allow the professionals to escape.

Behind the nearly blind driver and master bomb maker was a blue Lincoln Town Car sedan, at the moment driven by another "expendable," Mahmud Abouhalima. This vehicle would be their getaway car.

The men had been preparing for this day for months. In January 1993—weeks before the first al Qaeda attack in Yemen—they had mixed the dangerous chemicals in a cheap Jersey City apartment. The fumes were so powerful that they stained the walls blue.[5] One January night, neighbors saw a group of Arab men lugging away unmarked cardboard boxes. They moved the boxes into locker number 4344 at the Space Station rental storage facility just across the Hudson from the World Trade Center.[6] Inside the room-sized locker they built a virtual laboratory—complete with beakers, funnels, jars, glass tubes, transfer pumps, and vats of chemicals. This is where they built the bomb.

The next four hours of the then-largest foreign terrorist conspiracy on American soil remain a mystery. Perhaps they went to an as yet undiscovered safe house to pray and prepare. This is not an uncommon step in Islamist terror attacks. What is certain is that shortly after 9 A.M. they arrived outside Eyad Ismoil's residence.

After some discussion, Ismoil agreed to go with them. But first he wanted to take a bath. Out on the street, Yousef sprang his trap.[7] Citing Ismoil's experience as a taxi driver, he asked if he would drive the van.[8]

Ismoil assented. Another "expendable" was added to the cell. He had no prior involvement in the plot, beyond a few innocuous phone calls from Yousef, until that fateful morning. Their destination was the World Trade Center.

Shortly after noon, the van and the sedan drove some one hundred feet down the ramp beneath the Vista International Hotel and stopped along the south wall of the north tower. The place was carefully chosen. It would not arouse suspicion: trucks and vans often parked illegally there while their drivers hustled to the nearby elevator to make a delivery. But Yousef had chosen the spot for another reason, a reason that structural engineers puzzled out months later. The location was ideal for using the internal geometry of the building to focus the force of a blast.

Yousef opened the rear doors of the van and lit each of the four twenty-foot fuses. He slammed closed the doors and ran to the getaway car. With the fuses burning at one and one-half inches per second, they had only 160 seconds to escape.

For a moment, they were trapped like their intended victims. The exit ramp was blocked. Honking frantically, they shouted at the driver ahead of them. He told them to wait. Wait? Seconds ticked by. The truck ahead of them finally eased into traffic. The killers roared away.

Behind a two-foot-thick concrete retaining wall, on level B2 of the World Trade Center's parking garage, Monica Smith was hard at work.[9] She had no window in her office and couldn't see the yellow van on the other side of her office wall.

Smith's life revolved around the World Trade Center. An immigrant from Ecuador, she was making it in America. She had worked her way up to a position that gave her a quiet underground office and a middle-class income studying timesheets of the World Trade Center's janitorial staff. She even met her husband, a salesman, in the Twin Towers. On that fateful day, she was seven months pregnant with their first child, a boy. [10]

Then the Ryder rental truck exploded. The blast smashed through the concrete wall, grabbed her from her office chair and smashed her against a reinforced-steel concrete wall. The impact was so great that the knit pattern of her sweater was imprinted on her shoulder.[11] Flying chunks of concrete hit her body like bullets. In seconds she and her baby were dead.[12]

Tenths of a second later, five more people were murdered.[13] It happened so quickly that one maintenance man was killed before he could even close his eyes. The blast drove powderized concrete particles at him at more than 1,000 miles per second, far faster than the human brain's automatic reflex to close the eyelids. When firefighters uncovered his body days later, his eyes were still open and pockmarked by high-speed dust. A locksmith, six months from retirement, was found impaled by a pipe. A maintenance supervisor, in the midst of chewing his lunch, was discovered ripped apart.

On a floor above Monica Smith, Wilfredo Mercado had been looking over deliveries for the Windows on the World restaurant. He was sucked down five stories into the burning abyss and crushed under tons of falling rubble.

The explosion capsized cars, punched up through the anteroom of the Vista Hotel ballroom, showering broken glass into the tower lobby, and burrowed down through three levels of solid concrete, dropping building blocks into the tower's air-conditioning units on level B5. It broke loose a steel brace weighing fourteen thousand pounds and hurled it seventy-five feet. It blew debris through the turnstiles of a PATH train station on level B3. It set five floors of the sub-basements ablaze and tore through the cinder block walls of five elevator shafts, turning them into giant chimneys for acrid, black smoke.[14]

Miles of power cables and water pipes were severed in seconds. With the power out, the only light in the sub-basements was cast by the spear points of flame, devouring overturned cars and office debris. As the flames grew, the fire drew the air toward itself in a howling wind.

Inside the foundation lines of New York's tallest building, a crater sixty feet deep and 180 feet wide opened. As the air pressure equalized, the crater became a jagged mouth, sucking down cars and corpses and swallowing two million gallons of sewage and air-conditioning fluid.

The public address system was dead. The fire wardens on each floor knew nothing. Sixty stories up, some office workers thought they felt a tremor. An earthquake in New York? Then colleagues and customers from across lower Manhattan phoned them. Did you know that there's smoke coming out of your building? Within minutes those friendly phone calls were superfluous. Smoke soon invaded every corner of the tower's more than 8.8 million square feet.[15]

The evacuation was orderly. Until they got to the lower levels of the emergency stairwell, some bankers were still doing deals on their cell phones. As they descended, they fell silent. The smoke was chokingly thick. From the top, it was more than one-quarter of a mile down dark stairs. The climb down took hours. Some one thousand people were eventually treated for severe smoke inhalation.

Then came the many painful, personal readjustments. The wife of Wilfredo Mercado, the missing Windows on the World restaurant worker, came to this site every day. She asked the firemen the same sad question: Have you found my husband? One day, the rescuers stopped their shoveling and joined her in a hopeful prayer.[16] Sixteen days after the bombing,[17] buried under a mountain of smashed pipes and concrete blocks, they found her husband's body.

Monica Smith's husband and mother-in-law still burned with pain and anger years later. Her mother-in-law, Patricia Smith, sat three feet behind the World Trade Center bombing mastermind at his 1997 trial. "It was enraging," she told reporters. "I wanted to hit him with my cane."[18]

When he met reporters after the 1994 trial of the four "expendables," Monica Smith's widowed husband, Edward Smith, still had a searing, searching kind of grief: "I ask myself, what type of person shows no regard for human life and would bomb the most populated building in the world?"[19]

The first call to 911 came within seconds of the explosion. Firefighters were on the scene in less than two minutes. Trucks and crews kept arriving all afternoon. By the end of the day, the New York City Fire Department had sent some 750 vehicles and forty percent of its on-duty firefighters; it was the equivalent of a sixteen-alarm fire. At the time, it was the largest call-out of trucks and men in the fire department's history. Only the September 11, 2001, attack drew a larger response from the New York Fire Department.

Within an hour, the FBI established a command center at 26 Federal Plaza. FBI assistant director James Fox was in charge.

Some fire department officials suggested an electrical transformer had exploded. Or a PATH train had crashed. A bomb was unthinkable.

Amid the chaos and confusion, Fox gathered his agents, who were arriving from all over the city. Around him everyone had questions. If this was a bomb, who was the target? Could it be the New York governor's office on the fifty-seventh floor? Or President Clinton's limo in the parking garage? And what was the motive? Was it a bank heist gone bad? (The building held thousands of gold bars stacked neatly in the underground vaults.) Was it terrorists? And if so, which terrorists? The Serbians, the Iraqis, the Palestinians, a mysterious cult? Fox had no answers and no leads.

While the terrorist angle seemed the most promising, it was also the most confusing. Seventeen different callers had phoned city authorities, claiming credit for the attack. So many nations, factions, and cult groups had appointed America as their enemy that the investigation could plausibly go from the Balkans to the Himalayas.

At first, the Serbians seemed the most likely culprits. The World Trade Center bombing occurred less than twenty-four hours after the Clinton Administration announced that U.S. planes would air-drop supplies to the encircled Bosnian refugees. Five hours before the Trade Center attack, a bomb had been left at the front gate of the American Embassy in Zagreb, the capital of Croatia, an enemy of Serbia.[20]

Other agents suspected the Iraqis. In the course of a larger bombing, an American cruise missile had struck Baghdad's Al Rashid Hotel on January 17, nearly killing Saddam Hussein, who was opening a conference for Islamic fundamentalists. Perhaps the Iraqi dictator or one of his invited extremists decided to take revenge by bombing a New York hotel that catered to visiting dignitaries. Iraq had long been a major supporter of international terrorism and the Gulf War had left Hussein with a lasting hatred of America. He had repeatedly and publicly vowed to take his revenge.[21]

David Williams, the FBI's senior bomb expert, poked through the ruins and wiped the debris for traces of bomb residue. After a few hours, he went to see Fox at the command center. Williams announced that the World Trade Center had been bombed.

How could he be so sure? Fox asked.

"I have examined ten thousand bombings," Williams said.

"That's good enough for me," said Fox.[22]

The FBI investigation was then soon officially code-named "Tradebom."

THE WHITE HOUSE—On a Saturday morning, a day after the World Trade Center explosion, there was no sense of crisis in the White House. The bombers of the Twin Towers—the first-ever foreign terrorist attack on American soil—had changed little in the routine of Clinton. The sheer scale of the blast had not sunk in. The few presidential aides in the West Wing were casually dressed and focused on the president's economic policy. The few reporters hanging around the briefing room were there to cover the president's radio address that would focus on his economic-stimulus package. Later that day, Chelsea's friends would arrive from Little Rock to celebrate her thirteenth birthday; Hillary had planned a party on the second floor of the White House residence.

President William Jefferson Clinton sat in the Oval Office scribbling. He was preparing for his weekly radio address and, as usual, making last-minute revisions.

It was the thirty-ninth day of his presidency and, so far, it wasn't going well. The president's military salute—a few fingers sheepishly and momentarily touching his forehead—was faulted. National Security Advisor Tony Lake went to see the president about the "salute issue" and they had practiced for a few minutes in the Oval Office.[23] Now his military salute photographed well as he walked across the South Lawn to board *Marine One*, the presidential helicopter. Yet few press complaints were so easily resolved.

Clinton had lost his second attorney-general nominee, Kimba Wood, when nanny-payment problems raised a red flag. President Clinton's offhand remarks about Iraq and his subsequent "don't ask, don't tell" fudge on his controversial plan to integrate homosexuals into the military had also touched off rounds of critical newspaper stories. The Clinton Administration—the first Democrats in the White House since 1980—seemed to be crumbling.

Now Clinton was trying to regain the initiative. He was finally ready to announce the details of his economic stimulus package, the centerpiece of his 1992 campaign. Then the World Trade Center was attacked. Should he depart from his plans and his script and say something about the headline-making attack on New York's tallest towers? At first, he couldn't decide.

New York Governor Mario Cuomo telephoned the president while the Twin Towers were still being evacuated. Clinton and

Cuomo had a difficult relationship. Clinton had spent much of 1991 wondering if the New York governor was going to challenge him in the Democratic presidential primaries, and much of 1992 trying to get Cuomo's full-throated support.

But this phone call was surprisingly simple: Cuomo simply wanted to brief the president and get his assurance that New York State would enjoy the full support of the federal government. Clinton must have quickly realized that this was a common kind of phone call that governors made after disasters. He had made a few of these calls himself. Perhaps this was the reason Clinton didn't seem to fully grasp that this disaster was not natural, but manmade. That it was terrorism.

Cuomo told Clinton that a bomb had most likely caused the World Trade Center blast—a conclusion that the Clinton White House still chose to consider "speculation." After conferring with his aides, the president asked his press secretary, Dee Dee Myers, to put out the cautious line that the New York authorities "have reason to believe it was a bomb but are not definite."[24] This was a grudging admission of the obvious, but it gave Clinton time to decide how and whether to act.

Why was Clinton so anxious to discount the idea that the Twin Towers had been bombed? A bomb suggested a terrorist act. A terrorist act of this magnitude required a strong response. And strong action was politically dangerous if it misfired. So, from the day of the World Trade Center bombing until the last day of the Clinton Administration, the president demanded absolute proof before acting against terrorists. Ambiguity suited his purposes.

To preserve that ambiguity, either Clinton ignored the overwhelming evidence that the towers were bombed or the White House staff failed to keep him fully informed. Perhaps President Clinton had not yet been told that the FBI's top bomb expert, David Williams, believed that the World Trade Center was bombed or that the New York FBI investigation was proceeding on that basis. Or perhaps the president had not been told that the bomb was planted by terrorists, although the FBI had made that determination within hours.

The president knew that he would have to add something about the World Trade Center explosion to his Saturday radio address. But what? His staff had spent much of Friday working on the speech. Now, on Saturday morning, Clinton was doing some reworking of his own. Strangely, despite the mounting evidence, Clinton still wasn't willing to say that New York's tallest towers had been bombed.

While he worked on his speech, the president was told that FBI Director William Sessions was on the line. The president didn't relish this call either. Sessions, a Bush appointee, was plagued by petty scandals and Clinton planned to replace him.[25]

Clinton picked up the receiver. The director told the president that the FBI's New York office now felt confident that a bomb had caused the blast at the World Trade Center. The president probably wasn't listening very closely; he had come to see Sessions as a political time bomb, not a source of information about an actual bomb.

After a few minutes, Clinton hung up and went back to scribbling. He kept crossing out words and writing new ones—but "bomb" was not one of them.

Clinton's radio address reflected his beliefs about the World Trade Center attack. He treated it like a disaster, a humanitarian crisis. Like a twister in Arkansas. But not as an attack. Indeed the bombing was a sideshow, a distraction from what the president really wanted to discuss—his economic agenda.

This would be Clinton's first and last extended speech on the plot to topple the Twin Towers. Frankly, this is surprising. How does a president shrug away a major terror attack with a few words in a radio address heard by a fraction of the American people? The president's speech clearly demonstrated that he did not sense the importance of the 1993 World Trade Center bombing. Because they reveal so much, Clinton's remarks on the attack follow in full:

"Good morning. Before I talk with you about our economic program this morning, I want to say a word to the good people of New York City and to all Americans who've been so deeply affected by the tragedy that struck Manhattan yesterday." This opening suggests that Clinton didn't want to shift away from his campaign-winning "it's the economy, stupid" theme, referring to the attack as a "tragedy," a sad event, not an aggressive act requiring a strong response.

Clinton continued: "A number of innocent people lost their lives. Hundreds were injured and thousands were struck with fear in their hearts when an explosion rocked the basement of the World Trade Center. To their families, you're in the thoughts and prayers of my family and in the synagogues and churches last night; today and tomorrow, you will be remembered and thought of again and again." This is an admirable attempt at reassurance, reminiscent of Bush's consoling words following the September 11 attacks. But again, it misses the mark: these people were *murdered*, not struck by lightning.

The young president hammered away at his compassionate theme, anxious to leave no one out. "My thoughts are also with the police, the firefighters, the emergency response teams and the citizens whose countless acts of bravery averted even more bloodshed. Their reaction and their valor reminds us of how often Americans are at their best when we face the worst."

Next, Clinton came to the place where he had to report on his administration's actions and plans. These amounted to phone calls—and only phone calls. "I thank all the people who reached out to the injured and the frightened amid the tumult that shook lower Manhattan. Following the explosion, I spoke with New York's Governor Mario Cuomo and New York City Mayor David Dinkins to assure them that the full measure of federal law enforcement resources will be brought to bear on this investigation." This was a pivotal decision, though Clinton did not seem to realize its full implications at the time. The terror attack would be treated as a criminal matter, not a threat to national security. This approach would hobble Clinton's war on terror for years.

Clinton expanded on the law-enforcement theme, signaling that terrorists need not fear an armed response. "Just this morning I spoke with FBI Director Sessions, who assured me that the FBI and the Treasury Department are working closely with the New York City police and fire departments. Working together we'll find out who was involved and why this happened. Americans should know we'll do everything in our power to keep them safe in their streets, their offices and their homes. Feeling safe is an essential part of being secure.[26] And that's important to all of us."

Then, Clinton suddenly shifted the subject. "I also want to take this opportunity this morning to talk about another crucial aspect of our security, our economic security..."[27]

As the president shifted to discuss his economic package, which consumed the bulk of his speech, his voice warmed up and slowed down. It was clear to listeners, certainly those in the press, where the president's real interests lay. Almost every contemporary press account of President Clinton's Saturday radio speech leads with the details of the president's economic package and the support that he was garnering around the country.[28] And of course, the bulk of the radio address was on Clinton's economic plan.

But note that his remarks on the bombing were limited to reassuring the public and thanking the rescuers, the kind of things governors say after floods or tornadoes. Significantly, President Clinton said nothing about hunting down or punishing the perpetrators. Not even a ritualistic denunciation of "these cowardly acts" or a mention of the shock value of an attack on a skyscraping symbol of America.

Why were his words so thin? President Clinton believed that he had a historic opportunity to restore American prosperity and reposition the Democrats as the party of growth and hope. This was partly achieved over the next eight years, ironically with the help of a Republican-led Congress. Clinton also had an opportunity to transform his party on national-security issues—to overcome its 1960s-era hesitancy to use force and to remake it as a strong defender of freedom, justice, and security. Instead, Clinton shrank back. He had an opportunity to stop an escalating wave of terror attacks, guided by bin Laden, in the first weeks of his administration. But, tragically for the nation, he didn't see it.

Of course, presidents do not have the clairvoyance of historians. Yet, at the time, the president's political opponents may have seen more clearly the pivotal role the World Trade Center bombing would play in American history. On the day after the bombing, the then–minority whip of the House of Representatives, Newt Gingrich, said that the president should be "cautious" in cutting the defense budget, as Clinton planned to do. Citing the Twin Towers bombing, Gingrich said, "there's a very real requirement for human intelligence and military strength. Every time we have any display of weakness, any display of timidity. . . . There are people on the planet eager to take advantage of us."[29] These would prove to be prescient words—words, unfortunately, that Clinton did not heed.

Clinton's first historic opportunity to wage war on terrorism did not quickly drift away like a plume of smoke after the World Trade Center bombing. It lingered for days and weeks. Within days, evidence quickly accumulated that an Islamic terror cell, supported from abroad, had carried out the World Trade Center attack. There were front-page newspaper stories about the arrest of Mohammed Salameh and the presence of a network of dangerous Islamic radicals, with a hub in Jersey City. Yet the president appeared uninterested.

President Clinton did not visit the World Trade Center in 1993. Perhaps, if he had, he might have understood the enormity of the damage. What might have happened if Clinton had seen the immense crater or talked to the family of Monica Smith?

Four days after the attack, Clinton was across the Hudson River in New Brunswick, New Jersey, discussing job-training programs. There, he urged the public not to "overreact" to the World Trade

Center bombing.[30] But he didn't cross the river and see the damage for himself. [31]

It would have taken a few minutes, but Clinton did not bother.

Why didn't he go? One implausible rationale offered by Clinton officials is that unnamed New York officials urged the president to avoid the site.[32] One senior Clinton official—through an anonymous quote in the *Boston Globe*—noted that "Clinton had a full schedule in New Jersey, with no opening for a visit to the site in Manhattan."[33] Full schedule. The site in Manhattan. The sheer clinical distance of those words, days after the attack, speaks volumes.

Dick Morris, offers two more likely explanations. Clinton saw himself as a comforter who needed to reassure an anxious public (in New Jersey, he urged Americans to "keep your courage up and go about your lives"[34]) and he saw the attack as a criminal matter, not a terror strike. "In what is likely, in retrospect, to be judged the single greatest omission of his presidency, Clinton chose to treat the Trade Center attack as an isolated criminal act, devoid of serious foreign policy or military implications," writes Morris.[35] Clinton just didn't get it.

Over the next month, the president made four fateful decisions. He did not keep the bombing before the public with speeches and actions. He left the case in the hands of the FBI, which was headed by a man he did not trust and was waiting to fire. He treated the bombing as a law-enforcement matter, not a counter-intelligence investigation, thus cutting the CIA out of the fight against terrorism. And he did not even meet with his handpicked CIA director to consider alternative approaches to combating international terrorism aimed at Americans. This ensured future victories for bin Laden.

LANGLEY, VIRGINIA—Frustration was growing at CIA headquarters. The Counter-Terrorism Center was kept away from the World Trade Center investigation—even though the CTC was designed to be the center of information on terrorist threats. The State Department, the FBI, and the Secret Service had detailed personnel to the CTC to make sure that important information was shared, not hidden behind bureaucratic bulwarks. Indeed, one of the reasons that the deputy director of the CTC was an FBI official was to guarantee that information was shared among the institutions.

If the Clinton Administration wanted to conduct a joint counterterrorism operation to discover the full breadth of the 1993 World Trade Center bombing conspiracy and to take action against the perpetrators overseas, the CTC would have been the perfect vehicle. That is what it was designed to do. It also had a secret presidential "finding," written by President Reagan and still in force, which specifically allowed covert operations to smash terrorist cells.[36]

But the FBI, with the president's tacit acceptance, was treating the World Trade Center attack as a law-enforcement matter. That meant that everything the FBI gathered, every lab test result, every scrap of paper, every interview, every lead, every clue from overseas was theirs alone. No one outside of the FBI's New York office would see it for years.

How could the FBI keep the evidence from other terror-fighting agencies? This was actually standard procedure when the FBI conducted criminal cases, as opposed to strictly counterterrorism investigations. The FBI invoked rule 6E of the Federal Rules of Criminal Procedure. If the FBI shared the information with other federal agencies, then a judge could rule the evidence inadmissible in a court or require the government to share it with the accused terrorists, so that they could mount an effective legal defense. That would provide the accused terrorists with vital information about what the federal government knew and what it didn't. So Rule 6E was designed to prevent information sharing— and preserve the government's evidence for trial. "It is not that they [the FBI and CIA] don't get along—it's that they can't share information by legal statute" in criminal cases said Christopher

Whitcomb, an FBI veteran who worked on the 1993 World Trade Center bombing investigation.[37]

Jim Woolsey, the director of Central Intelligence, fumed. Any twenty-four-year-old junior agent in the FBI's New York office knew more about the largest-ever terrorist attack on American soil than he did. "It was frustrating," Woolsey told the author. "Nobody outside the prosecutorial team and maybe the FBI had access" to information about the case.[38]

The CIA's Counter-Terrorism Center itself could only follow a few scattered scraps of intelligence. And, even though they passed information on to the FBI, the CIA had no way of knowing if they were supplying the FBI with redundant data or vital clues.

As a result, both the CIA and the FBI missed several key connections between Ramzi Yousef and Osama bin Laden. Yousef had stayed in bin Laden-owned guesthouses in Pakistan, both before and after the World Trade Center attack. When he was finally arrested in 1995, Yousef had several pictures of Osama bin Laden (posing with machine guns) in his baggage and a business card from Khalid Shaikh Mohammed, a relative of bin Laden's, in his wallet.

The CIA would not learn the full details of the 1993 World Trade Center bombing until the FBI made its evidence public—at the end of the first trial in 1996. And even then, the critical evidence was supplied to the CIA by an independent investigator, Laurie Mylroie, who told the author that she photocopied it and handed it to the agency.[39]

NEW YORK—The FBI worked quickly. On the same day as Clinton's speech, investigators found the differential housing from the bomb van. A vehicle identification number stamped on it allowed them to trace it to the leasing agency in New Jersey. The manager said one Arab man had stopped to collect his $400 deposit. That man turned out to be Mohammed Salameh, who desperately needed the money to pay for a plane ticket. The few dollars Yousef had given him was for an infant's plane fare; without the money to upgrade the ticket he would be trapped. That was what Yousef wanted. This is how "expendables" are used.

The FBI arrested Salameh in a sting operation at the leasing office. His phone records and storage unit keys connected the rest of the dots. But Yousef escaped and the quick initial successes of the investigation masked missed clues of a wider conspiracy, including a number of intriguing connections between Osama bin Laden and the World Trade Center bombing.

For years, the New York FBI office knew about a growing network of Islamic extremists in the tri-state area, but until the 1993 World Trade Center bombing the agents couldn't even open a full investigation. Again, bureaucracy got in the way. To begin an investigation—according to both the official Department of Justice guidelines and various statutes passed by Congress—required that agents have evidence that a crime had been committed or was under way. Sometimes, supervisors would not approve an investigation even if there was evidence of criminal activity, if the crime seemed insignificant. In practical terms, that meant that the FBI could investigate terrorists after Americans were dead, but not before.

And, in 1993, the idea of punishing small, seemingly insignificant crimes as a way of preventing larger ones had not yet taken hold. The FBI was aware that many Islamic radicals were training with weapons at Connecticut and Pennsylvania gun ranges. Indeed, one of the 1993 World Trade Center bombers, Mohammed Salameh, was identified as one of those participants. But arresting these men on weapons charges or investigating the wider purposes behind such "training" was shrugged off as a minor affair. Target shooting is not a crime, while owning a gun without a proper permit is a minor one. The FBI was also barred from monitoring the mosque in Jersey City where the World Trade Center bombers met, on the grounds of religious freedom. All of these internal, bureaucratic restrictions made life easier for bin Laden's cells, both inside and outside the United States.

Still, individual FBI agents valiantly tried to make a difference. A number of special agents knew that some Brooklyn and Jersey City residents—many from the same two mosques that were frequented by Salameh and other bombers—were taking their "vacations" in Afghanistan to wage jihad, even years after the Soviet Union had retreated. Some New York agents considered investigating these men for violating the Neutrality Act, which makes it a crime for an American citizen to fight in another nation's war. But, the agents soon discovered, most of the suspects were legal residents or illegal aliens, not citizens. The Neutrality Act did not apply to them. So, in most terrorism cases before the 1993 World Trade Center bombing, the FBI could do little to counter the growing network of militants training and arming themselves in its midst.

And no one at the FBI—at headquarters or in the New York office—realized that one of the FBI's most-trusted informants was a "double agent," working for both the Feds and Osama bin Laden.

An Egyptian soldier named Ali Mohammed received a U.S. visa in 1985.[40] He later became a U.S. citizen and obtained a military security clearance. He seemed to have an encyclopedic knowledge of violent Islamic radicals and had been a very helpful source for both the CIA and the FBI. At the time, those agencies did not know why Mohammed was so well informed.

By 1987, Mohammed was working at the U.S. Army's warfare planning center at Fort Bragg. Part of his job was to lecture American soldiers about Muslim terrorists. He certainly knew his subject.

Mohammed did not mention that he was still an active member of the Egyptian Islamic Jihad. That terrorist group was run by Ayman al-Zawahiri, who soon became bin Laden's second-in-command. Nor did Mohammed mention that he had played host and tour guide to Zawahiri on his two visits to America.[41] Mohammed had also met Osama bin Laden many times in Khartoum and had trained bin Laden's bodyguards, according to his own admissions in court documents.[42]

Concedes Larry Johnson, a former CIA officer and a counterterrorism official at the State Department, "He was an active source for the FBI, a double agent."[43]

The FBI had good reason to be suspicious of Mohammed—if its agents had been paying attention.

When Rabbi Meir Kahane, founder of the Jewish Defense League, was gunned down by El Sayyid Nosair in 1990, the murder was treated as a hate crime, not terrorism. The New York Police Department eventually uncovered enough evidence to indict Nosair. The FBI monitored the case but did not intervene. "I was in charge of bureau operations at the time," Buck Revell explained, "and I never received any information that the assassin of Meir Kahane was connected with any sort of organization that might have a terrorist agenda."[44]

The FBI was in the dark because, tragically, the New York Police Department and the FBI's own special agents missed several important clues. In the course of the investigation of the Kahane murder, documents were seized from Nosair's apartment that, when finally translated years later, proved to be U.S. Army manuals—some marked "top secret"—that had been translated into Arabic by Mohammed. Since the police and the FBI had not yet translated the documents, they did not investigate exactly how Nosair came into possession of them. If they had, they would have learned that Nosair was introduced to Mohammed by a man named Khalid Ibrahim, who had run a fundraising operation for Osama bin Laden's various organizations since 1989.[45] They also would have learned that Mohammed had conducted weapons training—sometimes using semiautomatic rifles—for Nosair, Ibrahim, and Abouhalima. (Abouhalima drove the getaway car for the 1993 World Trade Center attack.)[46]

Abouhalima was also tied to Ibrahim's Alkifah Refugee Center in Brooklyn, where money for bin Laden was raised. Finally, Abouhalima was a part-time driver for Sheik Omar Abdel Rahman, the blind Egyptian cleric who was later convicted of "seditious conspiracy" in a wide-ranging plot to blow up the Holland Tunnel—when it was packed with rush-hour traffic—and other plans to destroy New York landmarks.[47]

Indeed many of the World Trade Center bombers met each other though the blind cleric's mosque, a dark, dirty series of rooms located over a cheap Chinese restaurant in Jersey City. The mosque where the bombers met was called Masjid al-Salaam, the "mosque of peace."[48]

But all of these connections eluded the FBI, in large part because the bureau did not translate Nosair's mysterious documents for several years and because of the bureaucratic barriers on their proposed investigations. Nor did the FBI fully investigate phone calls to Iraq and other Middle Eastern nations made by the World Trade Center bombers. So the terrorist conspiracy continued—under the nose of the FBI.

Meanwhile, Mohammed continued to work for bin Laden. He flew to Sudan to train bin Laden's personal bodyguard. According to U.S. district court documents, he also taught small-unit tactics and helped survey several U.S. embassies in East Africa in late 1993, which would be bombed five years later. Those blasts would kill hundreds in a few fiery minutes.

KHARTOUM, SUDAN—Osama bin Laden, safe and unsuspected, heard the news of the World Trade Center bombing at his palatial house in the Riyadh section of Khartoum. He was thrilled and ordered that special prayer services of thanksgiving be held that night.[49]

In some subsequent interviews, Osama bin Laden claimed he didn't know Yousef. "Ramzi Yousef, after the World Trade Center bombing, became a well-known Muslim personality, and all Muslims know him. Unfortunately, I did not know him before the incident," bin Laden told ABC News in 1998. "America will see many youths who will follow Ramzi Yousef."[50]

Bin Laden's claim that he didn't know of Ramzi Yousef before the 1993 World Trade Center bombing is probably another expedient lie.[51] Certainly, Yousef traveled in circles of people who knew bin Laden before the bombing and worked alongside al Qaeda operatives after the bombing. And bin Laden does not appear to have personally known the September 11 hijackers either. Today federal court indictments and an array of publicly available FBI documents list bin Laden's attacks on America. Nearly every such list includes the 1993 World Trade Center bombing.

Meanwhile, bin Laden was planning another attack, one far closer to home. As he celebrated the first World Trade Center bombing, bin Laden was waiting for a report from Abu Hafs, the commander of his military wing. Hafs had just returned from Mogadishu, Somalia.

CHAPTER THREE

THE BATTLE OF
THE BLACK SEA

MOGADISHU, SOMALIA—An American UH-60 Black Hawk helicopter swept over the crumbling skyline of Mogadishu sometime after 2 A.M. on September 25, 1993. It was known by its radio call-sign as Courage 53.

The fate of its five-man crew would not feature in the grim headlines that would emerge from Somalia a week later. Nor would it be found in the bestselling book *Black Hawk Down*, or the blockbuster movie that followed. (Only Lawrence E. Casper in his book, *Falcon Brigade*, noted the fate of Courage 53 and he was one of the commanders on the ground at the time.) The story of Courage 53 was a kind of "coming attraction" for the worst American military defeat since the Vietnam War.

Most likely, the air crew did not see the flash of the rocket-propelled grenade launcher fired from more than one hundred feet below, hidden somewhere in the tangle of dusty alleys.

But they felt it. A red ball flashed somewhere beneath the belly of the Black Hawk. Its fuel tanks exploded.

Inside, an inferno raged. The flames, in the words of an American senior officer on the ground in Mogadishu, were "responding to the one hundred-knot wind [rushing in] like oxygen to acetylene in a blowtorch."[1]

Two crewmen in the rear were eaten alive by the flames. A third crawled forward into the tiny cockpit. But there was no refuge. The fire surged forward and the searing heat reflected back off the curved canopy.[2]

The Black Hawk was a falling comet with five Americans aboard. As the warning horns blared and the fire raged inside, pilot Dale Shrader desperately fought to keep control. With a mangled tail rotor, the helicopter was spiraling downward. Shrader's training worked faster than his thoughts. He switched off one of the blazing engines and tried to compensate for the loss of the rear rotor by increasing the power to the main blades. It was no use.

The helicopter screamed across the roof of a ruined building, cut the neck of a telephone pole, and plunged into the street, plowing a furrow one hundred yards long. What was left of Courage 53 smashed into an embankment.

Somehow, the two pilots survived. Shrader clawed his way out of the burning hulk with a broken wrist. He found his copilot, Perry Alliman, blinded and burned, and pulled him to safety. Shrader ran back to rescue the other crewmen. But he was driven back by a series of explosions. The fire had found the ammunition on board. There were no other survivors.

Suddenly the street came to life. Somali militiamen appeared with AK-47s and grenades. Shrader shrank back into the shadows. But they were soon spotted. Shrader desperately radioed for help.

A man ran toward them with a grenade in his hand. Shrader fired his 9-mm pistol. The man disappeared. Other Somalis lobbed grenades, but the two airmen were lucky. For now.

The Somalis were reckless and relentless in their attacks. All around them, the pilots could see the muzzle flashes of hostile fire and hear the crack of bullets. In the darkness the attackers were a growing mass of faint shapes. Shrader fired his pistol to hold back the mob. Gradually, the Somali forces became bolder and more visible to the downed pilot. One ran toward the Americans, blindly spraying bullets from his AK-47. Shrader had one bullet left. He dared not fire too soon. The attacker kept coming. Bullet holes scored the bricks around the trapped pilots. Shrader squeezed off his last round, dropping the man.

Now the Americans were desperate. They were alone and out of ammunition. So far, their attackers had likely been "irregulars," a pickup team of volunteers armed with their own automatic weapons and grenades. Their tactics and their marksmanship suggested a lack of formal military training—though they were deadly enough thanks to years of street fighting in Somalia's civil war. But the forces of General Mohammed Farrah Aideed, an anti-American warlord backed by bin Laden, were mostly former Somali Army regulars. They were professional killers. Their shots would be better aimed and their assaults better coordinated. And they were never long in coming.

The gunfire died down momentarily.

"American boys! American boys!"[3]

Was it a taunt by his attackers or had a rescue party finally arrived? Cautiously, Shrader wandered out into an alley. He saw an armored personnel carrier and a soldier with a flashlight. His desperate radio message had gotten through. Shrader and Alliman were rescued by a United Arab Emirates patrol. America's United Nations allies and their armor had saved the day. It would not be the last time.

Later that day, American troops from the Tenth Mountain Division would fight their way to the wreckage only to find that the bodies of the three remaining airmen had been cremated inside the molten husk of the helicopter.[4] There were few remains to recover. Before the American soldiers arrived, an enterprising Somali had dragged part of the charred corpse of an American from the wreckage. He stuffed the burnt body parts into a food-relief bag. The next day, he dragged the bag through the streets and charged passersby for a look inside. Stenciled on the food bag was "Gift from the U.S.A."[5]

Courage 53 was the first American Black Hawk helicopter to be shot out of the skies of Mogadishu, but it wouldn't be the last. Like the Aden bombing and the World Trade Center blast, it was a warning shot that went unheeded at the highest levels of the Clinton Administration.

It was also the start of a grim pattern: A mighty Black Hawk brought down; its crew killed or cut off; a shortage of ammunition; bravery by the Americans and audacity by their attackers; dead Americans exhibited for sport; and finally, a rescue by America's Third World allies. The events chronicled in *Black Hawk Down* would precisely follow this pattern.

The most powerful nation on earth had sent away its tanks and armored personnel carriers months earlier. Local commanders made repeated requests to bring them back. As recently as September 14, 1993, Major General Thomas Montgomery had formally asked for the deployment of tanks and other armored vehicles. General Montgomery's commander, General Joe Hoar, and Colin Powell, chairman of the Joint Chiefs of Staff, scaled down, but approved, the request. But Clinton's Secretary of Defense, Les Aspin, vetoed it on September 23, just days before the Battle of the Black Sea. Aspin thought that the presence of American tanks would signal politically unacceptable "escalation."[6]

So the lessons of the loss of Courage 53—the vulnerability of the Black Hawks to rocket-propelled grenades and the importance of armor for ground operations in a largely hostile metropolis—remained unlearned.

Soon Aideed, the Somali warlord, backed by training from Osama bin Laden's most hardened fighters, would conduct a more deadly tutorial. Eight days later, the events memorialized in *Black Hawk Down* and in countless newspaper articles would unfold in more than twelve hours of bloody fighting.

LANGLEY, VIRGINIA—CIA headquarters sent the first major operations team to Mogadishu in June 1993. These agents recruited twenty major informants as well as a wealth of lesser snitchers. But the quality of the "actionable intelligence" was spotty, the *Washington Post* reported.[7]

CIA officers had introduced money as a "control factor" but it often bought lies, not information. Even when the reports were genuine, they often weren't helpful. The informants generally refused to go out after dark—denying American forces timely tactical information. That meant Aideed, the Somali warlord, would have to be captured in the daylight, ensuring that Special Forces, with their night-vision goggles, could not conduct an after-dark extraction. In daylight, Somali snipers could lurk unseen in the dark hollows of buildings while American forces had to work under a dazzling sun. So the shortcomings of intelligence greatly increased the risks to American peacekeepers.

And, like many intelligence informants, the Somali recruits were unpredictable and unstable. The CIA's top informant died in August 1993, when he shot himself in the head playing Russian roulette.[8]

While human intelligence was poor, signal intelligence was virtually nonexistent. The CIA and military intelligence operations teams learned little from monitoring Somali radio traffic, because the Somalis were clever enough to outwit high-tech surveillance with an ancient strategy. The warlords sent sensitive messages by courier—ensuring that America's costly listening devices and spy satellites could not monitor their communications. In the field, Somalis used burning tires to send smoke signals or banged on metal cans to send messages. Only occasional intercepts of the low-power radios used by enemy mortar crews for their daily attacks on Americans provided clues about the foe's movements and plans. Those intercepts provide tantalizing clues about bin Laden's involvement.

Back at headquarters, the Counter-Terrorism Center deployed a team of specialists to track terrorist threats to American forces in East Africa. The analysts were mostly worried about Stingers, a shoulder-launched missile that the CIA had indirectly supplied to the Afghan resistance in the 1980s. These weapons had brought down scores of Soviet helicopter gunships. The Stinger spelled the beginning of the end for the Soviets.

But a covert operation in the early 1990s to buy up Stingers in Afghan and Pakistani arms markets had largely failed. Hundreds of these powerful weapons were unaccounted for—and could turn up in Somalia. Al Qaeda operatives were believed to have transported Stingers to nearby Sudan in 1991. And an international black market could easily have supplied Stingers. What if those Stingers were used against America's Black Hawks?

Without helicopters, American forces in Somalia would be marooned in poorly defended isles—the New Port, the university, the old U.S. embassy, the old Soviet airport—surrounded by Aideed's murderous militiamen. Retreat or defeat would be the only real options.

So headquarters kept pressing the agents on the ground to look for Stingers. But investigating the clandestine shipment of Stingers would be nearly impossible, local CIA officials knew. Searching for Stingers was written off as a "CYA operation,"[9] another attempt by headquarters to shield itself from criticism if things went badly.

Besides, intelligence was having a hard enough time tracking small-arms shipments. In the first few months of 1993, when the U.S. Marines ran operations in Somalia, many weapons were confiscated and fewer people were seen toting machine guns. But the UN peacekeeping force deployed in the spring of 1993 had much more restrictive rules of engagement and spent little time disarming Somali militias. It was "too dangerous."

The result was a surge of small arms in the hands of khat-chewing militias.[10] "The Marines had laid down the law," Captain Lee Rysewyk, who had served in Mogadishu, wrote in an unpublished report the author obtained from Fort Benning, Georgia. "Now UN soldiers could no longer confiscate small arms.... Consequently, the Somalis dug up weapons from hidden caches or snuck them into the city in fifty-five-gallon drums, unchecked by UN soldiers."[11] Without the help of the allied soldiers on the ground, U.S. intelligence was unable to track the alarming increase in Somali firepower. It would prove easy for bin Laden to bring in men and arms.

As it happened, the warlords of Mogadishu didn't need Stingers. They had found another weapon, cheaper, closer at hand, and equally deadly: the simple Soviet-made rocket-propelled grenade launcher. This is the weapon that Arab Afghans had used to bring down Soviet helicopters. Now they would transfer their techniques to their anti-American allies in Somalia.

KHARTOUM, SUDAN—Osama bin Laden's house in Sudan is pinkish. The capital city of Sudan is a dusty settlement of winding roads and run-down buildings that straddle the confluence of the Blue and White Nile rivers. Khartoum was bin Laden's home for more than four years.

Jackknifing off the main road that passes the Khartoum Military Airport, where bin Laden kept his plane, a visitor turns onto a wide potholed dirt street. The road verges past empty lots and flows into the Riyadh neighborhood, a wealthy enclave of Sudanese and foreigners who made their money in the Middle East and came to Sudan to build multi-story concrete houses ringed by painted cement walls topped with razor wire or broken glass. Behind the gates lay hidden gardens kept green with expensive water and cheap caretakers. Sometimes a sunken swimming pool casts a glittering light on the palm fronds visible from the road or, in the harsh sunlight of the afternoon, a satellite dish winks back at a visitor.

On El Meshtal Street, a visitor finds bin Laden's walled compound.[12] The exterior walls are pink and faded to filth. The house is not the most opulent in this Sudanese version of Bel Air. It is a vaguely Art Deco affair, three stories high, with a ridge running up its front.

Everything about the exterior of the house indicates comfort. An aluminum-frame walkway topped with thin wooden slats assures shade from the driveway to the front door. Air conditioners hum. The shrubbery is thick and green. A water-hungry willow tree, planted at bin Laden's request, rises nearby.[13]

It was almost as if bin Laden had decided to make up for the hardships that he and his four wives had endured in Afghanistan during the 1980s. For bin Laden and his family, the house represented both the start of a new life and the continuation of the old. It was larger and more comfortable than their quarters in Afghanistan and Pakistan, but often used for the same purpose: planning terrorist attacks.

In Sudan, bin Laden commanded a commercial army of road-builders, airport-concrete pourers, animal-hide tanners, horse breeders, bridge builders, bankers, bakers, and farmers. But they were just the base of a larger pyramid of account managers, record-keepers, and moneymen. At its peak was a tall, bearded chief executive who used it all to finance the largest private terror network in the world.[14]

Flanking his house is a series of walled-in compounds. Bin Laden owned guest houses on both sides of the street. These were the homes of his top officers. Traveling terrorists would receive temporary accommodation at the guest houses beside his home. Bin Laden maintained an office on the second floor.[15] But he often preferred to sit on plastic chairs in the front yard and talk jihad with the men.[16]

For the past few years, bin Laden had been hoping to raise his status in Islamist circles. While he was regarded as a hero for his still murky but much-exaggerated role in fighting the Soviets in Afghanistan, that luster had faded. According to Sudanese government officials, bin Laden was seen as a fundraiser and pious Muslim, but not as an organizer of daring terror operations. One Arabic-language pro-Islamist newspaper, *Al-Quds al-Arabi*, reported that Sudanese officials regarded bin Laden then as "a moving bank."[17]

Bin Laden wanted to change that image. The Aden bombing that had failed to kill American soldiers had nevertheless succeeded in driving U.S. forces from Yemen. That was one success. He had driven the infidels from the birthplace of his father, Mohammed bin Awaz bin Laden. Bin Laden's loose links—including funding some of the plotters in the 1993 World Trade Center bombing—also raised his status. But these achievements were not enough. He was determined to be a major leader in the Islamist movement.

How would the expatriate Saudi millionaire make his mark? Being a "moving bank" for Sudan's Islamic revolutionaries only took one so far. Bin Laden saw his chance in nearby Somalia.

The American troops in Somalia were a perfect Islamist target. One window into bin Laden's thinking comes from Ayman Zawahiri, the head of Egyptian Islamic Jihad, and bin Laden's personal doctor (and ideological mentor by many accounts). Zawahiri listed the ideological enemies of his brand of militant Islam in a book called *Knights Under the Prophet's Banner*.[18] In addition to the United States and Russia, he cited six enemies of Islamism: "the United Nations, the friendly [to the West] rulers of the Muslim people, the multinational corporations, the international communications and data-exchange systems, the international news agencies and satellite media channels, [and] the international relief agencies, which are being used as a cover for espionage, proselytizing, coup planning, and the transfer of weapons."

Somalia combined almost all of these ideological enemies in one large, unsuspecting target. The peacekeeping effort was run by the United Nations. Somalia's Muslim rulers were friendly to the West (and in dire need of Western aid) and had welcomed American troops. The international news media and scores of relief agencies were thick on the ground. And, in the eyes of Islamists, these news organizations and relief agencies had helped turn the American government against the pro-Islamist Somali warlords.

Equally important, Somalia was within operational reach of bin

Laden's base in Sudan. It was close enough to reach by truck across one of the longest essentially unguarded frontiers in East Africa. Bin Laden had already established training camps inside Somalia, near the Kenyan border.[19] Finally, bin Laden had a good working relationship with Al Itihaad al Islamiya, a Somali Islamist terror group that he helped bankroll.

Bin Laden wasn't about to let this opportunity escape. To an Islamist with bin Laden's cast of mind, the American target in Somalia would seem like a gift from Allah.

While the public record on bin Laden's operations in Somalia is sparse, numerous interviews with American, Sudanese, and other intelligence sources reveal the details of bin Laden's initial combat with American forces. While these accounts are impossible to verify, the author was shown and had independently translated Sudanese intelligence documents that support much of what follows. On balance, it seems reliable. What emerges is the first detailed account of bin Laden's plot to kill American soldiers.

The Somalia operation began when bin Laden met with a man variously known as Mohammed Atef and Abu Hafs al Masry,[20] and known to his terrorist comrades as "the commander."

Bin Laden dispatched Atef to Somalia on a scouting mission sometime in early 1993, according to a Sudanese intelligence source. There he observed U.S. military operations and met with local members of Al Itihaad al Islamiya. Through that terrorist network, Atef (according to Sudanese intelligence) met with several Somali warlords, including Mohammed Farrah Aideed—the emerging nemesis of America.

One of the few known pictures of Mohammed Atef shows a man with a thick black beard, olive skin, and narrowed eyes, wearing a white turban. He was an Egyptian who had fought in Afghanistan in the 1980s and co-founded al Qaeda. By 1993, he was the head of the military committee of bin Laden's organization, and he was one of bin Laden's most-trusted subordinates. One measure of that trust was that Atef was designated to be bin Laden's successor, in the event of bin Laden's capture or death.[21] Another measure of that trust was that Atef personally supervised bin Laden's most important and dangerous operations, including Somalia.[22]

Atef's trips to Somalia were short and, upon his return, he always sped directly from the airport to bin Laden, the head of Sudanese intelligence told the author during a visit to Khartoum in March 2002. Shortly after Atef's first expedition to Somalia, bin Laden began to supply arms and training for Aideed.[23] Bin Laden sent a team of bomb makers and guerrilla-warfare specialists to help the Somali warlord, according to portions of Sudan intelligence files made available to the author on a 2002 visit to Khartoum.

Bin Laden's team was led by Mohammed Ibrahim Makawi, another veteran of the Afghan war and longtime bin Laden associate, according to the same intelligence sources. He is also known as Saif al-Adl al-Maduni. A former Egyptian army officer, Makawi was also linked to Zawahiri's Egyptian Islamic Jihad, suggesting that the operational coordination between the two terror groups—al Qaeda and Egyptian Islamic Jihad—is much older and much closer than has previously been reported.

Sudanese intelligence, which observed Makawi talking with bin Laden on several occasions, believes that he was designated to be Atef's successor. In his trips to Somalia, Makawi would transit through Nairobi, using a Yemeni passport. Most interestingly, he is believed to have been in Aden during the bombing of hotels frequented by U.S. troops in December 1992. He may in fact have been the operation's field commander.

One of Makawi's particular skills was the use of rocket launchers. Rocket launchers are designed to strike targets on the ground, usually tanks and bunkers. When the shoulder-slung weapon is fired, hot explosive gases are expelled from the rear of the tube. Soldiers are taught to keep the rocket launcher parallel with the ground; otherwise the explosive back-blast could burn them. Standard training does not envision firing up; such a maneuver would probably kill the shooter.

In Somalia, Makawi demonstrated an innovation that al Qaeda had developed in the Afghan war.[24] By crouching in a particular way and leaning at a forty-five-degree angle, a shooter can safely fire at objects in the sky. Another technique involved a shooter climbing trees to fire at helicopters.

Makawi also showed the Somalis how to tamper with the charge so that it would explode after traveling a shorter-than-usual distance. That allowed a battery of shooters to set up a low-hanging curtain of shrapnel just above the horizon. Combine these two skills and you have a perfect technique for bringing down helicopters.

From their experience in Afghanistan, bin Laden's men knew that the weakest part of a helicopter is the tail rotor. If shrapnel from a constant barrage of rocket-propelled grenades shredded the tail rotor, the helicopter would fall.

Other bin Laden associates, including Abu Obeida al-Bansheeri, taught the Somalis about the most effective use of mortars, which were regularly deployed against American troop barracks. Another al Qaeda operative, Mohammed Saddiq Odeh, who was later convicted of twelve counts of murder for his role in the bomb attack on the U.S. embassy in Nairobi, Kenya, told FBI agents that he had trained Somali militia to fight American and United Nations forces in Somalia.[25]

And bin Laden's men may have done more than teach. One U.S. Army Captain, James Francis Yacone, testified that U.S. military intelligence in Mogadishu intercepted radio signals from enemy mortar crews in Arabic.[26] Those Arabic commands provided targeting information, so that mortar crews could more accurately hit American soldiers. Several Americans were killed in mortar attacks in the course of the Somalia campaign and more than a dozen were wounded. Captain Yacone, the Black Hawk helicopter squadron commander, recalled, "The reason I remember the Arabic intercepts of intel being given to us was because that was thought to be unique, the fact that we were picking up Arabic, adjusting mortar rounds on us, so that led intel briefing to say, hey, there may be other people here training Aideed's clan."[27]

Few Somalis speak Arabic.[28] But bin Laden's men do.

Al Qaeda also seems to have engaged in shoot-outs with American troops. An October 4, 2001, report by the British government flatly states, "On 3 and 4 October 1993, operatives of al Qaeda participated in the attack on U.S. military personnel serving in Somalia."[29]

To assure secrecy, the team in Somalia made its progress reports in person to Atef, who made several trips to Mogadishu in the spring and summer of 1993, a senior Sudanese intelligence official told the author. These reports were then relayed to bin Laden. They had spent months planning a deadly surprise. Now they were ready.

THE WHITE HOUSE—Three days before President Clinton ordered his first military strike against terrorists, he was sitting in a parlor near the Lincoln Bedroom in the residence portion of the White House. It was after eight P.M. on June 23, 1993, and the fading summer light filtered in through large windows.[30]

Clinton had grown more confident. He no longer thought like a governor who treated terrorist attacks as natural disasters. But while he was willing to deploy American power, he was addicted to cautious half-measures and perhaps a lingering distrust of the U.S. military.

Seated around the president were National Security Advisor Tony Lake and his deputy Sandy Berger, Vice President Al Gore and his advisor Leon Fuerth, Secretary of State Warren Christopher, Chairman of the Joint Chiefs of Staff Colin Powell, Defense Secretary Les Aspin, Chief of Staff Mack McLarty, and special advisors David Gergen and George Stephanopoulos.[31] It was a war council.

In April 1993, Kuwaiti intelligence uncovered a plot to kill former President George Bush. Bush was in Kuwait to receive an award for liberating that nation during the 1991 Gulf War. But his Gulf War enemy, Saddam Hussein, had other plans. Iraqi intelligence had supervised the construction of a massive car bomb to be detonated near the forty-first president's motorcade. Kuwaiti police later arrested fourteen men, many of whom had links to Iraqi intelligence. President Clinton had ordered separate investigations by the CIA and the FBI to determine if the Iraqi dictator was indeed behind the plot. The dual investigations took months. While certainty is a very difficult thing to find in clandestine affairs, eventually, the accumulated evidence was "overwhelming," Lake told the author.

Clinton's questions were focused on "Is this truly a proportionate response?" and "How can we minimize the harm to innocent civilians?"[32] But his concerns had nothing to do with Catholic "just war theory" and everything to do with his 1960s antiwar skepticism about military force, and of course, his innate political caution. The ideas of "proportionate response" and "harm reduction" emerged from the chaos of 1960s antiwar efforts.

A tough-minded realist might have approached the matter differently. "Proportionate responses" are notoriously hard to calibrate, nor can a realist ignore the possibility that a single, knock-out blow can end a conflict that might otherwise continue to take innocent lives. While reducing the risk of harming civilians is essential, it often means that the perpetrators escape injury as well. That, too, tends to prolong hostilities. But such realist arguments were rarely aired in the Clinton Administration.

After hours of deliberations, President Clinton decided on a cruise-missile strike.

From the Oval Office on the quiet Saturday afternoon of June 26, 1993, the president gave the final order. Moments later, twenty-three Tomahawk cruise missiles streaked across the skies of southern Iraq toward Baghdad. Their mission: to lay waste the headquarters of the Iraqi Mukhabarat, Saddam Hussein's feared external intelligence service. It was after midnight in Baghdad and the target was deserted.

Saddam Hussein's punishment for plotting to kill a former American president was the destruction of an empty building in central Baghdad. Clinton wanted to minimize casualties. The missile strike was most likely not seen as a sign of strength by an Iraqi dictator who would casually order executions over lunch. Instead, it must have seemed like timidity and toothlessness.

The Iraqi dictator was not the only one of America's enemies to notice. Bin Laden soon learned of the attack, which made headlines in the Arab press. Bin Laden could not have missed Clinton's low-risk strategy. If the arch-terrorist tried to kill Americans, he risked little more than some empty buildings.

President Clinton was even less decisive with Somalia. He was not following the situation closely. Until the debacle in Mogadishu in October 1993, there was no meeting of the top decision makers to discuss the U.S. military operation in the country.[33] Their deputies were charged with making most of the decisions regarding Somalia. Lake told the author that he was "pissed off" when Secretary of State Warren Christopher later tried to pin the blame for the debacle on the deputies. In any administration there has to be a division of labor—and Lake himself was absorbed with the ongoing tragedy in Bosnia. And, of course, the deputies were acting within parameters set by their respective superiors, including Lake and Christopher. Still, Somalia was a looming problem for the Clinton White House. Clinton's political analysts recognized that any political benefit that could be wrung from that East African humanitarian adventure had already been extracted by the previous president, George H. W. Bush. He had sent U.S. troops to stop the attacks on aid convoys, whose goal was to feed the starving. The political liabilities were left for Clinton, in their view.

Now Clinton was stuck with what Bush's ambassador to Kenya, Smith Hempstone, had called a "tar baby." Hempstone warned

President Bush in the early days of Operation Restore Hope in Somalia, "Somalis, as the Italians and the British learned to their discomfiture, are natural-born guerrillas. They will mine the roads. They will lay ambushes. They will launch hit-and-run attacks."[34] This is exactly what happened.

The longer American troops stayed in Somalia, the more restive Congress and the American people became, but if Clinton withdrew the military quickly, he would be blamed for Somalia's collapse into anarchy. The Clinton Administration thought it had devised a brilliant political solution in the spring of 1993. The Somalia operation was turned over to the United Nations. But UN Secretary-General Boutros Boutros Ghali had demanded one concession: that a token force of some one thousand American combat troops would remain as part of the UN contingent.[35] This didn't solve President Clinton's political problem—American troops were still in harm's way and far from home, on a mission that most of the public thought had long since been accomplished. All the president had done was to reduce the potential number of American casualties, and reduce America's strength in a volatile region.

UN control added other problems. One was Boutros Ghali himself.[36] The UN Secretary-General was an Egyptian—indeed, he had been Egypt's ambassador to Somalia—and for that reason was viewed with deep suspicion by many of Somalia's clan leaders. Egypt, with its vast intelligence services and diplomatic corps, was blamed for intrigue in Somalia's long civil war. Boutros Ghali and the warlord general Aideed knew and despised each other. The UN Secretary-General simply didn't seem to be neutral.

Another problem was inexperience. The United Nations had never before deployed a large, combat-ready force under its own command in an active war zone. Usually, the United States handled such operations under a UN imprimatur. Turning operations directly over to the UN was a Clintonian innovation—and as things would turn out, not a particularly good solution.

Finally, the UN imported a slumgullion of language barriers and cultural differences into Somalia. By September 15, 1993, the UN had 18,800 troops from thirty-two countries—ranging from Bangladesh to Sweden—on the ground in Mogadishu, under the command of a Turkish general. The Nigerians, Pakistanis, and Malaysians theoretically shared the English language (at least among the officers) and a close understanding of Islam, but in practice they often disagreed bitterly.

Perhaps the Italians, the former colonial masters of Somalia, caused the biggest headaches. "The Italians paid off clan elders to not bother their troops, and even fed them information about UN operations," writes U.S. Army Captain Lee A. Rysewyk, who was part of Task Force Ranger in Mogadishu in October 1993. "The Italians guarding a checkpoint merely watched as six Nigerian peacekeepers got ambushed and killed not more than one hundred meters away,"[37] Captain Rysewyk notes. A Kuwaiti commander later approached Rysewyk to ask if he knew the details of the Italian side deal.[38] None of this inspired trust within the UN contingent, which had to work as one if it was going to succeed.

Meanwhile, back in Washington, the Clinton Administration was not paying attention. Inside the White House, the Somalia chapter was considered closed, but for a few housekeeping details. In a June 17, 1993, White House press statement, the president said that the mission in Mogadishu was "over."[39] At best, this was misleading.

There were many small crises in Somalia. Twenty-four Pakistani peacekeepers were ambushed and shot by Aideed's forces on June 5, 1993. The United Nations, with the Clinton Administration's agreement, put a $25,000 price on Aideed's head and authorized UN peacekeeping forces (including American soldiers) to arrest him for the deaths of the peacekeepers. President Clinton later told the press, "We cannot have a situation where one of these warlords, while everyone else is cooperating, decides that he can go out and slaughter twenty peacekeepers."[40]

U.S. planes bombed Aideed's compound for the next four days, yet the warlord survived. Another toothless gesture.

The decision to arrest Aideed was made without any formal meetings of the National Security Advisor, his staff, or the top staff of the Secretary of Defense. The president was told about the decision only after the UN resolution to arrest Aideed had already been drafted by the State Department and sent to the UN The president was not formally briefed and was not told that the effort to capture Aideed would fundamentally expand the U.S. role in Somalia. If the president wanted to be directly involved, he would have been. But his aides sensed that he wanted Somalia handled by subordinates. The presence of American troops in a hostile land was not enough to hold the president's attention.

At the same time, there was a dangerous gap between the White House's ideas and what was actually happening in Mogadishu. President Clinton and National Security Advisor Tony Lake, who had served as a diplomatic officer in South Vietnam, had a visceral and vivid understanding of the dangers of nation building. Both men wanted U.S. troops to leave as soon as possible, provided the situation could be stabilized and not portrayed as an American retreat. A viable exit strategy, Lake explained to the author, was not a well-planned pullout, but a clear idea and establishment of the "desired political end state."

But some Clinton appointees in Somalia, including the American representative to the United Nations in Somalia, retired U.S. Navy Admiral Jonathan Howe, held a different view. Admiral Howe was determined to arrest Aideed. After the UN authorized a reward for capturing Aideed, Howe ordered staffers to put up wanted posters all over Mogadishu. This only gave away the goal and drove Aideed into hiding. Next, Howe began lobbying the U.S. government to send in Special Forces to arrest Aideed. It was this kind of zealousness that led White House officials to privately refer to him as "Jonathan Ahab."[41]

Defense Secretary Aspin opposed using Special Forces for police work, as did Powell and several army generals. But Howe recruited the support of UN ambassador Madeleine Albright, the

State Department's Undersecretary for Political Affairs Peter Tarnoff, and other diplomats. Throughout the summer of 1993 the administration was divided about sending in Special Forces, while Aideed's murderous attacks continued.

The next crisis came on August 8, when a U.S. Army humvee drove down a rough road in southern Mogadishu. Concealed in a pothole was a land mine. A wire ran from the mine to a nearby building. A Somali spotter watched the vehicle approach. When the humvee was in position, he clicked the detonator. Four American military policemen were murdered. They were among the first Americans killed in Somalia. Again, Clinton did nothing.

Then, on August 22, another bomb exploded near a U.S. Army humvee. Six Americans were wounded and their vehicle was completely destroyed. Clearly, Aideed's al Qaeda-trained men were serious about killing American troops.

President Clinton received the news while on vacation in Martha's Vineyard. He was furious and told his National Security Advisor, Tony Lake, that it was time to take action. Again, there was no meeting of the National Security Council or a gathering of the principals. That Sunday afternoon, August 22, a quick, casual phone conversation set larger events in motion.[42]

Within hours the U.S. Army Rangers and America's elite Delta Force—combined as "Task Force Ranger"—were formally ordered to Mogadishu.

Within six weeks, the mission was widely seen as a failure. By October 1993, Task Force Ranger had made six raids to arrest Aideed or his top officers. All failed to nab Aideed. Before the last raid, Courage 53 was shot down. But no new orders came from Washington.

Ominously, the Somalis noticed that the Rangers conducted all six raids using the same tactics, the same equipment, and the same order of events. This repetition was supposed to ensure quick approvals from headquarters and from the Clinton White House, but it proved to be an enormous strategic blunder. "If you use the same tactic twice, you should not use it a third time," Aideed colonel Ali Aden later told the *Washington Post*. "And the Americans already had done basically the same thing six times."[43] It would soon become clear just how much Aideed's men had learned—and how much the Clinton team had not.

Clinton officials working with the UN in Somalia misread the president's views and the United Nations' original mission in Somalia. They seemed to believe that peacekeeping in Somalia was akin to the American occupation of Germany and Japan after World War II. There, overwhelming military presence might have allowed the U.S. to remake those societies into prosperous, peaceful democracies. But Somalia was different in every respect. It had not been defeated by war, but by hunger. Its central government could not be replaced by the United Nations, because warring warlords had destroyed it more than two years earlier. There was nothing to replace. Unlike with the triumph over the Axis Powers in 1945, in Somalia powerful rival clans had emerged before the Allies arrived. And they were hostile.

A cycle that one could call "the tragedy of nation building" had begun. War destroys human beings, but it does not extinguish human nature. An occupier has but a short interval to remake a tyrannical state, during which the vanquished is inclined to put aside his passions and rebuild. As the immediate memory of misery fades, politics returns. Inevitably, at least one faction finds its interests injured and its wrath unslaked.

Meanwhile, the hubris of the "nation builders," those ambitious administrators from overseas, grows. They imagine that countries are like gardens that can easily be rearranged into more congenial patterns. Especially in Africa, any decent-minded visitor soon sees a hundred seemingly simple changes that would make life gentler, richer, cleaner, or safer. Give that visitor manpower and money and the temptation becomes all but irresistible to make improvements. In Somalia, the legions of international nonprofits, federal bureaucrats, and even some military men had largely succumbed to this temptation. It is precisely these improvements, for which rival factions get no political credit, that fuel discontent and war.

Over time, the differences between the outraged faction and the ambitious administrators yawns wider, like the slowly opening jaws of an alligator. In Somalia, in 1993, those jaws were about to clamp shut on the U.S. Army Rangers.

MOGADISHU, SOMALIA—Major General William Garrison, the Delta Force commander, thought he might have caught a lucky break. At about 1 P.M. on October 3, 1993, an intelligence officer reported that, according to an informant, a meeting of Aideed's top officers was set for later that afternoon. General Garrison called his superior, General Joe Hoar, on a satellite phone. After a brief discussion, General Hoar approved yet another operation to capture Aideed, or at least his top commanders.

Everything went according to plan. The helicopters arrived over the target on schedule. As the Black Hawk helicopter blades stirred up a blinding brown cloud of dust and garbage called rotorwash, Delta Force commandos slid down ropes hanging from the helicopters and burst into the building.

Meanwhile four groups of Army Rangers "fast-roped" down three-inch-thick spongy cables into positions near the four corners of the building, establishing a defensive perimeter. Only a few Somalis were taking potshots. Most were poorly aimed. Within twenty minutes it was all over. Twenty-two leaders in Aideed's organization were captured in one fell swoop. A Delta Force trooper radioed the base, giving the code word for operational success: "Laurie."[44]

Mission accomplished. Or so it seemed.

The convoy of humvees and half-ton trucks arrived on schedule. Since the helicopters couldn't land in Mogadishu's narrow streets, these vehicles would provide the way home. As they loaded the prisoners, the shooting started in earnest. The machine-gun fire suddenly increased and seemed to come from all directions. Rocket-launched grenades exploded all around them.

Hundreds of smoke trails from rocket-propelled grenades sliced through the air. They exploded in a continuous barrage. The helicopters were using an orbit known as "racetracking," but that oval pattern took them repeatedly through showers of rocket-propelled grenades. Pilots tried to vary their route while rear gunners fired their massive machine guns. But there were too many targets, too many exploding bombs.

Soon the odds caught up with helicopter Super Six One. A rocket-propelled grenade shattered its tail rotor, using the very technique bin Laden's men had taught. The Black Hawk shook and spun out of control. Chief Warrant Officer Cliff Wolcott desperately tried to pull back on the power control levers,[45] but nothing could keep the bird in the air.

A radio officer monitoring the Ranger operation at the Quick Reaction Force headquarters recorded a startling transmission: "We got a Black Hawk crashed in the city... six-one, six-one down."[46]

It dived nose first into a cluster of shacks along an alley known as "Freedom Road." Super Six One lay on its side, wedged among crumbling buildings. The two pilots died on impact. Five others aboard—two crew chiefs and three Delta Force snipers—were able to crawl out of the wreckage.

Strangely this exact scenario—with Super Six One playing the doomed aircraft—had been rehearsed a week earlier.[47] Now the trained-for rescue plan swung into action. A Ranger "chalk" (equivalent to a squad) led by Lieutenant Tom DiTomasso ran toward the crash site. A fifteen-man search-and-rescue team was dropped down to treat the wounded and secure the area. But their intensive training had not prepared them for the Somali reaction.

Within minutes, Somalis swarmed toward the crash site, carrying machine guns and rocket launchers. The enemy included women and children. Soldiers saw women firing machine guns at them and others carrying ammunition for enemy mortars. Boys fired rocket-propelled grenades. "When you shot a guy, the next joker would just come over and try to pick up the weapon," one solider told Colonel David Hackworth. "The same thing with the RPGs. They would pick up the RPGs, reload and fire."[48]

The Somalis kept coming. They meant to finish off the survivors.

Within minutes, a second Black Hawk was shot down. At least four members of the crew, including the pilot, Michael Durant, were still alive. Helicopters passing over saw several crewmen moving or waving. Now General Garrison, the head of Task Force Ranger, was in a moral quandary. The Rangers simply didn't have enough men to defend two crash sites—and were sure to lose men simply getting to the sites. Indeed, the rescue convoy got repeatedly lost on the way to the first crash site. By 4:30 P.M., there were no good choices.

Hovering near the second crash site, Master Sergeant Gary Gordon and Sergeant First Class Randall Shugart, two Delta Force snipers, made a third request to go in. This time, Lt. Col. Thomas-Matthews changed his mind. They were sent in.

The two snipers, Gordon and Shugart, jumped into the yellow dust cloud. They ran through the empty streets and found the wreckage of the Black Hawk.

Until the American snipers arrived, the Somali attacks had been mostly isolated bursts of gunfire from long range. But now the regulars had come. The volume of fire stepped up and the shooting became more accurate. The Somalis came in waves. Bullets pinged nearby and grenades boomed. The snipers shot dozens of them but the enemy kept coming. Shugart positioned the wounded pilot, Michael Durant, against a wall of the downed helicopter and gave him a rifle with five rounds. Then the Somalis charged again.

The Black Hawk had massive machine guns mounted in the rear with thousands of rounds of ammunition, but the guns ran on electric power. And the bird's batteries were dead. There was no hope of holding off the Somalis now.

The two snipers and two crew members were hacked and beaten to death in a bloody struggle. Durant fired all five rounds and then placed the useless rifle across his chest. For some reason, the pilot was spared. He was held prisoner for the next eleven days.

The two Delta snipers were posthumously awarded the Medal of Honor, the first awarded since the end of the Vietnam War.

Back at the first crash site, the pilot of an MH-6 "little bird" helicopter squeezed down into an alley. Steering with one hand and firing his service revolver with the other, pilot Karl Maier hovered near the first crash site, while his copilot ran to carry away two of the wounded survivors. In minutes, the wounded were loaded and the MH-6 shot skyward.

But retrieving the dead was more difficult. The search-and-rescue team couldn't pull the corpse from the cockpit, which had crumbled on impact. Their emergency-saw blades snapped against the helicopter's armored door panels. The "jaws of life" would have helped, but they were in a storage locker at a base three miles away.

At this point the Rangers were defending one dead body at the first crash site. The Somalis thought they were trapped.[49] And they were—not by Somali militiamen but by their own sense of honor. In the early hours of the battle, the Rangers could have run the gantlet in their heavy trucks and escaped—if they were willing to abandon the bodies of their comrades. But they were not. Their code of honor held them fast. The fifth stanza of the "Ranger Creed" contains this line: "I will never leave a fallen comrade to fall into the hands of the enemy."[50]

This creed was not an abstraction to the Rangers. Of the thirty-eight lessons of the Battle of the Black Sea drawn by Captain Rysewyk, in an unpublished report obtained by the author, only number seventeen is in bold typeface: "Never leave a fallen comrade to fall into the hands of the enemy."[51] The Rangers were not about to leave.

When the corpses of other American soldiers from the second crash site fell into the hands of the Somalis, they were dragged through the streets with ropes and hacked to pieces for crowd-pleasing souvenirs. The Rangers were fighting and dying to make sure this would not happen at their crash site.

Back at the Quick Reaction Force base, Colonel Casper ordered the 125 members of Charlie Company, Second Battalion, Fourteenth Infantry Regiment, to board a convoy of five-ton trucks lined with sandbags for protection. They were the cavalry.

But in a deadly hail of gunfire, rockets, and grenades—with every tire shot flat, every bullet-resistant window spiderwebbed with the impacts of bullets, the armored doors of several humvees dented inward from rocket attacks, the trucks coated with the blood of wounded soldiers—the convoy was forced to retreat.

If the Quick Reaction Force had had armored vehicles, such as the Bradley Fighting Vehicle, they could have traveled through the Somali attacks unscathed. Instead, two soldiers were killed and twenty-two were seriously wounded on the convoy.

The need for tanks was obvious. But there were no American tanks. To save the Rangers, General Garrison would need armored vehicles from the Pakistanis and the Malaysians, nations that were not worried about the public reaction to the presence of their tanks in Somalia. It also meant hours of negotiation with these UN partners. The tanks would not roll until 11:15 P.M., almost eight hours after the battle had begun.

As night fell, Task Force Ranger was in trouble. It was surrounded. Ammunition was running low. Most men had been issued only seven thirty-round magazines for their M-16s, and only two hand grenades each.[52] Ammunition was air-dropped in regularly, but it was never enough. There were hundreds of attackers.

All night long in the battle zone, the communication officers manned their Sabre MX radios. They continuously said, "Request fire mission, over" and gave new coordinates each time. Without the constant supporting fire from aircraft, the Rangers would have been overwhelmed and killed.

After seven hours of continuous battle, eighteen Malaysian armored personnel carriers and four Pakistani M-48 tanks, followed by an American line of trucks, roared through Mogadishu.

All bodies were recovered. The Rangers were on their way home by 4 A.M. Eighteen Americans were dead and eighty-four wounded.

THE WHITE HOUSE—While the Black Hawks were shot down and Task Force Ranger encircled by Somali militia, Hillary Clinton was worried about pro-life protesters in Washington, D.C.

The president, like all of his recent predecessors, was due to attend a Catholic Mass to bless the opening of the U.S. Supreme Court on the first Monday of October. It was an annual ritual and one of the few in which the president would mix with the justices of the high court.

Sometime after midnight, the president paged George Stephanopoulos. The special advisor could hear Mrs. Clinton in the background urging the president to cancel an invitation that he had accepted weeks earlier.[53]

Stephanopoulos had a different fear: a headline reading "Clinton snubs Catholics," a key voting bloc.[54] Finally the president agreed to go. But it was the kind of last-minute indecision that didn't bode well.

Fearing that the president might still forgo his visit to St. Matthew's Cathedral, Stephanopoulos went to the White House early the next morning. He was determined to prevent a political crisis. Instead, he immediately found out about a rapidly developing national security crisis.

Hardline Communists in Moscow were storming the main television station and the Russian parliament. CNN carried the pictures live. To get a briefing on the Moscow crisis, Stephanopoulos phoned Tony Lake, the national security advisor, who was still at home.

Through Lake, Stephanopoulos learned about a third crisis. At about eight that morning, Lake had been told that a mission had gone wrong in Somalia.[55] Several Rangers were dead. Nearly one hundred soldiers were surrounded by thousands of gunmen. It was only going to get worse.

When Stephanopoulos found the president, he was carrying a red folder from the Situation Room. It was marked "Somalia."

"Ready for the questions?" Stephanopoulos asked.

"About Somalia?"

"No, Russia."[56]

There were plenty of crises to go around. They went to the church without a word to the press.

An hour and a half later, President Clinton was back in his limo, gliding toward the White House. Mrs. Clinton was sipping bottled water and linking her health-care project to that day's sermon about "the common good." The anti-abortion protesters were few and silently held up their signs.

As they drove away from the church, the president approvingly quoted Congressman Barney Frank's joke about conservatives who believe "that life begins at conception and ends at birth."[57] At the same time, the president knew from the red briefing folder beside him that American lives were ending in Mogadishu.

In the white-walled Oval Office, the president sat at his large "partner's desk." He had heard the latest reports from Somalia. So far, six Americans were dead. Many more were wounded.

When the briefing ended, the president exploded. "We're not inflicting enough pain on the fuckers," he said. "When people kill us, they should be killed in greater numbers."[58]

The president turned to Lake, who had grown accustomed to Clinton's sudden, volcanic temper. "I can't believe that we're being pushed around by these two-bit pricks."[59]

As the president calmed down, he grew contemplative and introspective. The American people, he told Stephanopoulos, are "basically isolationist."[60] The president believed that the American people would not support operations in Somalia if it meant body bags. It would be days before the president would choose between striking back and pulling out.

SAN FRANCISCO—The day after the Battle of the Black Sea, Clinton was in a room at the Fairmont Hotel, a landmark tower perched on San Francisco's Russian Hill. His trip to California was a part of a multi-million-dollar campaign fundraising tour. When he turned on the television, he saw what ordinary Americans had been seeing for hours: CNN footage of dead Americans dragged through the streets of Mogadishu while a crowd of Somalis joyfully jumped up and down, shouting "God is great."

The president took action. He ordered that new images of defeat and disaster in Somalia be kept from the world's television networks. Eight videotapes of the battle made by a P-3 Orion reconnaissance plane circling overhead were quickly marked "classified."[61] The president did not want to see those tapes broadcast on CNN.

The White House also concentrated on damage control. Administration officials were packed into marathon meetings. They debated whether the president should cut short his fundraising trip to California. It didn't look good. But canceling the tour would look like panic. In the end, the president came back to Washington one-half hour earlier than planned, and participated in a lengthy series of conference calls. "It strikes me as dumb at a minimum to put U.S. troops in helicopters in urban areas where they could be subject to ground fire," he said.[62] Yet it was *he* who had ordered them to go.

To control the story, the administration debated sending two Pentagon press flacks and, most unusually, a White House press officer to Mogadishu. The Defense Department initially opposed the idea. It was unprecedented to send a White House press officer to a battle zone. But eventually the White House prevailed. A media relations expert from Hillary Clinton's health-care war room, Jeff Eller, was paged by the White House switchboard. He was then connected to *Air Force One*. David Gergen, a senior advisor to the president, told him, "The First Lady and the president have given their approval. Go ahead and go."[63]

Twenty-four hours later, Eller was in Mogadishu wearing a flak jacket and helmet. But his was a hopeless task. No amount of spin could overcome the televised images of dead Americans.

In public, the president accepted full responsibility for the losses in Mogadishu. In private, he blamed his staff, the UN, and the press.

"Why didn't I know this was going on?" he asked his advisors, meeting in the Situation Room. "Who was running this here? Why wasn't I told?"[64]

A fierce battle was fought within the administration and Congress. Lake vigorously fought back calls for an immediate removal of all U.S. forces from Somalia. "You'd be painting a bullseye on every America soldier everywhere in the world," he told the author. He debated Christopher in the Oval Office as Clinton looked on and later made his case to delegations of Democratic lawyers in the White House's Roosevelt Room.

After two days of meetings, an internal compromise was hammered out. President Clinton would publicly announce that U.S. troops would leave Somalia no later than March 31, 1994. It was a victory of sorts for Lake. That was the earliest date the military believed it could move the ships into place to haul away all of the men and equipment. In the meantime, American troops would be reinforced with 1,700 soldiers and 104 armored vehicles and new helicopter gunships. Then they would withdraw on schedule. It was not supposed to look like retreat.

President Clinton tried to sell the decision to the press and the public. As with many Clinton statements, it was carefully calculated to be technically true while omitting any responsibility for policy mistakes. "If we were to leave today, we know what would happen. . . . Our leadership in world affairs would be undermined at the very time when people are looking to America to help promote peace and freedom in the post–Cold War world. All around the world, aggressors, thugs, and terrorists will conclude that the best way to get us to change our policy is to kill our people. It would be open season on Americans."[65]

KHARTOUM, SUDAN—Osama bin Laden saw the Somalia disaster for what it was. As with the Aden bombing ten months earlier, bin Laden's "holy warriors" had driven the world's sole superpower from a poor, Muslim land with a single night of attacks. The outcome of the "Battle of the Black Sea" would only confirm his view that Allah had granted him a triumph. He called Somalia his "greatest victory."[66]

Bin Laden was still exultant and confident in his vision of American weakness when he sat for an interview with an ABC News camera crew five years later, in 1998:

"Our boys went to Somalia and prepared themselves carefully for a long war. . . . Our boys were shocked by the low morale of the American soldier, and they realized that the American soldier was just a paper tiger. He was unable to endure the strikes that were dealt to his army, so he fled, and America had to stop all its bragging."[67]

He plainly saw Clinton as a weak giant, and America as more feckless and less fearsome than the old Soviet Union. These would prove to be very dangerous lessons to teach him. But these were the lessons that bin Laden learned from Clinton's strategy of carefully calibrated attacks followed by rapid retreats.

Just across the Red Sea, in his native Saudi Arabia, bin Laden saw several more American targets. Now, it would be open season on Americans.

CHAPTER FOUR

THE SEPTEMBER 11 PRACTICE RUN

MANILA, THE PHILIPPINES—Even with a $2 million price on his head, Ramzi Yousef had eluded American intelligence for almost two years.

He was too infamous to retire. And he liked the dangerous life too much to try. Like his habit of wearing sunglasses at night,[1] being a terrorist was a part of who he was. He once had a business card printed up that featured his name in bold print. Below was his job title: "international terrorist."[2] It was probably the only honest identification that he ever carried.

So he kept making bombs. His specialty was a difficult recipe involving liquefied nitroglycerin, the explosive ingredient in TNT. Liquid bombs are extremely volatile, as Yousef painfully knew. In September 1993, he was taken to two separate emergency rooms in Karachi, Pakistan. He had mysterious burns on his hands and face. He claimed that the injuries were caused by the explosion of a butane lighter. Pakistani investigators now believe that Yousef was conducting a test explosion of one of his trademark liquid bombs—which misfired.[3]

As he recovered from his bomb wounds, Yousef holed up in a series of dingy rooms. The thin, bearded terrorist was twenty-seven years old and still hoped to commit some memorable atrocity.

Eventually, a representative of Osama bin Laden recruited him for perhaps the boldest series of terrorist plots ever conceived before September 11, 2001. If the plots succeeded, four thousand Americans would be killed in eleven simultaneous explosions, Pope John Paul II would be murdered, and President Clinton would die in a cloud of poisonous gas. Yousef even had sketchy plans for a finale: flying bomb-laden planes into the CIA headquarters, the Pentagon, the White House, and the World Trade Center.

If this sounds like a test run of the September 11 atrocities, it probably was. And that was no accident. Both series of attacks—in Manila in 1995 and in New York and Washington in 2001—are believed to have shared the same operational commander, a colorful al Qaeda agent named Khalid Shaikh Mohammed.[4]

There are other ominous parallels. Twice in 1993, Mohammed summoned a U.S.-trained Kuwaiti airline pilot named Abdul Hakim Murad to Pakistan and questioned him extensively about pilot training and aircraft operation.[5] At those meetings, Murad said he suggested to Mohammed that al Qaeda use jumbo jets to destroy landmark buildings. So the outlines of what became the September 11 attacks seemed to have been simmering inside al Qaeda for at least eight years—virtually the entire duration of the Clinton Administration.

Sometime in October 1994, Mohammed began to build a cell to carry out his plan. He recruited Murad, who in turn recommended his old friend Ramzi Yousef. The two had met in Palestinian activist circles in the 1980s, although neither was Palestinian. Each soon flavored his spoken Arabic with a distinctive Palestinian accent. Fueled by anti-Israel and anti-American sentiment of student youth groups, each drifted into terrorist circles. Yousef went on to become a "professional," while Murad remained a fellow traveler who went to the United States to train as a commercial airline pilot. After attending three aviation schools and doing poorly, he was finally awarded his pilot's certificate in 1992. He might have gone straight, but he maintained his links with the then-fledgling al Qaeda organization. Soon, he was sucked in.

Next, Mohammed recruited Wali Khan Amin Shah, an Afghan-Beluch who was one of the founders of Konsojaya, a Malaysian business started in 1994 to fund terrorist operations across East Asia.[6] Shah had trained in bin Laden's camps and was trusted by the organization. Even better, he had an extensive Rolodex of terrorists across East Asia and could plausibly pose as an investor.

Mohammed chose to base the new cell in the Milate district of Manila, the capital of the island archipelago of the Philippines. It was a neighborhood of seedy nightclubs and cheap hotels that attracted a large, transient Arab population; the plotters knew that they could blend in.[7]

The team was expert. These men knew how to handle automatic weapons, mix chemicals, and build bombs. But to carry out this ambitious wave of bombings and assassinations, the terrorist team would need large covert transfers of money, a secure escape route, and a pile of false documents to evade capture. Most of all, they needed the approval of Osama bin Laden.

Though intelligence analysts and U.S. government prosecutors believe that it is safe to conclude that bin Laden did in fact finance and coordinate the Philippine attacks, no definitive proof has yet been made public. But there is little doubt that bin Laden was behind them; indeed he was later indicted in a U.S. district court in New York for the Philippine plots.

One way of establishing bin Laden's connection was to follow the money. Investigators later traced the Philippine terror cells' funds to two high-level al Qaeda operatives. The operation's budget passed through an Abu Dhabi bank account seemingly controlled by Khalid Shaikh Mohammed, the operation's commander.

Another spur of the money trail ends in a bank account used by the Manila-based International Islamic Relief Organization, a phony charity that was run by Mohammed Jamal Khalifa, one of bin Laden's brothers-in-law. Khalifa was also believed to be the financial connection behind the 1993 World Trade Center bombing and other attacks. He was one of the few men that bin Laden trusted to launder relatively large sums. He met with Yousef in Manila in 1994. Khalifa had brought Yousef to the Philippines before, in 1991, to train Abu Sayyaf—a terrorist band on the southern Philippine island of Jolo—and other Muslim terror groups.[8]

If the team was compromised, bin Laden made sure that they would have a secure base to flee to. Bin Laden is believed to have contacted Abu Sayyaf. Its links to bin Laden were long-standing; the group is run by a longtime associate of bin Laden, Abdurajak Janjalani, and is named after another longtime associate of bin Laden, from his days in the Afghan jihad. Like other terrorist operations on the Pacific Ocean island archipelagoes, the murderous Abu Sayyaf was funded partly through donations by a bogus charity controlled by bin Laden's brother-in-law Khalifa, who lived in Manila in the mid-1990s. With bin Laden's funds, Abu Sayyaf became notorious for kidnapping American missionaries and beheading them.

The forged papers were prepared, probably by a special unit within al Qaeda. With twenty-one different aliases[9] and at least sixteen different passports, Yousef arrived in the Philippines sometime in November 1994.

In Manila, he linked up with Waly Amin Shah, a Muslim militant whose fingers were deformed from making faulty bombs. Yousef had similar burns on his hands. But these men shared more than the scars of their trade. They each had a passion for a decidedly un-Islamic nightlife. In Manila, they would drink and watch naked girls swing from brass poles. On other nights, they went to discos in shiny, open-necked shirts and chatted up local girls. Abdul Hakim Murad arrived the day after Christmas and promptly joined in the bacchanalia.[10]

Khalid Shaikh Mohammed set the tone. While infidel culture might be sinful, he immersed himself in it. He held meetings in go-

go clubs. When he wasn't trying to take dancers home, he pursued a non-Muslim Filipina dentist. He once rented a helicopter, buzzed over her office, and phoned her on his mobile phone.[11] *Look out the window*, he told her, and *wave*. To celebrate the six-year anniversary of the explosion of Pan Am Flight 103 over Lockerbie, Scotland, he called together the entire cell and their girlfriends for a party.[12] They all happily drank alcohol.

Of course, fundamentalist Muslims do not drink alcohol, frequent strip clubs, or even listen to rock music. All music and dancing is forbidden in the severe Salafist strains of Islam. For the followers of bin Laden's Salafist sect, even allowing a woman to accidentally bump against you was forbidden. Soliciting a lap dance was out of the question.

In fact, nothing about the lives of the Manila terrorist cell members suggested that they were Muslim fanatics trying to impose a puritanical Islamic state. Such a state would probably punish them more harshly for their lifestyle than Western governments would for their crimes.

If this lifestyle was an elaborate cover, it nevertheless seemed to be a disguise they enjoyed. Curiously, many of the September 11 hijackers were spotted in strip clubs in Florida. Perhaps this lifestyle was a motivational tool, a little advance payment of the martyr's paradise that they were promised.

Yousef and Murad seemed to live in a karaoke bar on A. Mabini Street in Manila. Philippine investigators found pornography on their computers and, in Shah's one-room bachelor pad, Rough Rider brand condoms.[13]

The terrorists were hardly raffish charmers. An audio file on Yousef's laptop computer provides an arresting view of their lives. On that recording, Shah's Filipina girlfriend, Cindy, said sweetly, "I love you."

He responded, "Shut up, you bitch."[14]

It was but a flash of their cruel side, a momentary fluttering of the curtain that reveals the darkness backstage. In the coming months, they hoped to show the world a sustained scene of carnage: the deaths of thousands of people trapped aboard passenger jets.

THE WHITE HOUSE—Less than a month after the 1993 World Trade Center explosion, President Clinton became obsessed with capturing and convicting Ramzi Yousef. His fingerprints had been found on the Space Station storage unit where the World Trade Center bomb was built and witnesses in custody had fingered the mysterious mastermind. Like Abu Nidal in the 1980s, Yousef had become the new face of terrorism. He had to be caught, preferably before the 1996 presidential election.

The president made capturing "the world's most dangerous man" the personal responsibility of Richard A. Clarke.[15] To the outside world, appointing a little-known National Security Council staffer to lead a global manhunt for a terrorist mastermind seemed unusual.

Why not a general, a cabinet secretary, or an elder statesman? The thinking inside the Clinton Administration was simple and clever: this was a secret war. If it failed, no one would know and the president would not be blamed. If it succeeded, the president would get the credit.

This may have seemed like shrewd politics, but it carried hidden risks. Terrorist-fighters often run into bureaucratic and political roadblocks, both at home and abroad. If the president openly declared war on the World Trade Center terrorists, he would have had the political clout needed to overcome most internal resistance. Few lawmakers or bureaucrats want to get in the way of a popular president with a political mandate to punish notorious killers. Resisting the president would be particularly hard for the leaders of Clinton's Democratic Party, who controlled both houses of Congress at the time. They would have to give him whatever he wanted and ply their own agendas at the margin. Even the press would have to give the president a pass: Who can quibble with catching terrorists? Overall, a public war on terror stood a better chance of success.

But a public war brings political risks. If the president tried to get Yousef and failed, Clinton's supporters in Congress and the press could turn on him. His Republican opponent in the next election could mock his failure. Clinton knew this well. On the campaign trail, he had attacked then-President Bush for failing to arrest the legendary Colombian cocaine king Pablo Escobar.[16] He didn't want to suffer arrows drawn from his own quiver.

The political equation had a seemingly obvious solution: the president would wage a *secret* war. If the anti-terror effort succeeded, Clinton would get the credit. If it failed, few would know enough to fault the president. For this clandestine manhunt to work, the president would need someone highly competent and virtually unknown to the White House press corps. Enter Richard Clarke.

In fact, he was perfectly cast for the part. Clarke was so colorless that even his office seemed to project more personality than he did. A few yards from the West Wing of the White House, Clarke's office suite was on the third floor of the Old Executive Office Building. It was a succession of blue-carpeted rooms[17] that had long been the center of international intrigue. The same office suite once housed Colonel Oliver North, who made his name by facing down a congressional committee over the "Iran-Contra scandal." The main room of Clarke's office suite still bore the scars of Colonel North, who broke White House rules by constructing an unauthorized plywood second level, beneath the main room's sixteen-foot ceiling, to accommodate more covert operatives. The "loft" still stands. In the Clinton years, it was occupied by America's ever-growing counterterrorism team, led by Clarke.

No one would mistake Clarke for a Tom Clancy hero. A career federal bureaucrat, he doesn't pack a pistol, or race around in convertibles. A tall, trim man in a bland suit, Clarke could be mistaken for a middle-aged, mid-level employee at the Department of Energy.

Appearances aside, he was now America's de facto counterterrorism czar. It was his job to fight and win the president's private war. In the first two years of the Clinton Administration—while the Director of Central Intelligence, Jim Woolsey, had trouble securing a one-on-one meeting with the president—Clarke regularly briefed Clinton on terrorism. By April 1993, he was leading the global manhunt for Yousef.

Though Yousef's trail had gone cold, Clarke kept pursuing leads and forcing agencies to pool information. Through sheer force of will, he coordinated an alphabet soup of federal agencies: the National Security Agency, the Central Intelligence Agency, the Federal Bureau of Investigation, the State Department, and the Defense Department, among others. Imagine what he could have accomplished if Clinton had publicly endorsed his efforts.

For almost two years, Clarke was blunt, tough, and unrelenting. His most frequent refrain was: "Well, where is he?"

Eventually, it paid off.

MANILA, THE PHILIPPINES—It was the black smoke that gave them away.[18]

Spilling out of the kitchen window in the sixth floor of the Dona Josefa apartment building,[19] the thick smoke quickly brought complaints. The building security guard phoned the fire department, which didn't answer. So he phoned Manila police station number nine.

Captain Aida Fariscal took the call.[20] She had already changed out of her uniform into a loud print dress and flip-flops, and was about to go off duty. But something made her suspicious. She dispatched a patrolman. He was back in minutes. "Nothing to worry about," he told her. "Just some Pakistanis playing with firecrackers."[21]

But Fariscal, one of the few women to make watch commander in the Manila police force, tended to trust her instincts.[22]

She had good reasons to be suspicious. It was 11 P.M. on the night of January 6, 1995. Exactly a week later, Pope John Paul II was scheduled to arrive in the city. The papal nunciature, the Vatican embassy where the pope would sleep, was less than two hundred yards away. The pontiff's bulletproof vehicle was scheduled to drive right past the apartment building. President Clinton also had announced plans to visit the Philippines en route to an economic policy summit in East Asia.

She put her uniform back on and marched down Quirino Avenue.

The Dona Josefa apartment building is one of those typical Third World buildings, made from concrete and designed to look modern. Its lobby smelled smoky.

The hotel security guard filled in the details. Two men, who had rented the room a month earlier using Arab names and a Moroccan address, had run out of the lobby, claiming that some firecrackers had exploded.[23] Firecrackers had never generated so much smoke in Fariscal's experience. She asked the guard to unlock their apartment.

When the door to unit 603 swung open, Fariscal found a bomb-making factory. There were plastic beakers, coils of colored electrical wire, boxes from German and Pakistani chemical companies, a whitish foul-smelling liquid soaked into sponge-like bricks of cotton, and four brand-new hot plates.[24] In the kitchen, they found a burned hot plate and smoke damage on the walls. She quickly decided she needed a search warrant.

Abdul Hakim Murad and Ramzi Yousef had been hiding out in a nearby bar for the past hour, debating what to do. Their apartment was littered with evidence of a vast terrorist conspiracy. And in a hole in the wall, they had left behind a stock of forged passports and loads of cash that would be needed to make their escape. Clearly, someone had to destroy the evidence and recover their money and travel documents.

Murad soon began creeping back toward the Dona Josefa apartment building. Entering the open-air lobby, he spotted the uniformed police. A middle-aged policewoman with a ponytail was talking to the security guard. Murad turned to run, but he didn't get very far. He tripped on the roots of an overturned palm tree. Before he could stand, a patrolman grabbed him from behind. "I'll give you $2,000 to let me go," he said.[25] It didn't work.

Then the hotel security guard spotted Ramzi Yousef. "There's the other one."[26] He pointed outside to a bony, bearded man talking on a cell phone. Fariscal sent the other patrolman bounding after him. But Yousef scurried through the growing crowd of pedestrians and onlookers and slipped away.

Within hours, the National Philippine Police had a search warrant and had begun to unravel one of the most devious terrorist plots ever conceived. Simply cataloguing everything in apartment 603 took days. They found Yousef's Toshiba laptop and chemistry textbooks with handwritten recipes for bombs taped to some pages. A hole in the wall held a cache of sixteen passports, including a Norwegian one that matched one of Yousef's known aliases. In November 2002, Philippine intelligence found that the Norwegian passport was purchased in Peshawar, Pakistan. Yet more evidence suggesting bin Laden's involvement.

The plot to kill the Pope was evidently very far along. They found a photograph of John Paul II, a Bible, and a crucifix. The answering machine yielded a message from a tailor: Murad's Catholic priest's cassock was ready for a final fitting.[27]

Murad was taken to a special facility used by Philippine intelligence, in Camp Crame, Quezon City.[28] He was interrogated for days. Eventually, he admitted that he planned to pose as a priest, approach the pope's motorcade and, when the pontiff reached out to shake his hand, detonate a bomb hidden under his vestments. The murder would shock the globe's more than one billion Roman Catholics and give Murad the two things he said he most desired: fame and martyrdom.

But why did the terrorists need to make so many bombs for a single suicide operation?

The answer took months to uncover. By decrypting and translating documents on the hard drive of Yousef's computer—including files he had deleted—investigators were able to piece together the terror cells' plans and activities over the past few months. They had never seen a terrorist plan of such scale.

The al Qaeda cell called it "Project Bojinka." *Bojinka* is a Serbo-Croatian word meaning "loud bang." (Al Qaeda was active inside the former Yugoslavia in the early 1990s.) Yousef and the others had been carefully preparing the project for months. Yousef had to devise a new type of bomb and test it until it worked. Next, he had to discover how to defeat airport security. He would prove diabolically clever on both counts.

The new bomb was small enough to hide inside a standard travel-size bottle of saline solution, used to clean contact lenses. Inside the bottle were the unmixed ingredients of a liquid nitroglycerin bomb. Other components were hidden in other innocuous small bottles. The timer was a modified Casio wristwatch, the kind with the plastic band that sells for less than $10.[29] The power source for the bomb was a nine-volt battery, small enough to hide in the heel of a shoe. The metal battery would never be found, he reasoned, because airport metal detectors stop at a passenger's ankles. In all of these observations about the gaps in airport security, he was entirely correct. (Indeed, these gaps may still exist today—even after the September 11 hijackings and the attempt by al Qaeda operative Richard Reid to ignite a bomb in his shoes.)

Yousef was fanatic about testing his creations and callous about the innocents harmed by his experiments. He smuggled the first version of his new bomb into a Manila movie theater, planted the bomb under the seat, and walked out. The timer worked as expected and the blast followed his calculations exactly. Many people were injured, but the maimed and wounded were side effects.[30]

But could he get the bomb aboard an airplane? For his next experiment, Yousef bought a ticket on a Philippine Airlines flight from Manila to Tokyo, which (crucially) stopped at the Philippine island of Cebu. As he expected, airport security did not find the bomb components. He slipped right through the metal detectors.

Once the flight was aloft, Yousef locked himself in the tiny airplane bathroom and began mixing the chemicals for his bomb. Next, he set the timer on the Casio watch—it included a standard alarm function—and wired the battery. When the alarm sounded, the bomb would explode.

He carried the device back to his seat in a lunch bag and stuffed it under his seat. He deplaned at Cebu. The plane continued on toward Tokyo. A Japanese engineer took Yousef's seat on the flight's final leg.

No one heard the watch's tiny alarm beep. Seconds later, an ear-shattering blast rocked the cabin. The explosion punched a man-sized hole in the fuselage. The wind roared in. Amid the screams and smoke, a flight attendant noticed two small hands on the edge of the hole in the hull. The Japanese engineer had been almost cut in two and the top half of him was struggling to stay inside the plane.[31] The stewardess tried to pull him back in. But it was no use.

After forty harrowing minutes, the pilot made an emergency touchdown on the island of Okinawa. Against all odds, he had saved the lives of his crew and passengers—except for one.

Yousef could not have cared less about the poor engineer, the brave pilot, or the trapped passengers. He had proved to his own satisfaction that he could easily smuggle the bomb aboard, make it, set it, and safely escape. Now, with "Project Bojinka," he would shift to mass production.

The Manila cell painstakingly identified eleven planes, mostly United and American Airlines flights, which would make at least one stopover before landing in the United States.[32] According to the plan, Yousef would board and set bombs on four separate flights—with each hidden bomb set to explode at the same time. His accomplices would conceal bombs on seven other flights. At zero hour, all eleven planes would explode simultaneously somewhere over the Pacific. As many as four thousand people would die. That is roughly the death toll of the September 11 attacks.[33]

ISLAMABAD, PAKISTAN—The two-story SuCasa guest house must have been grimly familiar to Yousef. He had spent years in similar places and now he was on the run again.

He had checked in the night before, a month after he disappeared from the Philippines, and resumed his furtive routine. He had successfully evaded capture for thirty-two days. The hard part was supposed to be over; he had slipped past airport security and border checkpoints on two continents. Now he just had to lie low and wait. He was already working on his next attack, which involved placing high-tech explosives in remote-controlled toy cars.

"We moved assets into the area," Tony Lake said dryly; at the time, the FBI was hot on Murad's trail. As Philippine intelligence grilled Murad, Yousef's erstwhile comrade, he revealed that he was originally supposed to rendezvous with Yousef in Karachi, Pakistan, after the attacks.[34] FBI investigators realized that Yousef was unlikely to go to the rendezvous point in Karachi, but Pakistan was nevertheless a strong lead. The FBI advertised a reward for Yousef across the country. The bureau printed posters and matchbook covers with Yousef's face. Maybe one of his acquaintances would turn him in.

Ishiatique Parker, a South African–born Muslim student, walked out of the guest house at about 9:30 A.M. on February 7, 1995.[35] He must have been nervous. He had come to Pakistan to study in a *madrassa* and found himself in the company of Ramzi Yousef. He had heard about the $2 million reward for information leading to the arrest of Yousef and convinced himself to become an FBI informant. The night before, his young wife had reluctantly agreed. Now she was waiting nearby. If Yousef ever learned of Parker's treachery, he knew he would be killed in the most painful way possible.

The FBI did not make it easy for him. He had hoped to give them the address of Yousef's hideout and collect the money. But they wanted him to knock on Yousef's door and make sure he was there, and then leave, giving the agents a pre-arranged signal.

Now Parker emerged from Yousef's room, squinting in the sun. He doffed his skullcap and raked his fingers through his hair. That was the signal: Yousef was inside.

Pakistani Special Forces smashed down the door. Barefoot and startled, Yousef was looking down the barrels of a collection of automatic weapons. The field commander of the 1993 World Trade Center bombing was quickly shackled and dragged away to face American justice. FBI agents filtered into Yousef's hotel room, searching and securing everything as evidence. Most notably, they found photographs of Osama bin Laden posing with an AK-47.

THE WHITE HOUSE—Alone in his dark kitchen in his Maryland home, Tony Lake picked up the telephone.[36] It was just past 1 A.M. on February 8, 1995.

He noticed something unusual about the way that the caller said "hello."

Counterterrorism czar Richard Clarke sounded excited. He almost never sounded excited.

Clarke said, "We've got him."

Lake pumped his fist in the air. Then, wedging the phone between his shoulder and chin, Lake clapped so that Clarke could hear it. Lake was ecstatic. "Going after terrorists is usually a drawn-out, sometimes ambiguous process," Lake told the author, recalling the call from Clarke. "In brief moments of success, you get a surge of adrenaline and something like joy. And this was such a moment."

Ramzi Yousef had been caught. The president had scored an enormous victory against terrorism. America was safe again. Or so it seemed inside the Clinton White House.

NEW YORK—The FBI agents purposely diverted the helicopter to fly over the skyline of southern Manhattan.

Ramzi Yousef had been talking freely, even bragging, to the two agents with him. He mistakenly believed that anything he said on the helicopter would be inadmissible in court, as long as it wasn't written down. So the FBI men kept the terrorist talking.

But the special agents knew that federal prosecutors always liked to see things written down. The agents would take turns slipping away to scribble notes.

Now the terrorist was about to get his comeuppance. One of the agents pointed at the World Trade Center. "You see that? They're still standing," he said.

"They wouldn't be, if I had enough explosive," Yousef said coolly.[37]

He was later convicted for the World Trade Center bombing and sentenced to 240 years in a "supermax" security prison in Florence, Colorado.

QATAR—The operational commander of "Project Bojinka," and financial manager of the 1993 World Trade Center attacks, Khalid Shaikh Mohammed, did not escape through luck and skill. He was helped by at least one Arab government and by the lack of focus at the highest levels of the Clinton Administration.

Sudanese officials told the author that Mohammed briefly returned to their country in 1995, but was soon discovered.[38] The Sudanese intelligence agency, known as the Mukhabarat, paid him a visit. He was told, politely, to move on. Sudan already had enough trouble from Western governments with its emerging reputation as a rest stop for terrorists. It didn't need any more wanted men in its capital city. He was given a few weeks to find a safe haven—outside of Sudan.

Sudanese intelligence later told a Cairo-based FBI legal attaché about Mohammed's visit to their country.[39] More important, the Sudanese revealed the terrorist's next destination: Qatar.

By October 1995, Mohammed was cornered. The FBI had tracked him to an apartment building in Qatar. The special agents had even confirmed his presence by using an undisclosed "surveil-lance technology" and provided the government of Qatar with his street address and an apartment number, Clinton's counterterror-ism coordinator, Richard Clarke, told the author. They were told to wait in a certain hotel until the paperwork was complete.

Mohammed's arrest and transfer to an American prison should have been a legal formality that only took a few days. Qatar has a long-standing extradition treaty with the United States. FBI Direc-tor Louis Freeh even phoned top Qatar officials to emphasize the importance of the case. But days dragged into weeks. The Qatari authorities insisted on processing the formal extradition request as slowly as legally possible.

Whatever the cause, when the FBI agents finally received a valid extradition order, they raced over to Mohammed's apartment. It was empty.

How did he get away? Qatar's minister of religious affairs had tipped off Mohammed and provided him and a traveling compan-ion with false passports, according to Robert Baer, a former CIA official.[40] They are believed to have fled to Prague, where Mohammed assumed the identity of "Mustaf Nasir."[41] Baer, who at the time was a CIA case officer working in the region, said that Hamid bin Jasim bin Hamad, a disgruntled member of the King-dom of Qatar's ruling family, had told him about the arrangement.

Mohammed is widely believed to have been the operational commander behind the September 11 attacks. He was pho-tographed meeting with several of the September 11 group com-manders, in January 2001, in Kuala Lumpur, and he was linked to a shadowy figure known as Mustafa Ahmed al-Hisawi. Whoever al-Hisawi is, it is a matter of record that someone with a Dubai iden-tity card with his name on it opened a bank account at a Standard and Chartered Bank branch in Dubai in the United Arab Emirates.

Al-Hisawi used that bank account to transmit tens of thousands of dollars to Mohammed Atta and other September 11 hijackers.

On or about September 10, Atta and others wired back the unused balance of the funds to the same account. After the account was drained, Khalid Shaikh Mohammed disappeared from Dubai.

Mohammed's 1995 escape from Qatar was probably the Clinton Administration's first missed opportunity to prevent the tragic events of September 11. It wouldn't be the last.

LANGLEY, VIRGINIA—Director of Central Intelligence James Woolsey was unable to personally brief Clinton about bin Laden— or any other threat to America's security.

Never once during his two-year tenure atop the CIA was Woolsey granted a one-on-one meeting with Clinton. Even semi-private meetings were rare. They only happened twice, Woolsey told the author: one in January 1994 and the other in October 1994. In these two meetings, the president was accompanied by National Security Advisor Tony Lake, Deputy National Security Advisor Sandy Berger, and Woolsey's deputy director. "I don't recall the president ever saying that he didn't want Woolsey there," Lake told the author. But he never invited him, either. Woolsey's ability to forge a bond with Clinton and speak his mind about emerging threats to America was severely limited. Clinton was apparently uninterested in learning about emerging threats from his director of Central Intelligence. "It wasn't that I had a bad relationship with the president," Woolsey told the author. "It just didn't exist."

Of course, Woolsey also saw Clinton across the room in dozens of National Security Council meetings. Woolsey was extremely lim-ited in what he could tell the president in these gatherings. In addi-tion to the National Security Council staff—some of whom had top security clearances—Clinton liked to invite in six to eight White House domestic policty staffers, including two or three public-rela-tions officials, all of whom lacked high-level security clearances.[42]

This is highly unusual behavior for an American president. Most presidents have scores of one-on-one meetings with their directors of Central Intelligence and often call upon their expertise in making important foreign-policy decisions. So why did Clinton freeze out his own handpicked director?

Clinton has never commented publicly on the issue, and, initially, Woolsey said he was mystified by Clinton's behavior.

Then a series of off-the-record interviews by the author revealed what might have been Clinton's secret motivation for giving his director of Central Intelligence the silent treatment. In a second interview, Woolsey confirmed this never-before-reported account. In February 1993, Director of Presidential Personnel Bruce Lindsey approached Woolsey and said he had a candidate for the CIA's general counsel post.

"I've got a general counsel and she's great," Woolsey replied.

"Do you know where this is coming from?" Lindsey was letting him know that the unnamed candidate was a personal pick of President Clinton.

"No," Woolsey said, missing Lindsey's point. "But I'm keeping my general counsel."

It took Woolsey weeks to figure out what Lindsey had implied. By then, Clinton had already repeatedly refused to meet with him. He never learned who the "friend of Bill" was.

Lindsey told the author that he recalled talking to Woolsey about a possible vacancy at the CIA's general counsel office, but says that filling that post had "no effect" on President Clinton's relationship with Woolsey.

Woolsey's account is credible because it was standard Clinton practice to insinuate "friends of Bill" within the administration. One such example was the president's decision to make his long-time friend Webster Hubbell, the former mayor of Little Rock, Associate Attorney General, making him Clinton's eyes and ears within the Justice Department.[43] Hubbell later resigned from the department, pled guilty to two felony charges of defrauding his Arkansas law firm, and fought a series of legal efforts to compel him to testify before an independent council. Perhaps Clinton was considering a similar move at the CIA, and Woolsey inadvertently blocked it.

In the wake of his fateful conversation with Lindsey, Woolsey repeatedly tried to establish a rapport with the president. In February and March 1993, he accompanied the CIA briefing officer to the White House for the daily intelligence briefing. He hoped the president would invite him in, as was customary in past administrations, but Clinton, aware that Woolsey was waiting outside his office, never asked him in.[44]

Often, the briefing officer himself would not be welcomed into the Oval Office. Clinton would simply have the sealed briefing folder carried in by a junior White House staffer. The president was a "speed reader," Woolsey was assured.[45] Ten or twenty minutes later, the team from the CIA would be told that the president didn't have any questions. It was time to go.

These White House visits soon became a humiliating ritual known to many inside the Clinton Administration. When a small plane accidentally crashed on the White House lawn in 1994, West Wing staffers joked that it was Woolsey trying to see the president, according to Woolsey, in an interview with the author.

After a few frustrating months, Woolsey stopped schlepping to the White House, and decided the president could send for him if he was needed. Clinton never did.

Meanwhile, Woolsey was fighting other bureaucratic battles— instead of bin Laden. The CIA was critically short of translators who spoke or read Arabic, Farsi, Pashto, and the other languages of the great "terrorist belt." That belt begins on the dirty beaches of Somalia, arcs up the river valleys of Sudan and Egypt, across the desert flats of Saudi Arabia and the Persian Gulf states, over the dry plateaus of Syria and Iraq, past the wastes of Iran, through the mountains of Afghanistan and Pakistan, and ends in the cold steppes of Central Asia. In the world's most terror-prone region, the CIA was essentially blind, deaf, and dumb.

Partly as a result, the intelligence community was able to decipher and translate less than ten percent of the volume of telephone and other intercepts gained from its extensive networks of spy satellites and listening stations.[46] Indeed, throughout the Islamic world, even many radio and television news reports went untranslated. While state-run broadcasts from the Communist bloc were a prime source of intelligence during the Cold War, in the Clinton years the CIA did not have the same capability against militant Islamists. And that deficiency was largely Clinton's fault.

Woolsey hoped to fix these dangerous deficiencies, but he ran into congressional roadblocks. Senator Dennis DeConcini, a Democrat from Arizona, repeatedly blocked any attempts to boost the CIA's budget for Arabic translators.

Woolsey and DeConcini came to viscerally dislike each other. The senator told the author that he lost faith in Woolsey when he defended the secret construction of a $300 million National Reconnaissance Office headquarters in Northern Virginia. When Woolsey privately warned the senator against speaking publicly about sensitive intelligence information, DeConcini was outraged. He said he phoned both Clinton and Lake, threatening to demand Woolsey's resignation on the floor of the U.S. Senate unless Woolsey apologized. Woolsey never apologized, and DeConcini never forgave him. As a result, Woolsey estimates that two-thirds of all his meetings on Capitol Hill were about undoing spending cuts proposed by DeConcini, then a key Senate Appropriations Subcommittee chairman. Woolsey had made a powerful enemy and America's security would pay the price.

When Woolsey suggested spending a few million dollars to hire Arabic-language translators in 1994, the feud with DeConcini intensified. DeConcini said he would only approve the request if it was a presidential priority. "I wanted to be sure," DeConcini told the author, "that Woolsey was not out on his own, like a cowboy."

If Woolsey did have Clinton's ear, it is unlikely DeConcini would have blocked the CIA's efforts to hire more translators.

Would the senator have given the CIA the money if Clinton wanted it? DeConcini did not hesitate. "Absolutely."

Some might be tempted to blame DeConcini alone. To be sure, without congressional approval, it would be illegal for the CIA to shift even one dollar from one part of its estimated $30 billion budget to hire translators.[47] But DeConcini called the president at least once and National Security Advisor Tony Lake many times, and never received a definitive response on whether hiring Arabic translators for the CIA was a presidential priority. With no such assurance, DeConcini felt confident in rejecting it. A Democratic senator does not lightly defy a Democratic president over a relatively small spending measure needed for national security, DeConcini insisted. But if Clinton wasn't interested, DeConcini would not be defying the president. The senator would have a free hand to thwart Woolsey. Without absolving DeConcini, Woolsey seems to acknowledge this point: "This was DeConcini's way of using the fact that I had no particular access to the president to turn down my request."

So Clinton's ostracism of Woolsey had weakened his hand in Congress and weakened the CIA at a critical time. Then the fecklessness of Clinton and his White House would only make matters worse. Over the next few months, the senator said that he called the president at least once and could not get a clear answer on the translator appropriation. He also phoned Lake many times, but never received a definitive response. Apparently the White House did not think hiring CIA translators to monitor terrorist states was very important.

On the day that the appropriations subcommittee was voting on the CIA budget, Lake finally called DeConcini back about the translators. "It wasn't the eleventh hour," DeConcini said, "it was the twelfth hour." Did the White House want the funds? As DeConcini recalls, Lake responded tentatively, "Well, we want some of that."

"Well, it's too late," DeConcini said. Lake, he recalls, did not object or argue. There would be no funding for the translators.

"I don't bear him [Woolsey] any ill feeling," DeConcini said. "He just wasn't in a position to get what he wanted. I guess the term would be 'screwed by the White House.'"

So a bureaucratic feud and President Clinton's indifference kept America blind and deaf as bin Laden plotted.

WASHINGTON, D.C.—Inside the federal bureaucracy, identifying the bin Laden threat was a glacial process.[48] The CIA had been investigating bin Laden since the 1992 attacks in Yemen. The agency suspected his role in the attacks on U.S. forces in Somalia in 1993, and had come to believe that bin Laden was behind the 1995 bombing in Riyadh. Bin Laden's connection to the 1993 World Trade Center bombing was most likely unclear to the CIA because the FBI was not able to share information about the case due to grand-jury secrecy rules and rule 6E of the Federal Rules of Criminal Procedure. Still, CIA analysts suspected bin Laden was bankrolling the assembly of a terrorist army using Islamic radicals he had met during his ten-year sojourn in Afghanistan.

Meanwhile, the FBI in its New York and Washington offices had uncovered traces of bin Laden's operations inside the United States and, after sifting the rubble left by his bombers, in Saudi Arabia in 1995. "His name just kept popping up," one FBI investigator recalls. "It was like every time you turn over a rock and there it was."

At the White House, National Security Council analysts were painstakingly piecing together the information gathered by the CIA, the FBI, and other intelligence services. But little information about the investigation seeped out of the FBI—which suited the Clinton White House just fine. "They [the FBI] were very loath to supply information to the White House," Lake told the author, "and we were very loath to ask about it" in order to protect the legal standing of the criminal investigation. Still, bin Laden's name was slowly welling up through the layers of the national security bureaucracy. Clinton's National Security Advisor Tony Lake believes he probably first heard bin Laden's name in 1993, mentioned as part of a web of Islamic militants loosely connected to the World Trade Center attack. If the arch-terrorist was known by senior members of the Clinton White House in the administration's first two years, Lake suggests, he was seen as simply another name in a shadowy network of terrorists, and no more.

By 1994, bin Laden loomed larger. Lake says he was first briefed specifically about bin Laden "sometime in 1994."[49] If Lake's recollection is correct, his bin Laden briefing precedes all known references to bin Laden in publicly available U.S. government documents, which first mention the Saudi terrorist in 1995.[50]

Lake could not be more specific about the timing of the bin Laden briefing, which is not surprising, given the long hours and numerous crises of the job.[51]

But if he is right that the Clinton Administration identified bin Laden as a threat "sometime in 1994," that's almost two years after the CIA and FBI learned of bin Laden's evil designs.

More important, Lake's comment strongly suggests that President Clinton was first briefed about bin Laden "sometime in 1994."

What happened in 1994 that made bin Laden important to the White House?

The answer is that in 1994, an FBI counterterrorism team returned from the Philippines with the details of "Project Bojinka." The CIA and the FBI briefed the National Security Council's Richard Clarke. This was something too big to ignore. President Clinton himself had been a target.

RIYADH, SAUDI ARABIA—No one saw the Chevrolet Caprice Classic glide into a parking spot alongside a three-story glass and concrete building that housed the Office of the Program Manager of the Saudi National Guard. And no one noticed the driver hurry away.

It was a busy street of upscale shops, air-conditioned offices, and apartment buildings in the fashionable al-Olaia district of Saudi Arabia's capital city. And at 11:30 A.M. on November 13, 1995, there were some perfectly ordinary reasons for the street to be empty. Most of the pedestrians had heeded the loudspeaker's call—what sounds like a mournful wail to Western ears—and rushed indoors to wash for midday prayers.

Of course, the Americans would still be working. They didn't leave their offices for prayers, and this time their lack of Islamic observance was an integral part of the plan to kill them.

American military planners spent their days worrying about the safety of embassies and bases. Millions of dollars had been spent hardening the defenses of embassies and other government buildings against terrorist attacks—including placing concrete planters to stop truck bombs, building blast resistant walls and doors, and constructing safe zones within buildings. The U.S. military and the officers of the State Department's Office of Diplomatic Security did not consider their nondescript tower in central Riyadh a potential target.

Certainly it was not an obvious target. It did not fly an American flag. It was not even the property of the U.S. government. The closest connection to American interests was the Vinnell Corporation, a military contractor based in Fairfax, Virginia, that is now a subsidiary of Northrop Grumman. Vinnell leased several floors of the building and had been a service provider for the armed forces and the CIA for more than three decades.[52] By the 1990s, Vinnell's office in Saudi Arabia was a lucrative and safe place to earn a living in a sunny clime. Many of its employees were retired U.S. Army officers who still cropped their hair to regulation length, out of habit, and whose responsibilities entailed training the Saudi armed forces.

Its mission was never considered to be controversial or dangerous. So there was no guard, no row of concrete potted plants, no steel-reinforced blast wall, and no reason to think they were needed.

What the Americans in Riyadh did not know, and perhaps could not know, was that they had been watched by a meticulous terrorist strike force for the past two years.

What made that force dangerous was not only its evil intent, but its patience. This quality, this willingness to lie in wait, sets bin Laden's organization apart from virtually every other terrorist apparatus. Most terror groups plan quickly and mount dozens of nearly spontaneous operations each year. Al Qaeda inculcates patience from the first days of training. Recruits are divided into small groups and urged to shout *ayahs* (verses) of the Koran in unison. Early in his training, an al Qaeda operative named Mohammed Rasheed Daoud al-Owhali recalls repeatedly chanting this Koranic verse: "I will be patient until patience is worn out from patience."[53] Nothing better summarizes al Qaeda's methods.

Osama bin Laden's spies had scrutinized dozens of targets in Arabia, according to the testimony of al Qaeda operatives in U.S. federal courts. Early on, the French and British embassies were rejected as targets. Security there was too vigilant. The Saudis, at the urging of French and British diplomats, had closed all of the streets that bordered their embassies and official buildings. A car or truck, packed with hundreds of pounds of explosives, simply couldn't get close enough to pierce the outer walls. It was a simple matter of physics: the force of a blast falls off by a square of the distance.

By mid-1994, al Qaeda was planning to attack the U.S. embassy in the Saudi capital city. A meeting of the executive council of al Qaeda, held in Khartoum, broke down into finger-pointing and shouting. One faction, mostly composed of experienced bombers from Egyptian Islamic Jihad, strongly favored a bold, reckless plot to ram a bomb-laden truck into the front gate of the American embassy. A Saudi faction, who had spent many hours studying the U.S. embassy, opposed the plan.[54] Usually, the Egyptian faction would have been expected to win the argument in al Qaeda's consultative council. Longtime bin Laden associates believed that he had fallen increasingly under the spell of the Egyptians—especially his personal doctor and second in command, Ayman al-Zawahiri—generally favoring them with leadership roles and higher pay.

But bin Laden ultimately vetoed the project. He noted that the distance between the front gate and the main embassy building was more than sixty feet. The office windows were narrow slits barely two feet wide. The explosion would not be able to cross the distance and punch through the narrow windows with enough force to kill very many Americans. Al Qaeda needed a softer target.

They found it on a narrow shopping street in downtown Riyadh. The Saudi National Guard office building, where one hundred Americans worked, loomed over the sidewalk—well within striking distance. The street was open to car traffic, and it was unguarded. It satisfied all the technical requirements. With any luck, hundreds would die. And, if the bomb was timed to explode during midday prayers, no practicing Muslims would perish.

To someone of bin Laden's cast of mind, the target was almost poetic. It enabled him to strike simultaneously at both the Americans, who had "occupied" the Arabian Peninsula during the Gulf War, and the Saudi royal family, which considered the National Guard its own Praetorian Guard.

At about 11:30 A.M., retired U.S. Army Lieutenant Colonel Greg Turner swiveled his high-backed office chair away from his magnificent picture window and went back to work. That burst of industriousness probably saved his life.[55]

Seconds later, a 220-pound car bomb exploded. The window became a wall of moving blades. If Turner had been facing it, he would have been cut to pieces. Instead, the back of the chair was embedded with many shards of glass.

"I remember adjusting my glasses—then I had no sense of anything until I pushed a window frame off my shoulder," said Turner.[56] Bleeding and missing an ear, Turner stumbled across his office floor to the twisted metal staircase that led to the street.

A second, smaller explosion followed. The heat of the blast had ignited the fuel of parked cars. By the end of the day, five Americans were dead and some sixty Americans and others were wounded.

KHARTOUM, SUDAN—Less than an hour before the blast in Saudi Arabia, bin Laden had given his final approval by satellite telephone. The call had come from his modest farm, some twenty miles south of Khartoum, along a potholed road littered with plastic shopping bags.

Gutbi el-Mahdi, Sudan's then–head of intelligence and a friend of bin Laden's, told the author that the terror mastermind had done much of the initial building of the farmhouse himself. It was a small concrete structure, coated with dust, and had no electricity or running water. El-Mahdi explained that bin Laden wanted to "return to a simple life," to go back to nature. El-Mahdi hints that bin Laden was reconsidering his life of terror in 1995. "He was," el-Mahdi said, "a very pious Muslim."

But bin Laden was not Thoreau setting up camp on Walden Pond, according to a mid-level Sudanese intelligence official who read daily reports on bin Laden and his unsavory visitors. Egyptian terrorists, Saudi dissidents, and even Iraqi intelligence agents were observed visiting the farm. The mid-level agent, who spoke on the condition of anonymity, says bin Laden never slowed his global terrorist efforts. In fact, the farm was purchased to avoid foreign-intelligence surveillance (mostly British) of bin Laden's home and offices in Khartoum. Bin Laden oversaw construction of the small house to ensure that no electronic bugs were mixed in with mortar. He forbade power and telephone lines in order to guard against other forms of eavesdropping. And the farm was remote enough that no stranger could approach without being seen. It was the ideal safe house from which to plot a global war on America.

But bin Laden forgot about America's intelligence satellites, which can intercept virtually any wireless phone call on earth. On November 13, 1995, the National Security Agency intercepted an ominous call to bin Laden.

When bin Laden came on the line, the caller gave what appears to be pre-arranged coded reference to a forthcoming attack. Bin Laden became emotional, implored God to bless the caller, and declared, "This is not the first or the last. The rain starts with one drop and it soon becomes a downpour. Things will be ready."[57]

THE WHITE HOUSE—Over the next few days, the Clinton Administration would learn that the Riyadh bombing was the work of Osama bin Laden. The satellite evidence was overwhelming. The pattern, by now, was clear: bin Laden had declared war on America in December 1992.[58] He had ordered the bombing of hotels housing American troops in Aden, financed the 1993 World Trade Center bombing, underwritten savage attacks in Mogadishu in the summer and fall of 1993, and authorized "Project Bojinka" in 1994. Ramzi Yousef had worked for him. And now, with the U.S. presidential campaign heating up, bin Laden had murdered Americans in Saudi Arabia.

America had been attacked by a terrorist determined to wage war. Now President Clinton had to decide whether to fight back.

CHAPTER FIVE

SHOWDOWN
IN SUDAN

ROSSLYN, VIRGINIA—President Clinton's first opportunity to defeat Osama bin Laden came late in the afternoon of March 3, 1996, in an Arlington, Virginia, hotel suite. It was the first attempt by the Clinton Administration to deal decisively with the arch-terrorist. It lasted less than thirty minutes.[1]

At first, everything went according to plan. Sudan's then–Minister of State for Defense Elfatih Erwa[2] flew in for a secret meeting with Timothy M. Carney, the U.S. ambassador to Sudan, and David Shinn, Director of East African Affairs at the State Department.[3] Both Carney and Shinn were State Department veterans. Also present was a middle-aged man who was a member of the CIA's Directorate of Operations (Africa division) at the time and is still active with the agency today.[4]

Erwa and the CIA knew each other well. He had worked closely with the CIA and Britain's MI-6 during the 1980s to help counter Soviet influence in East Africa. He also had arranged for Israel to use Sudan's airport in Khartoum and a makeshift airfield in Aruse, near Port Sudan, to spirit persecuted Jews out of Ethiopia to Israel in 1985.[5] So, in 1996, it was natural for Sudan's president, Omar Hassan al-Bashir, to personally direct Erwa to approach his old friends at the American intelligence agency.[6]

99

After agreeing to the meeting, the CIA gave Erwa very specific instructions. These instructions were "typical tradecraft," one U.S. government official familiar with intelligence practices told the author. Erwa was to approach the front desk and rent an unreserved room (making a reservation might tip off a hostile intelligence service). Then, he was to take his room key, ride the elevator to the appropriate floor, unlock and enter his room, and wait to ensure that he wasn't being followed. Finally, he was to step back into the hall, climb the stairs to another floor, and knock on the appointed door.

Erwa followed his instructions. He rapped softly at the door. [7]

After the opening pleasantries, the CIA representative handed Erwa a two-page "non-paper"—a document without government letterhead that is designed to be deniable.[8] While Shinn says that he "approved the concept" of the non-paper, he added that the document itself was drawn up by the CIA. At the top, the document was titled "Measures Sudan Can Take to Improve Relations with the United States."

Item number one dealt with (largely imaginary) threats to intelligence and diplomatic personnel at the U.S. embassy in Khartoum. Citing security concerns, U.S. Secretary of State Warren Christopher had ordered all American personnel to leave the embassy in Khartoum in February 1996. Later, the CIA would have to "withdraw" more than one hundred of its reports on Sudan when its main source—a rebel sympathizer earning $100 per report—failed a routine polygraph test.[9] The "threats" to the U.S. embassy were partly based on these later-discredited reports.

Item two: Osama bin Laden. The first part of item two demanded information on bin Laden's network inside Sudan. "Provide us with names, dates of arrival, departure and destination and passport data on mujihideen that Usama Bin Laden[10] has brought into Sudan."[11]

The CIA believed, and its representative told Erwa at the time, that some two hundred al Qaeda terrorists were holed up in Sudan.

(The actual number, the author learned in Khartoum in 2002, was as high as 583.)[12]

Other items dealt with closing the offices of known terrorist organizations, including Hamas and Hezbollah.

As he read the two-page memo, Erwa did not speak or reveal his thoughts through facial expressions. "He was a pretty good poker player," Shinn told the author.[13]

Finally, Erwa looked up. "We can't close the Hamas office. You see them as terrorists; we see them as a Muslim charity."[14]

Privately, Erwa was surprised by the mention of Osama bin Laden. The arch-terrorist's name had never come up before in his discussion with American government officials. But he kept his surprise to himself and made a mental note to follow up with the CIA on the subject of bin Laden. Despite some press reports, "Bin Laden" was not mentioned *aloud* at this meeting, according to Erwa, Shinn, and Carney.

Erwa did not have the power to negotiate. He was simply a high-level courier of sensitive information. He said that he would talk to Sudan's president about providing the information on bin Laden and other items in the memo. He would receive a decision in a few days and meet again with the CIA officer later that week. At the next meeting, Erwa would be empowered to make an extraordinary offer.

Five days later, Erwa again met with the CIA operative. This time, the two State Department officials, Carney and Shinn, were not present. Erwa and the CIA officer were alone as they decided the fate of Osama bin Laden.[15] It would not be the last such secret meeting, but it was the most heartbreaking.

Sudan offered to arrest and turn over bin Laden at this meeting, according to Erwa. He brought up bin Laden directly. "Where should we send him?" he asked.

This was the key question. When Sudan turned over the infamous terrorist Carlos the Jackal to French intelligence in 1994, the CIA covertly provided satellite intelligence that allowed Sudanese intelligence to capture him on a pretext and escort him to the VIP lounge at the Khartoum airport. There, he was met by armed members of French intelligence and flown to Paris in a special plane. Would the CIA pick up bin Laden in Khartoum and fly him back to Washington, D.C.? Or would bin Laden go to a third country?

The CIA officer was silent. It was obvious to Erwa that a decision had not yet been made. Or perhaps his offer was not quite believed. Yet, the Sudanese official was still hoping for a repeat of the French scenario. Finally, the CIA official spoke.

"We have nothing we can hold him on," he carefully said.[16]

Erwa was surprised by this, but he didn't let on. He was still hoping for a repeat of the French scenario, a silent and quick operation to seize bin Laden and bring him to justice. With any luck, Sudan would be on better terms with the U.S. and be in position to deny that it had turned over the terror master to the infidels.

He explained that three Sudanese intelligence services—the Mukhabarat (external intelligence), Internal Security, and Military Intelligence—had been watching bin Laden since he had settled in Sudan in 1991. Initially the arch-terrorist had been welcomed by Hassan al-Turabi, the Islamist intellectual who founded the ruling National Islamic Front. But Sudan's government officials became suspicious when they observed bin Laden meeting with members of Egyptian Islamic Jihad and other Egyptian terrorists committed to the violent ouster of the Egyptian government. At the time, Egypt was a mortal enemy of Sudan. That suggested that bin Laden might be using Sudan as a staging area to attack Egypt—a move that could lead to war. So bin Laden was watched. His front companies and other operations were penetrated by informers. Bin Laden was shadowed and secretly photographed. And the government of Sudan kept detailed records of the passports, visas, and identity cards of every foreigner who visited bin Laden. "Let us watch bin Laden for you," Erwa suggested.

The CIA officer seemed to find the offer tantalizing, according to Erwa. Sudan's files on bin Laden and his network were extensive. Sudan had dossiers on all of bin Laden's financial transactions, every fax he sent (the Mukhabarat had even bugged his fax machines), and every one of bin Laden's terrorist associates and his dubious visitors. If Sudan's surveillance was as good as Erwa claimed, bin Laden's entire global terrorist network would be laid bare. And the CIA would be able to track the movements of his foot soldiers and lieutenants across the Middle East.

There were good reasons to believe that Sudan was serious about taking action against bin Laden. Sudan was anxious to be rid of the man they once called "the moving bank." The government had squeezed him for all it could, demanding bribes, kickbacks, and especially "loans" to pay for roads, airports, and other infrastructure projects. When it was time for bin Laden to be paid back (with a profit), the government pled poverty and compensated him with money-losing state-run enterprises.

That is how bin Laden ended up owning a tannery and an animal hide business, along with other failing ventures, in Sudan. Once bin Laden took possession of these "assets," he lost even more money.

By the time the Sudanese had squeezed bin Laden dry, he had become a political liability. His terrorist activities had isolated Sudan from the United States and much of the developed world. Sudan's internal politics were moving against the terror master too. President Bashir was in the midst of a power struggle against Hassan al-Turabi, the Islamist leader. Bin Laden supported Turabi with cash and a potential armed cadre of Muslim militants. If Bashir could rid himself of bin Laden, he could simultaneously restart Sudan's relationship with the United States and vanquish his chief internal political rival.

Over the next few months and years, Sudan would repeatedly try to provide its voluminous intelligence files on bin Laden to the CIA, the FBI, and senior Clinton Administration officials—and would be repeatedly rebuffed through both formal and informal channels. This was one of the greatest intelligence failures of the

Clinton years—the result of orders that came from the Clinton White House.

As the Clinton Administration was weighing whether to seize bin Laden or take the opportunity to obtain valuable intelligence on his global network, the CIA's own intelligence on bin Laden was shockingly poor.

Human intelligence on al Qaeda was virtually nonexistent. *Washington Times* investigative reporter Bill Gertz uncovered a memo written only a few months after Sudan offered its intelligence on bin Laden. The July 1, 1996, CIA memo was marked "TOP SECRET UMBRA," meaning only the case officers, analysts, and officials specifically cleared to read the documents marked "UMBRA" could have access to this sensitive document. (Very few CIA officials and National Security Council staffers have access to all top-secret documents; most who have security clearances can read documents from only a handful of passwords.) The July 1996 memo reveals how ignorant America was about its emerging nemesis. "We have no unilateral sources close to bin Laden, nor any reliable way of intercepting his communications," the report said. "We must rely on foreign intelligence services to confirm his movements and activities."[17]

This frank report reveals that as early as 1996—five *years* before the September 11 attacks—the CIA and other senior policymakers knew about bin Laden-related intelligence failures. When it came to rectifying the cause of these failures, however, little was done.

THE WHITE HOUSE—It is unclear that Sudan's offers to either arrest bin Laden and hand him over to American justice or to watch the arch-terrorist were ever passed on to the White House. Tony Lake told the author that "he doesn't remember" any such offer. Sandy Berger hotly denied to the author that there ever were any offers from Sudan, calling them a "fantasy." Richard Clarke told the author he had never heard of any such offer and in his job he would have. Besides, the Sudanese were asked to arrest a particular al

Qaeda operative and failed to, he said. Their credibility was shot. Michael Sheehan, who then handled terrorism on the National Security Council and was later the State Department's coordinator for counterterrorism, dismissed the Sudanese "offer" as a "p.r. job."

What's going on? The most likely possibility is that the CIA's director of operations agent never told his superiors or the White House about Sudan's offers. The CIA's station chief in Sudan had persuaded CIA Director John Deutch less than a month earlier to take the unusual step of closing the CIA station in Sudan on the grounds that it was "too dangerous." Any veteran CIA staffer would have realized in March 1996 that it wasn't a good career move to pop up and recommend a covert operation with the Sudanese as partners. Yet something had to be done about bin Laden in Sudan. Over the next ten weeks, the Clinton Administration debated the options. Essentially, there were five:

1) do nothing,
2) ask that bin Laden be extradited to Saudi Arabia or expelled to another country,
3) trust Sudan to spy on or capture bin Laden,
4) attempt to assassinate bin Laden, or
5) transport him to the U.S. to stand trial.

The Do-Nothing Option

Doing nothing was the first option to disappear.

By March 1996, the Clinton Administration had awakened to bin Laden's terrorist designs on America and understood the risks of doing nothing. If it didn't act and bin Laden murdered Americans during a presidential election year, Clinton would look ineffectual and weak.

The 1994 congressional elections had shocked the Clinton White House by delivering both houses of Congress to the Republicans, for the first time in forty years. Clinton knew that it was just a matter of time before Republicans began criticizing his record on terrorism. Congressional oversight committees were learning— from information seeping out of the intelligence agencies—what the president already knew. By 1995, both Democrats and Republicans on the House and Senate Intelligence Committees recognized the danger bin Laden posed and were surprised by the Clinton Administration's failure to act.

Clinton expected withering salvos from the new Republican majority unless he did something soon. Senator Richard Shelby, a Republican from Alabama, was chairman of the Senate Intelligence Committee at the time. He told the author that he first heard of bin Laden in 1995.[18] Soon, lawmakers would begin asking hard questions about terrorism and the president's plans to combat it. No one in the Clinton White House wanted to troop up to Capitol Hill and say, "We're doing nothing." In its 1995 Patterns of Global Terrorism report, the State Department, for the first time, mentioned bin Laden, calling him "a major financier of terrorism."[19]

The Saudi Option

The most logical option was to arrest bin Laden in Sudan and ship him to Saudi Arabia. He had committed crimes in that country and was dedicated to the violent overthrow of the Saudi government. Indeed, the Saudis had repeatedly asked for American help in removing bin Laden from Sudan. The Clinton Administration would spend weeks trying to persuade the Saudis to take custody of him. But statecraft with the Saudis is always a complicated business, a tangled skein of imperatives and impossibilities.

The government of Saudi Arabia had been growing increasingly apprehensive about bin Laden since his return from Afghanistan in 1989. Saudi intelligence soon learned that bin Laden was meeting with terrorist acquaintances from Afghanistan and Pakistan in the Jeddah office of the bin Laden construction business.

When, in April 1991, bin Laden hurriedly packed up his belongings, his wives, and his children and fled to Sudan, Saudi authorities were alarmed. He was now completely outside their control. Bin Laden's sudden departure underlined the widening gap between himself and Saudi rulers.

Over the next few years bin Laden was linked to bombings and terrorist attacks in Yemen and Somalia, both considered to be in Saudi Arabia's backyard. In addition, Saudi intelligence believed that he was funding Saudi dissidents in and out of the kingdom.

By 1994, Saudi patience was exhausted. Prince Turki al-Faisal asked one of bin Laden's half-brothers to visit him in Khartoum. At first, it seemed like a simple family visit. But quickly, bin Laden learned that his half-brother had a message for him, according to a Middle Eastern intelligence source. He begged bin Laden to switch from his hostile course. It was hurting the family's construction business—which was primarily with the Saudi government—and was hurting Saudi Arabia. When these entreaties failed, bin Laden was allegedly cut off from all family funds. Of course, before he was purportedly cut off, bin Laden had secreted away millions.

Next, a Saudi intelligence agent visited bin Laden and warned him that Saudi Arabia was considering strong measures against him.[20] Still bin Laden remained obstinate.

The Saudis gradually escalated their pressure against the terrorist. By July 1994, he was stripped of his Saudi citizenship. Now bin Laden had lost his family, his business, and his passport. Then it got worse.

Sometime in 1994, Prince Turki al-Faisal is believed to have ordered bin Laden's execution, a Sudanese intelligence source told the author.

The details of the first Saudi assassination attempt on bin Laden's life in the summer of 1994 are hazy but undisputed. Indeed, the assassin might have succeeded if he'd gone directly to bin Laden's house in the Riyadh neighborhood of Khartoum. Instead, according to a Sudanese military intelligence source,[21] the killer first went to a mosque where bin Laden sometimes prayed.

He burst in and showered the crowd with bullets from his AK-47. Then, incredibly, he fled and hailed a taxi. The police chased the cab, as the gunman fired out of the passenger window. The pursuit ended about two thousand yards from bin Laden's walled compound. There, the would-be assassin engaged in a shoot-out with bin Laden's guards and police. Wounded, he was apprehended by the local police. Bin Laden was not home at the time.

But the assassination attempt had a profound effect upon bin Laden, according to Gutbi el-Mahdi, who was Sudan's intelligence chief in 1994.[22] He no longer went to horse or camel races and other public gatherings. He isolated himself and increased the number of his bodyguards. His rage against Saudi Arabia and America grew exponentially. Then came the Riyadh bombing in November 1995. It didn't take the Saudis very long to establish bin Laden's role in the attack. The blow was designed to simultaneously strike both American and Saudi interests and reflected bin Laden's main complaint against the kingdom: the presence of infidel troops in the land of the two holy sites of Islam, Mecca and Medina.

Sudan's President Hassan al-Bashir met with Saudi officials while on a *hajj* in Mecca in February 1996. He was eager for better relations with the Saudis and knew they wanted bin Laden. So he offered to seize bin Laden and transfer him to Saudi authorities in the VIP terminal at Khartoum Airport. But there was one complication—at least according to the Saudis. Considering Saudi Arabia's increasing hostility to bin Laden, the Saudis should have welcomed this offer, but things are rarely simple and direct in the oil kingdom. The Saudi intelligence chief, Prince Faisal, later wrote: "In 1996 the president of Sudan offered to hand him over to the kingdom if we agreed not to prosecute him. We turned down that offer; we wanted bin Laden to face trial."[23]

Mahdi Ibrahim, at the time Sudan's ambassador to the United States, told the author that his government had indeed offered bin Laden to Saudi Arabia in 1996, but flatly denied that there were any conditions on the secret offer.

Janet McElligott has represented the government of Sudan in Washington,[24] and knows the details of the Sudan's offer to Arabia. She says bluntly, "The deal between Bashir and the Saudis never had any provision not to prosecute Osama. The Saudis are the ones who did not want to have a trial because it would upset the Wahhabi sect and encourage further militants within the kingdom. The Sudanese just wanted him gone at this point." The Saudis wanted bin Laden "neutralized," McElligott told the author, but they didn't want the responsibility of doing it themselves.[25]

Whatever the conditions, or lack of conditions, on the Sudanese offer to hand bin Laden over to the Saudis, two things are clear: Sudan wanted to rid itself of bin Laden and the Saudis didn't want to take him.

In March and April of 1996, the Clinton Administration repeatedly tried to get Saudi Arabia to accept bin Laden from Sudan. The strange Saudi pattern was repeated. The Saudis pressed President Clinton for help in removing bin Laden from Sudan, but the Saudis repeatedly refused to take custody of the wealthy terrorist. They didn't want him; they just wanted him to go away.

Why would the Saudis be willing to assassinate bin Laden but not take him into custody? Saudi Arabia is an oligarchy ruled by some four thousand princes and a panoply of clerics. Saudi politics involve an endless search for consensus among these oligarchs. As American diplomats and businessmen soon learn, there is no central authority in Arabia. "It is a dictatorship run by committee," a Saudi lobbyist told the author. Every important matter is exhaustively discussed, and without consensus, nothing happens, and even when something happens, it is in a maddeningly incremental way.

Arresting bin Laden, who was still widely admired in Arabia for fighting the Soviets and for his religious piety, threatened to disrupt that fragile consensus. It was likely that his detention would become public. He had allies among the wealthy, many of whom he had grown up with, and with the hard-line clerics, whom he had befriended and funded. Putting bin Laden on trial would invite a wave of terrorist attacks from bin Laden's minions and hirelings inside the kingdom. On the other hand, a secret assassination would be politically deniable for the Saudis—if they pulled it off properly. So in the strange world of Saudi politics, assassination was far easier than arrest.

It is not that the Saudis were wholly uncooperative with America. Shortly after the assassination attempt in 1994, the Saudis finally shared their intelligence files on bin Laden with the CIA.[26] The following year, Saudi Defense Minister Prince Sultan established a joint intelligence committee with the United States to share information on bin Laden and al Qaeda.[27]

But because the Saudis would not take bin Laden into custody, he was America's problem now.

The Sudan Option

Trusting Sudan to watch or imprison bin Laden didn't seem plausible. Osama bin Laden enjoyed friendly relations with scores of senior Sudanese officials. Could a host become a jailer?

Actually, yes. In 1996, Sudan's strategic planners—Minister of Information Ghazzi Selehedin Attaboni and then–Foreign Minister Ali Osman Mohammed Taha put into action a plan to overthrow their onetime mentor, Sudan's Speaker of the Assembly, Hassan al-Turabi. The ouster of bin Laden and his "undesirable factions" was vital to their plan to topple Turabi.

But the Clinton Administration, especially its Africa expert on the National Security Council, Susan Rice, had not paid sufficient attention to the internal shifts in Sudan's politics and was intensely suspicious of anything Sudan offered to do.

A closer look at Sudan's political history would have produced a more accurate, nuanced view. Located south of Egypt and straddling the immense Nile River, Sudan is Africa's largest country and its strangest case. Since the end of British colonial rule on January 1, 1956, the country was blessed with a largely effective and honest civil service based on the British model—and yet cursed with a shockingly brutal civil war. The war, which pits the educated, Muslim North against the rural, Christian, and animist South, has raged with interruptions ever since independence.[28] More than two million have been killed in the past two decades alone. Only disease and malnutrition kill more.

War has erased material progress. In the South, old Anglican hymnals are perfectly preserved in well-kept brick churches, while power plants, roads, and bridges are allowed to erode away. When a half-ton truck is shattered by a land mine near the city of Yei, children crawl over the hulk, scavenging for parts. The North is rich only by comparison. Most of the roads in the capital city are sand and rubble. Until recently, unless you had a private generator, you had no lights at night.[29] Even the presidential palace is a marvel of fraying carpets and falling plaster. By 1996, economic hardship was forcing Sudan to reconsider its policies and tolerance of terrorists.

Following the bloodless June 30, 1989, coup that brought the National Islamic Front to power, it increasingly became a center of Islamic extremism. Sudan announced a new terrorist-friendly visa policy: Arabs did not need visas to live in Sudan. The motive was to bring in Arab money. The result was to make Sudan become a dumping ground for former Arab Afghans looking for a new, perfect "Islamic state."

Terrorists from all over the Arab world moved to Khartoum. Hamas, Hezbollah, and the Palestine Liberation Organization opened offices. Many others, including Egyptian Islamic Jihad, moved into cheap hotels or small houses. Even Carlos the Jackal— one of the world's most wanted men—moved in. Why not? Sudan was one giant safe house.

Early on, the Clinton Administration's view of Sudan shifted from a tragic backwater to a "viper's nest of terrorists," in the words of then–UN ambassador Madeleine Albright.[30] Every report out of Sudan made policymakers more suspicious and fearful.

As if to emphasize that Sudan was fast becoming another Iran, its government began sponsoring what Western diplomats invariably called "terrorist conferences" in 1991. They were held twice a year until 1996.

Hassan al-Turabi, the Speaker of Sudan's National Assembly, who hosted the conferences, called them "venting sessions." Few in Washington were fooled. Muslim militants from some eighty countries were welcomed to Turabi's biannual Popular Arab and Islamic Conferences with a lavish opening night banquet. In a Khartoum hotel, terrorist leaders talked freely about jihad, railed against Jews and Americans, and fantasized about creating a single Arab, fundamentalist Islamic state, stretching from Spain to Central Asia and Indonesia. The conferences were a call to arms, with networking opportunities for arms sales and bomb training. Here is how the only American journalist present at a 1995 conference, Ethan Bronner, described the speeches: "The theme was straightforward: the West, led by the United States, had defeated the Soviet Union through the exploitation of Muslim forces in Afghanistan. Now the Americans, with their sick culture of sex and hamburgers, were moving to phase two, establishing their hegemony as the sole and unstoppable superpower. Look around, speakers said. Palestine was overrun by Jews armed with nuclear weapons, Iraqi children were being starved, Kashmir was bleeding, Chechnya destroyed, Algeria imploding, Bosnia disintegrating. The United Nations and Amnesty International were tools of the West, the media run by Zionists."[31] All of these themes would later emerge in al Qaeda press releases and statements. Bin Laden was photographed at one of the conferences by a Western intelligence agency.[32]

Sudan was added to the U.S. State Department's list of state sponsors of terrorism in October 1993. It had officially entered the rogues' gallery.

By early 1995, Sudan allowed some twenty-three terrorist training camps to open, many of which were run by graduates of bin Laden's camps in Afghanistan.[33] These camps were closed in 1996.

Beginning in early 1995, Paul Quaglia, the CIA station chief in Khartoum (now retired), became convinced that bin Laden's men were likely shadowing American intelligence officers on the streets of Khartoum. Quaglia claimed that his agents had twice been threatened in 1995, once by a large knife-wielding man and another time by a pair of men with claw hammers emerging from a city dump.[34] (The men with the hammers were simply scavengers in the dump, Sudanese officials told the author.) There were no injuries reported in either case.

But the Sudanese noticed. Abul Gamri and an unnamed part-ner—both connected to bin Laden—attacked an American intelli-gence officer in Khartoum, according to Sudan's Minister of Information Ghazi Selehedin Attabani, and the Sudanese acted against the assailants.[35] "That is why we drove him [Abul Gamri] out of Sudan. Okay?" Attabani told the author in March 2002.

Still, one deportation did not allay Washington's unease, and Quaglia used these threats to lobby persistently for closing the embassy.[36]

Then, at a meeting of the United Nations General Assembly, a Secret Service agent approached National Security Advisor Tony Lake. The protective service had received intelligence from the CIA that a Middle Eastern terror group (not al Qaeda) with a tan-gential link to Sudan had dispatched assassins to murder Lake in Washington, D.C. Lake told the author that he doubted the reports from the beginning.

But the Secret Service immediately stepped up its efforts to protect him. He was chauffeured around the nation's capital in a bulletproof limousine and the vehicle was regularly swept for hid-den bombs. Lake and his family were moved into Blair House, an executive branch property near the White House, and to another safe house. These assassination threats later proved to be false, but the sense of menace from Sudan lingered over members of the National Security Council.

Sometimes it emerged as humor, as Lake told the author sometime in 1995. Sudan's foreign minister was in Algiers, the capital of Algeria, at the same time as Lake. He sent Lake a one-sentence message through a State Department diplomat: "Tell Mr. Lake I am not trying to kill him." When Lake heard the message, he laughed. His return message: "I'm not trying to kill you either."

A new low point in U.S.-Sudan relations was reached in November 1995. The U.S. ambassador to Sudan, Tim Carney, met with Sudan's President al-Bashir and Speaker al-Turabi. Carney told the president and the speaker about threats to American diplomatic personnel and reminded them that a U.S. ambassador was murdered in Sudan in the 1970s. He cited the growing numbers of terrorists in the capital. Finally, he handed them a typed letter, devoid of letterhead or signature. It warned that the U.S. government knew of Sudan's designs against America and threatened an "extremely damaging" response if Sudan struck at American officials.

When Carney handed them the letter, he noticed that they were not surprised. The previous U.S. ambassador, Donald Petterson, had delivered a similar letter two years earlier. Little had changed.

When Carney was traveling in February 1996, Quaglia won his internal battle. At a meeting of the emergency crisis group, consisting of the CIA Khartoum station chief and the head of the State Department's Diplomatic Security Service, it was decided to recommend closing the U.S. embassy in Sudan. It wasn't a hard sell. The African city was a hardship post—mosquitoes and disease lingered over the dusty metropolis, the drinking water was unsafe, citywide blackouts were a nightly occurrence, and alcohol consumption was illegal. A city full of terrorists made a bad situation worse.

But for all the hardships, and despite the warning he had delivered to the Sudanese government, Carney did not want the embassy closed. He raced back to Khartoum to try to undo the decision made by the CIA station chief and the head of the State Department's Diplomatic Security Service. He believed that shuttering the embassy would be an enormous diplomatic and national security disaster—and he was right. Without diplomatic cover, American intelligence would be unable to track terrorists in Khartoum or cross-check intelligence reports with local sources. And no American would be on the ground to witness an extraordinary shift in Sudan's politics—in a tentatively pro-American direction.

Carney sent a confidential cable to Washington. He made his case for keeping the embassy open but included the arguments of those, including Quaglia, who strongly urged the opposite course. Strictly speaking, Carney was the ambassador and had no obligation to include the arguments against his own position. It was sure to weaken his case with the State Department in Washington. So why did he do it? The author asked Carney in May 2002. "Vietnam," he said. He remembered his frustration as a young State Department staffer during the Vietnam War, and he had promised himself that if he was ever in a leadership position, he would include the views of subordinates who disagreed with him. He wanted Washington to have both sides of the story.

The debate about closing the U.S. embassy in Khartoum reached all the way to Secretary of State Warren Christopher. The last two decades had seen the deaths of almost two dozen diplomats. No one in the Clinton Administration wanted to be responsible for more deaths of embassy personnel. And, if the worst happened, the cable warning that lives were at risk in Khartoum was sure to surface in congressional hearings. Carney was ordered to evacuate the embassy by the morning of February 7, 1996.

After the embassy was "vacated" of Americans but not closed officially, Carney would commute to Khartoum from the U.S. embassy in Nairobi, Kenya, more than five hundred miles away. A skeleton crew of local, mostly Southern black Sudanese hires, would stay on.

It was less than a month later that Sudan allegedly made a secret offer to arrest bin Laden and turn him over to U.S. authorities. U.S. government officials did not know what to make of it. Could Sudan be trusted?

Absolutely not, believed a large faction inside the National Security Council. To this day, a Senior Clinton official doubts that Sudan's May 1996 offer was serious: "It's like an alcoholic saying he won't have another drink."[37]

Meanwhile, at the State Department and in some offices at the CIA, another school of thought was developing. Sure, Sudan was a rogue state, but the U.S. government deals with rogue states all the time. Why not test their words by demanding action?

These kinds of backroom deals with odious regimes were common during the Cold War—which is one of the things about them that some Clinton officials found intolerable. But sometimes such deals work, as Sudan's transfer of the infamous Carlos the Jackal to French intelligence agents at Khartoum airport in August 1994 demonstrated. Indeed, the Clinton Administration had seized Ramzi Yousef in Pakistan with a similar secret deal with Islamabad, which was hardly a liberal democracy at the time.

"Given the enormous variety of terrorist groups and objectives," former CIA counterterrorism expert Paul Pillar writes, there might even be some cases in which "agreements with terrorists might reduce terrorism."[38] Certainly, capturing bin Laden in 1996 would have been one such case.

But even the so-called realists at the CIA, like Pillar, and at the State Department, including Carney and Shinn, wondered if Sudan was really willing to arrest bin Laden. There were a few encouraging signs that it was moving away from its terrorist past. In September 1995, it had ended visa-free travel for Arabs, making it harder for terrorists to enter or stay in the country. And Sudan had already offered to turn bin Laden over to the Saudis.

Certainly, Sudan had strong incentives to move in a pro-Western direction. United Nations and United States sanctions were choking the already feeble economy of Sudan. President Bashir, who wanted to sell Sudan's cotton and gum arabic to the world, needed foreign investors to develop its oil and natural gas fields, and knew Sudan's politics had to change if he was to succeed. And if he wanted to loosen the grip of his rival, Hassan al-Turabi, the militant who ran Sudan's National Assembly, he would need to dispatch bin Laden first.

The most encouraging sign that Sudan might be changing came on the night before the formal departure of American diplomats on February 6, 1996. Carney and Shinn, who was visiting Sudan at the time, were invited to dinner at the home of Sudan's then–Foreign Minister Ali Osman Mohammed Taha.[39] There, they were in for a few surprises.

Taha's home was in the Riyadh neighborhood of Khartoum—a half mile from Osama bin Laden's walled compound. Carney drove past a neon-lit mosque, where bin Laden sometimes led the Friday prayers, and stopped outside a two-story concrete house ringed with sheet metal.[40]

Cut into the sheet metal wall was a small gate. Beside it, Carney saw the only sign of the Foreign Minister's power: two tall men in light-blue safari suits cradling AK-47s.

Once inside the gate, Carney was surprised. The grounds and the house were modest, even by Sudanese standards. The house had only two public rooms. One room had three metal-frame beds used as couches in the daytime. The other chamber had two brown couches arranged in an L shape. The concrete walls were painted beige; the torn brown carpet on the floor was held together by duct tape. Here, dinner would be served on a low coffee table, with the American ambassador and the vice president eating with plates in their laps.

The conversation quickly turned to terrorism. Carney reminded Taha that Washington was increasingly nervous about the presence of bin Laden, who seemed to be financing Egyptian Islamic Jihad and many other terrorist groups across the Middle East.

Taha said that Sudan was very concerned about its poor relations with the United States. "If you want bin Laden," Taha said, "we will give you bin Laden." A month later, bin Laden was formally offered to the Clinton Administration through the CIA.

The Assassination Option

Killing Osama bin Laden would be difficult and risky, and would require a presidential "finding" to be legal. Such a finding ordering the death of a terrorist that few in America had heard of—and doing so in an election year—was an unattractive option and apparently was never seriously discussed in 1996, according to senior Clinton officials interviewed by the author.

But two years later, Clinton did sign three secret "findings" ordering bin Laden's death. Intelligence officials would admit to Evan Thomas, writing in the *New York Times* in February 2002 that "the CIA has been trying to kill Osama bin Laden since at least 1998."[41] Why the change in Clinton policy?

In 1996, President Clinton did not fully grasp that America was already at war with Muslim terrorists—in part because American casualties were perceived as "low." On average, twenty-six Americans per year were killed by terrorists between 1990 to 2000.[42] By contrast, "Americans were more likely to die from lightning strikes, bathtub drownings, or poisoning by plants and venomous animals than at the hands of terrorists," noted Clinton's former director for counterterrorism, Daniel Benjamin, and Steven Simon, Clinton's former senior director for counterterrorism on the National Security Council.[43]

This is a strange rationale. Lightning strikes, drownings, poisonings, and animal attacks are all either acts of nature or accidents. The stronger analogy would be to a murder case. But all murders and attempted murders are investigated and the killers, if found guilty, punished. That analogy would have led the Clinton Administration to act, which it was loath to do.

By this strange and rather unique reasoning—comparing bin Laden to a murderer or an international mobster would have been more accurate than comparing him to an accident or a force of nature—bin Laden had not yet killed enough Americans to merit his own death sentence.

The Trial Option

What about taking bin Laden into custody and putting him on trial? This option, while seemingly the most straightforward, revealed a serious philosophical division within the Clinton Administration.

There are essentially two ways to fight terrorists: through covert action led by special forces and the CIA's Directorate of Operations or through international legal agreements led by the Department of Justice and FBI investigators.

So far, Clinton had seen terrorism as a legal problem. Within an hour of the February 1993 World Trade Center explosion, the FBI was in charge of what became America's largest counterterrorism operation to date—and the CIA was effectively shut out. The Clinton Administration had made an enormous strategic gamble and, as subsequent events would reveal, the wrong one.

The FBI's leadership of the World Trade Center investigation, code-named "Tradebom," set a powerful precedent. The Clinton Administration treated terrorism as a criminal matter and would fight killers with painstaking forensics, DNA samples, secret indictments, and surprise arrests.

Through patient police work and daring diplomacy, the FBI was able to grind out some successes. Operation TERRSTOP led to the arrest and conviction of most of the 1993 World Trade Center bombers; the mastermind of that bombing, Ramzi Yousef, was captured in 1995. These successes confirmed the Clinton Administration's view that law enforcement, not covert action, was the way to stop terrorists.

The backgrounds of the president and his top national-security advisors also disposed them toward a law-enforcement approach. President Clinton, Deputy National Security Advisor Sandy Berger, and many senior CIA officials were all trained as lawyers. For them, legal procedures were familiar and seemingly less risky than covert actions. The wheels of justice, unlike the march of covert war, proceeded according to fixed rules.

More important, law seemed to solve many of the problems posed by covert action. These problems can best be phrased as questions: How can one be sure that a particular terrorist is actually guilty of attacks on Americans? Is he genuinely a threat? When can a terrorist be removed from one country and transported to another and how should this be done? And what should happen to the terrorist once in the hands of America or its allies? International criminal law provides simple answers to these questions. The suspect is considered a threat once a prosecutor has amassed enough evidence to charge him and, until found guilty by a court of law, is presumed to be innocent. International agreements allow authorities to arrest and extradite the accused across national boundaries. The fate of these individuals is determined by a judge and jury.

Another benefit of fighting terrorists with lawyers—from Clinton's point of view—was political. The judicial process would insulate Clinton from any political criticism. The president could not be blamed for legal decisions that he cannot by Constitution, custom, and law even influence, let alone make. Whatever the outcome of the case, Clinton could not be criticized.

Covert action, by contrast, concentrates all the significant decisions in the president's hands. The president and his national security team must decide—often using incomplete information, informed guesses, and surmises—if a particular individual terrorist has actually carried out an attack on Americans and then must develop a plan to either snatch him or persuade an allied intelligence service to do so.

Covert operations have many risks that law enforcement does not. If a secret operation fails, targets the wrong man, kills or injures civilians, or costs American lives, then the blame is the president's alone. The wrath of Congress and the press would be intense and unavoidable.

For the Clinton Administration, the pitfalls of secret operations were not abstract but real and terrifying. Most of its senior members had suffered from the political fallout from a failed operation in Mogadishu, Somalia, in 1993. That incident had forfeited the lives of eighteen U.S. Army Rangers, wounded more than eighty other American soldiers, killed upwards of three hundred civilians, produced thousands of hours of cable television news coverage and hostile congressional hearings, and, ultimately, resulted in the resignation of Secretary of Defense Les Aspin. No senior member of the Clinton Administration, and certainly not the president himself, wanted to repeat the experience.

Finally, Clinton's senior officials came of age in the 1960s and 1970s, when the FBI was criticized for monitoring Martin Luther King Jr. and other Americans and the CIA was pilloried for its efforts to assassinate foreign leaders, topple foreign governments, and arm resistance movements. A certain disdain for intelligence operations undoubtedly lingered.[44]

But the glaring flaws in using lawyers and FBI agents to fight terrorists soon became evident.

Foreign governments often refused to cooperate or did so haltingly (as in the 1995 Riyadh bombing, where the Saudi government beheaded the suspects before the FBI could question them).

Even when overseas law enforcement tried mightily to cooperate, as the Kenyan and Tanzanian governments did in the aftermath of the 1998 U.S. embassy bombings in those countries, it lacked an intimate knowledge of America's arcane rules of evidence. If the "chain of custody" is broken—say a bomb fragment is stored in an unlocked container in a police station or taken home by a police officer—it would be considered "tainted evidence" on the theory that it could have been tampered with and therefore cannot be used.

And foreign policemen would overlook evidence that they themselves did not have the ability to evaluate. For months Yemeni police refused to turn over a hat recovered from one of the bombers of the USS *Cole*. They did not understand that the FBI had the ability to test the band inside the hat for DNA evidence to positively identify one of the perpetrators.

As a result, a lot of evidence and testimony that might be considered very valuable to intelligence agencies had to be discarded. Indeed, law-enforcement officials are not even supposed to directly communicate with intelligence officials. The results of the Clinton Administration's legal approach were obvious: all overseas FBI investigations of major al Qaeda attacks from 1995 to 2001 ended inconclusively. The effectiveness of law enforcement against terrorists stops at the water's edge.

Even if the hurdles of an investigation overseas could be overcome, bin Laden still had to be indicted in a U.S. federal district court. To get an indictment, Justice Department lawyers would have to present compelling evidence to a grand jury and the jury would have to vote to indict bin Laden. The problem was that most of the information that the FBI and the CIA had gathered on bin Laden by 1996 would be inadmissible in court. Much of it was assembled by foreign police forces, which didn't observe the details of America's legal code, and was therefore inadmissible. Still other evidence was gathered by the National Security Agency and was too secret—in what it would reveal about America's spy satellites—to be released in public. Some of the government's assembled information wasn't actually evidence—in the courtroom sense—at all, but a suspicious pattern of activity discovered by a CIA analyst. In short, the Justice Department lawyers believed that they did not have enough evidence to ensure a conviction—which is their internal test regarding whether or not to seek an indictment.

Since the Clinton Administration was locked into the law-enforcement mode of fighting terrorism, its inability to indict bin Laden made it impossible in their eyes to take him into custody. What seemed, to the Clinton Administration, like a logical and safe decision would ultimately make the world far more dangerous for Americans.

When explaining the administration's failure to act, Sandy Berger, among other Clinton officials, has repeatedly argued from this law-enforcement rationale—and also indulged some very Clintonian blame-shifting. "The FBI did not believe we had enough evidence to indict bin Laden at that time," Berger has said, "and therefore opposed bringing him to the United States."[45]

This is the most persistent excuse for failing to seize bin Laden: the U.S. government simply did not have enough evidence to convict bin Laden at trial. Clinton Administration officials, including Berger, feared that an acquittal would only strengthen the arch-terrorist's standing in the Middle East while further wounding the scandal-plagued president. The prospect of a military tribunal, as George W. Bush advocated for dealing with terrorists, was never considered, according to one senior Clinton official.

But the lack of evidence against bin Laden in 1996 is possibly one more example of Clinton spin-doctoring. An advisor to the George W. Bush Administration, who has studied intelligence files on bin Laden, told the author that there was "more than enough evidence to convict bin Laden in 1996." He couldn't be specific.

There was another way to seize bin Laden, but it went unexplored. In intelligence parlance, it is called a "rendition"—an extralegal transfer of a prisoner from one country to another. One anonymous American intelligence source, commenting on the government's reluctance to snatch bin Laden in 1996, told the *Village Voice*: "We kidnap minor drug czars and bring them back in burlap bags. Somebody didn't want this to happen [with bin Laden]."[46]

Unlike the French, who sent in a covert team to take possession of Carlos the Jackal, one of France's most wanted terrorists, the Clinton Administration was not willing to use covert action against bin Laden. At least, not yet.

The Expulsion Option

Finally, only one option remained: Asking Sudan to expel bin Laden. When General Erwa asked Ambassador Carney where the U.S. wanted bin Laden sent, Carney gave him the official line from Washington: "Anywhere but Somalia."

Bin Laden later told *Al-Quds al-Arabi*, the London-based Arabic language newspaper that is generally pro-Islamist, what his options were in May 1996: "Iraq is out of the question. I would rather die than live in a European state. I have to live in a Muslim country and so the choice is between Yemen and Afghanistan."[47]

Yemen made it quite clear that bin Laden would not be welcome in their desert republic, despite his family ties to the country. Afghanistan beckoned. For bin Laden, it was like starting over— returning to the land that made him a legend.

NAIROBI, KENYA—Outside Ambassador Carney's temporary office in the U.S. embassy, on May 20, 1996, a small fax machine came to life.[48]

Curling out of the old machine was a letter for Carney from Sudan's Foreign Minister Ali Osman Mohammed Taha. The letter simply said the "Egyptian elements" would depart Sudan in three days, a coded reference to Osama's bin Laden imminent departure.

In fact, bin Laden had been contacted by the Sudanese Mukhabarat almost a week earlier. He was told that Sudan was "no longer safe for him" and that his presence was causing the government immense diplomatic and economic problems, Fatih Erwa told the author.[49] Bin Laden had heard this before, but this time he knew it was real.

On May 18—two days before Ambassador Carney received the fax warning him of bin Laden's imminent departure—the Saudi terrorist had boarded a chartered plane with his wives, children, some 150 mujihideen, and a cache of small arms. His stated final destination was Jalalabad, Afghanistan, by way of Pakistan.

News accounts that suggested that Washington had advance notice of bin Laden's movements and could have seized the plane when it refueled in Qatar are false, according to Carney, Berger, and other Clinton Administration officials.[50]

The story of bin Laden's expulsion from Sudan has never been told in full before. According to a Sudanese intelligence source, bin

Laden purposely wrecked his plane in order to make a clean getaway.

On the runway of one of Khartoum's airports bin Laden carefully loaded his three wives, four daughters, and two sons into a small plane. A plane taxied as if to take off, and suddenly its landing gear breaks locked up, smashing the nose into the tarmac.

Unseen by Sudanese air traffic controllers,[51] who do not have radar, a mysterious plane hovered high overhead. It was unseen until it suddenly swooped down.

This second plane landed near bin Laden's wrecked craft. Bin Laden and his family quickly boarded this plane and it roared off into the sky. The ever-paranoid bin Laden believed (truthfully) that Sudanese intelligence had placed a tracking device on his airplane; the second plane allowed him to fly away unseen and untracked. Sudanese intelligence knew bin Laden's movements for six years. Now, no one would watch him. He would be invisible and deadly.

Back in Nairobi, and after bin Laden had left Sudan, Ambassador Carney conferred with Washington and responded with a fax of his own. In that letter, he asked the government of Sudan to freeze bin Laden's assets in their country.

Unfortunately, there were no assets left to seize. "He liquidated everything, and he left with his money," Erwa said. "We [the government of Sudan] didn't confiscate anything because there was no legal basis. Nobody had indicted him."[52]

Still, the myth of bin Laden's millions grew. The CIA was told by its informants, drawn from groups and countries opposed to the current Islamic government in Sudan, that bin Laden was able to redeploy millions of dollars to safe havens outside Sudan. Sudanese officials dispute this, and there are reasons to believe that they are telling the truth. The Sudanese government owed bin Laden millions of dollars for road and airport construction projects and was never able to pay. Bin Laden, these officials say, complained bitterly that Khartoum's defaults were threatening to bankrupt him.[53] And before he fled Sudan, he was unable to sell the money-losing state-owned tannery factory the government had dumped on him. The Sudanese government seized the factory and then sold it as an asset to the state-owned pension fund.

Even given the apparently calamitous state of bin Laden's fortune in Sudan, members of Clinton's National Security Council, including then–Deputy National Security Advisor Sandy Berger, believed that bin Laden would suffer more if he was forced out. Without his businesses and training camps, Berger and other officials involved in the 1996 decision believed, bin Laden would be financially and militarily weakened.

This proved to be a mirror image of the truth. Bin Laden's businesses, as noted above, were largely money-losers; forcing him out of Sudan actually cut his losses. And, without companies to manage, he was free to focus full-time on terrorism. Losing the training camps in Sudan did not amount to much, either. He had never closed his extensive network of training camps in Afghanistan and Pakistan. Now he would be on-site to make sure they ran at full tilt.

Steven Simon was Clinton's director for counterterrorism on the National Security Council during the secret negotiations with Sudan concerning the fate of bin Laden in 1996. Five years later, he described his calculations to a *Washington Post* reporter. "I really cared about one thing, and that was getting him out of Sudan. One can understand why the Saudis didn't want him—he was a hot potato—and, frankly, I would have been shocked at the time if the Saudis took him. My calculation was, 'It's going to take him a while to reconstitute, and that screws him up and buys time.'"[54]

Buying time must have seemed important in May 1996. The presidential elections were less than seven months away. But the Clinton Administration was also, unintentionally, buying time for bin Laden. In the coming years, bin Laden would be stronger, smarter, and more lethal than ever.

CHAPTER SIX

THE FRIEND
OF BILL

1996

NEW YORK—Bill Clinton's face was pink and his mouth was dry. Standing between the Stars and Stripes and the blue New York state flag in an anteroom off the ballroom of the Waldorf Astoria hotel in midtown Manhattan, the president was doing what he did best—shaking hands and smiling for pictures at the head of a line of wealthy campaign contributors in October 1993.

Political veterans dismissively refer to this fundraising staple as "grip and grin." But for Clinton it wasn't a dull chore but a full-body contact sport. He wasn't just a tired politician hand-pumping another receiving line of check writers. He was a smiling, hugging, back-slapping, and eye-crinkling machine, lavishing ergs of energy on each donor.

It was an experience that few could ever forget. Campaign donors describe meeting the president in remarkably similar terms: Bill Clinton grabs your hand, pulls you in close to him, less than six inches away, puts his right hand on your shoulder, looks you in the eye, and tells you that he needs you.[1] He means it and you believe him because...he is now your friend. For some donors this "friendship" was so believable and intense that they were actually shocked and hurt to learn later that it was simply a fundraising technique.

127

Not since Lyndon Baines Johnson has any president devoted so much personal energy to retail politics. Like that of LBJ, another Southern Democrat with humble origins and towering ambition, Clinton's personal energy in greeting strangers was overwhelming. It was the secret behind his legendary ability to raise vast sums of money and it was the fountainhead of his enormous political appeal among Democratic Party activists and donors. It is partly why they stuck with him in the depths of the scandal.

In time some of those party activists would come to learn that Clinton resembled LBJ in many other ways. Like LBJ, he had fierce loyalty to the aides that defended him and a volcanic anger to those who had failed him in some small way. He was committed to enacting the agenda of the liberal wing of the Democratic Party, but like LBJ, his efforts were often coupled with methods that liberals found unsavory: everything from suspicious campaign donations and cronies on the payroll. Johnson and Clinton also became known for their unusual personal habits: LBJ swam nude in the White House pool and summoned aides for face-to-face meetings while he was on the toilet, while Clinton enjoyed oral sex in the Oval Office and groped a campaign contributor who came looking for a job. Both had a history of cheating at sports where winning did not matter: Johnson hunted deer with a spotlight while Clinton unashamedly demanded unlimited mulligans from his golf partners. And both Johnson and Clinton could be dazzling on domestic policy while utterly feckless on foreign affairs.

During the Vietnam War, Johnson vacillated, hamstringing military commanders with ever-more complicated rules of engagement. Yet he lacked both the tenacity to win and the will to negotiate an honorable peace with Ho Chi Minh. Clinton's secret war on terror—which he kept secret partly to avoid LBJ's fate—also brought forth a tangle of red tape, a plethora of half-measures, and an inability to fight to win or to leave the Middle East to its fate.

Finally, both presidents raised campaign dollars from sources with sometimes disquieting personal agendas. LBJ relied on the ranchers in south Texas, most of whom feared that the Civil Rights Act might give their migrant workers the "wrong" idea. Clinton took donations from diverse sources, including the divorced wife of a fugitive financier, Marc Rich, who is alleged to have illegally traded with the government of Iran during the 1980 hostage crisis; a Loral Corporation Chief Executive who wanted an exemption from national security regulations so that his firm could sell technology to the Communist Chinese; and a shady entrepreneur named Roger Tamraz who wanted to build an oil pipeline through Central Asia, which would enrich the Taliban, who were then hosting bin Laden.

On the receiving line that night in October 1993 were some forty couples, each of whom had written $10,000 checks to meet the president and, incidentally, to support the reelection efforts of U.S. Senator Daniel Patrick Moynihan, a New York Democrat.

Among them was a self-made millionaire named Musawer Mansoor Ijaz, an American of Pakistani origin with combed-back jet-black hair, a groomed mustache, and the ability to write large checks. He had developed the CARAT computer system that enabled his clients, institutional and private investors, to make hundreds of millions of dollars. As a result, within four years of leaving a Harvard-MIT graduate program, he was worth millions.

Ijaz remembers the moment that he first met Clinton precisely. Clinton grabbed his hand and pulled him close. The sudden intimacy was overpowering. At that moment, it seemed that the president was delighted to finally meet him. "We need more people like you in the Democratic Party," Clinton boomed. The implied compliment surprised and delighted Ijaz.

Then the president spotted Ijaz's wife at the time, Yasmine. The leader of the Free World smiled at her and said, "Well, he-lllo." (The president would later similarly compliment Ijaz's current wife, Haifa.) Five years before the Monica Lewinsky scandal broke, Clinton's tone did not cause a nervous titter. Few campaign contributors knew or suspected that the president had a wandering eye, despite the Gennifer Flowers scandal, which came to light on the campaign trail. Instead, Clinton's attention to women was often seen as flattering.

Clinton's eyes darted back to Ijaz. "Do you have a business card?" he asked. The President of United States was asking for *his* card. It was a trademark Clinton move, but it touched Ijaz.

Ijaz stuffed his hands inside his jacket pockets and his suit pants, and patted himself all over. Where did he put it? The line was starting to push a bit. "Okay," Clinton said. "I'll get it from you later."

"No," Ijaz insisted. "I'll find it." At last, he did. Triumphantly, he handed it to the president. Impressed by Clinton's instantaneous interest in him, Ijaz was elated and ready to embark on one of the most unusual adventures in private diplomacy in American history.

Ijaz's odyssey was fueled by campaign donations—on a massive scale. Between October 1993 and October 1996, he would contribute some $250,000 of his own funds to the Democratic Party's various campaign committees, and raise almost as much again from American Muslims.[2]

He repeatedly invited his friends and business associates to his penthouse, with its floor-to-ceiling glass doors and wraparound terrace overlooking New York's skyscrapers, to hear prominent Democrats, including Hillary Rodham Clinton and Vice President Al Gore. Everyone who had crowded into Ijaz's open-plan penthouse had paid $5,000 to $10,000 for the privilege. Ijaz helped raise more than $200,000 from these events alone.[3] By 1998, Ijaz says he raised (from all sources) some $900,000 for the Democratic Party.

As a major donor, he quickly became a "friend of Bill." President Clinton would send him personal notes and invite him to attend White House parties. Top administration officials would welcome him into their offices, reply to his confidential memos, and call him on secure telephone lines. Hillary Clinton celebrated her birthday at Ijaz's home in 1999, along with fifty Muslim-American campaign contributors.

In turn, Ijaz would eventually bring the president several secret offers from foreign governments to disrupt terror networks and to arrest Osama bin Laden. The first came from Sudan.

Every administration receives a trickle of informal reports from traveling executives. Perhaps a government minister dropped a hint during a business meeting or a chemical plant seemed to be producing something unusual. Sometimes these tips would be quietly investigated by the CIA. More often, a White House official would listen politely as the executive breathlessly told him something that he already knew.

But in the Clinton years, the involvement of business executives in overseas intelligence and foreign relations reached a whole new level. In some cases, check writers became unofficial ambassadors, setting U.S. policy toward their favorite countries. There were many men like Ijaz. Others used their access to promote oil deals and to win export licenses—while Ijaz wanted to use his access to fight radical Islam. Private diplomacy by campaign donors was tolerated and even encouraged by the White House. As long as the money kept pouring in.

Of course, private diplomacy has its risks. Donors may have secret agendas that differ sharply from the administration's or from the interests of the nation. Or they may subtly misrepresent government policy to foreign leaders and accidentally scuttle promising diplomatic initiatives. In a worst-case scenario, foreign officials may believe that a visiting executive speaks for the United States. This is a particular problem in the developing world, where policy is often made on the basis of personal connections and the friend of the president is often more powerful than a cabinet member. The leaders of developing nations often assume that Washington works the way Islamabad or Khartoum does. This is why most administrations zealously guard their sovereign right to conduct foreign policy and forbid private diplomacy.

Used adroitly, private diplomacy can have benefits. It allows the president more options than he might have through official channels. If a private initiative succeeds, the president can claim credit.

If it fails, he can back away and say it was never the policy of his administration. Still, using businessmen as private diplomats must be done carefully.

Ijaz believes that the Clinton Administration never adequately weighed the benefits and costs of private diplomacy. "They never understood," Ijaz told the author, "what I as an American Muslim, who understood Muslim extremism, could do for them."

Certainly, Ijaz liked the role. There was the intellectual challenge. It fit well into his jet-set lifestyle. And he did it all proudly wearing his badge of honor, a lapel pin with the Great Seal of the United States on it that Clinton had given him on the president's fiftieth birthday.[4] As an unofficial envoy, Ijaz would travel regularly to Sudan, Pakistan, India, Singapore, Indonesia, and the United Arab Emirates. He would then report back to Clinton's chief of staff or the National Security Advisor. The author has seen scores of Ijaz's confidential memos and e-mails to White House officials, as well as responses from Chief of Staff John Podesta and National Security Advisor Sandy Berger.

Some of Clinton's national security aides now revile Ijaz as a Walter Mitty living out a personal fantasy; they cannot bring themselves to admit that he was good at getting foreign leaders to offer new proposals. Sandy Berger, Clinton's second National Security Advisor, told the author that he was suspicious of Ijaz's motives, which he couldn't identify. He hinted that Ijaz wanted to make money in nations like Sudan that were listed by the U.S. State Department as "state sponsors of terrorism." At the time, Sudan suffered from both U.S. and UN sanctions—making investment all but impossible for an American citizen to invest there.

Left unsaid was why Clinton allowed Ijaz to play the part and why Berger continued to send National Security Council officials to see him, as late as September 2000. Ijaz returned from his foreign travels bringing official offers to Clinton, regarding peace initiatives between India and Pakistan or the possible capture of bin Laden. Indeed, e-mails, letters, and other documentary evidence examined by the author indicate a consistent pattern of engagement between the Clinton Administration and Ijaz right up until Election Day 2000.

Indeed, as events unfolded, it became clear Ijaz's motives were not financial, but personal.

A few days after his father died in July 1992, Ijaz received a videotape. He pushed it into the slot in the face of his VCR. His father, dying of both brain and lung cancer, had recorded a message for him. Eleven years later, he can still remember his father's last words to him: "You're the only son we have who, no matter what pond we threw you in, you learned how to swim and survive. And now you have to survive the biggest test, because I didn't finish my work here [on Earth]. You have to finish that work. And that work is to save my country."

By "my country," his father meant Pakistan. He wanted his son to save it from the Islamists and the terrorists who were destroying it.

Mansoor, the oldest of five children, had spent much of his childhood striving to win his father's affection and attention. Yet his father was as remote from him as a subatomic particle, a distant man, a scientist even in his family life. "One of the very few times he ever said he loved me was in his dying video," Ijaz said.

But Ijaz now had a mission. "The political transformation of my life really happened at my father's death."[5] That transformation coincided with Bill Clinton's rise to power, and accelerated during Clinton's unacknowledged duel with Osama bin Laden. Ijaz facilitated a number of real offers from foreign governments to stop bin Laden—offers the Clinton Administration did not accept. And the issue was not Ijaz, but the Clinton Administration's refusal to work with the government of Sudan. The search by Berger and others for Ijaz's motivations distracts from the more fundamental questions that they should have asked: How significant were the offers? And why weren't they accepted? After all, even a small chance of stopping bin Laden might have saved thousands of lives.

While the outlines of Ijaz's odyssey have appeared in a few places in the press, the full story is presented here for the first time. It illustrates the Clinton Administration's tragic inability to overcome its dogmatic opposition to working with the government of Sudan and its failure to seize the extraordinary opportunities provided by its greatest Muslim fundraiser. Failing to grasp the series of offers from the leaders of Sudan, Clinton later said, "was the greatest mistake of my presidency."[6]

Mansoor Ijaz has an immigrant's sense of patriotism. Born in Tallahassee, Florida, Mansoor Ijaz graduated from the University of Virginia with a degree in physics in 1983. Next he studied at the Massachusetts Institute of Technology and Harvard Medical School, graduating in 1986 with a Master's degree in Neuro-Mechanical Engineering. Later, Ijaz moved to Wall Street. He joined International Investors, then the world's largest gold mutual fund, to help analyze the effects of the Chernobyl disaster on their portfolio's holdings. That's where he met Klaus Buescher.

Buescher, a legendary fund manager, gave him an education about Wall Street and human nature. And Ijaz needed it. Freely admitting that he was "arrogant," Ijaz didn't work well with people he thought were intellectually inferior or who thwarted him. "Having found a solution to a problem, I would become completely dismayed that people who I thought were my friends could not see even the smallest aspect of what I was talking about and wanted to just put up artificial barriers to solving the problem," he said. Ijaz can be relentless when he believes he's right. Opposition seems to energize him. "I don't suffer fools—at all."

In the Clinton years, the same dynamic would play out with the National Security Advisor of the United States—with disastrous results.

PESHAWAR, PAKISTAN—Mansoor Ijaz first heard the name "Osama bin Laden" in April 1996, more than two years after he first met President Clinton.

He had been shuttling between Pakistan and New York to start a series of independent private schools that he hoped would counter the role of the madrassas, radical schools that teach the ideology of the Taliban and bin Laden. The schools are funded with money from radical Islamists throughout the Gulf. Many madrassa graduates are illiterates who can recite the Koran but not read it; they are fit for no job but jihad. Without an alternative educational system, Ijaz feared, the next generation in Pakistan would be poor, Islamist, and anti-American. That is very far from what his father had hoped. So Ijaz set out to create schools that would prepare students for careers, not terrorism.

Everywhere the financier went in the poorer regions along the Pakistan-Afghanistan border in 1996, he heard about a wealthy bearded Saudi in gold-fringed white robes who lived in Sudan. And Sheikh Osama, as he was called, was coming back to Pakistan. In the spring of 1996, Ijaz says, he could feel "the glee in the radical religious networks in Pakistan because they were anticipating bin Laden's arrival for months." Bin Laden would return to Pakistan in May 1996.

And the leaders of the madrassas—who esteemed bin Laden— were attending annual conferences on radical Islam in Khartoum, Sudan. Bin Laden also attended these conferences, which were organized by Hassan al-Turabi, the leader of Sudan's parliament.

Ijaz began to realize that if he was going to win his struggle against the radical Islamic schools in Pakistan, he would have to go to Sudan.

NEW YORK—In June 1996, Ijaz received a phone call from a family friend named Lutfur Khan, a Canadian citizen who hailed from one of the biggest land-owning families in Pakistan. Khan once owned a controlling interest in Arakis Energy, which planned to produce oil in Sudan. (Ijaz never invested in Khan's company or did business with Khan in Sudan or any other country that Ijaz talked to the Clinton Administration about. When Khan saw Ijaz's June 10

Wall Street Journal opinion piece on political problems in Pakistan, he wondered whether Ijaz would go to Khartoum and write a similarly frank article about Sudan. Khan had been badgering Ijaz to visit Khartoum since January of that year. In numerous phone calls, he told Ijaz that "the Sudanese are not what the American government says they are."

Sudan was listed by the U.S. State Department as a state sponsor of terrorism and had played host to bin Laden for close to five years. Now the Sudanese government, Khan told Ijaz, feared that their support of radical Islamist networks was beginning to turn on them. They wanted to find ways to work with the U.S. in order to remove both American and United Nations sanctions that choked Sudan's weak economy.

Ijaz had his own parallel interests in Sudan. He believed that if he could meet that country's leaders, face-to-face, Muslim-to-Muslim, he could persuade them to stop encouraging the dangerous ideology of the Pakistani madrassas. He knew that Sudan's leaders would see him; his Canadian friend had substantial business interests there and Ijaz was a "friend of Bill."

Ijaz agreed to go with Khan to Sudan. But first, he wanted to see a friend in Washington.

WASHINGTON, D.C.—The U.S. State Department sits on a tree-shaded hillock overlooking the gleaming white marble of the Lincoln Memorial in a neighborhood known as Foggy Bottom. The name inspires a lot of jokes.

But on this July afternoon in 1996, Ijaz says that a State Department official was surprisingly direct. On the fifth floor of the sprawling 1950s structure, an unusual meeting between a major Clinton campaign donor and a key State department bureaucrat was in progress.

Mansoor Ijaz was meeting with the U.S. State Department Sudan Desk Officer Steve Schwartz. Schwartz was in charge of monitoring all events in the largest nation on the African continent, in whose vast expanses, the Clinton Administration believed, were hidden twenty-two training camps for every major Muslim terrorist organization in the world. Perhaps no one at the State Department knew more about Sudan at the time than Schwartz.

As Ijaz recalled, the meeting started with a small surprise. Ijaz said he was planning to meet with Hassan al-Turabi, the speaker of Sudan's parliament. The State Department had long regarded Turabi as the locus of terrorist activity across the Muslim world.

"You've got that kind of access?" Schwartz said. "That's pretty interesting."

During the bulk of the meeting, Schwartz counseled Ijaz on the finer points of obeying U.S. sanctions on Sudan and warned him to expect the worst: fear, poverty, disease, tapped phones, and civil war. But the most surprising news was saved for the end of the meeting, when Schwartz, according to Ijaz, said, "So you're going to see Turabi, right?"

"Yeah."

"Well you tell Turabi something from us. We're watching every step he takes. He moves one step out of line, just one step out of line, we're going to have his ass."

Reached at a U.S. embassy office in Pretoria, South Africa, Schwartz recalled meeting Ijaz, but he told the author that he categorically denies asking Ijaz to deliver a threat to Turabi. He did, he recalls, emphasize to Ijaz that the U.S. was seriously concerned about terrorism in Africa's largest nation. State Department officials who have worked with Schwartz over the years say that they have never heard Schwartz use profanity or make threats. Ijaz stands by his account.

When he was asked to deliver what he believed was a threat, Ijaz realized that somewhere along the way, American-Sudanese relations had gone seriously wrong. But Ijaz's education in the Clinton Administration's strange policies toward Sudan was only just beginning.

KHARTOUM, SUDAN—"Let me just tell you one thing up front. I am an American. I do not believe that my government is telling such a big lie that you guys can sit here and claim that you are not doing anything wrong," Ijaz said.

Looking at him was Hassan al-Turabi, the speaker of Sudan's parliament and the intellectual leader of the National Islamic Front, which had seized power in Khartoum in 1989. Turabi hoped to create a model Islamic state, where the Koran would prevail as law, and peace would reign as a gift from Allah. Instead, the civil war with the Christian and animist South dragged on as it had (with pauses) since 1955. Sudan remained one of the poorest nations on earth. Sudan's open-door policy for Muslim terrorists, pushed by Turabi, meant that the nation was increasingly isolated in the world.

Turabi and Ijaz were sitting in Turabi's home, which was well-appointed by Sudanese standards and designed to signal his status as a kingmaker in national politics. To Western eyes, it was an exercise in poor taste. A wall-to-wall tan carpet covered the concrete floor with duct tape covering its many rips.

Ijaz and Turabi sat on cream-colored overstuffed chairs facing each other. Beside Turabi sat Sheikh Ibrahim Sanousi, a key advisor. Lutfur Khan, the Canadian businessman who had invested in Sudan's fledgling oil industry, sat next to Ijaz.[7]

The meeting began pleasantly enough. Tea was served and Turabi engaged his guest in an academic argument about the true meaning of jihad in Islamic thought. Turabi's version of jihad was that Muslims should conscript nonbelievers into Islam because the Koran says that Islam will be the religion of all people on the Day of Judgment. Turabi just wanted to move up the timeframe. Ijaz sharply disagreed. From there, the conversation drifted into the morality of suicide attacks to achieve Islamic ends. Next, they talked about bin Laden. Turabi said that he respected him as a devout Muslim and a good businessman.

But Turabi did not like him as a person, Lt. Gen Gutbi el-Mahdi, a Sudanese friend of Turabi, told the author. El-Mahdi headed Sudan's intelligence services in the 1990s. Mahdi recalls Turabi commenting bitterly about bin Laden's lack of conversational range. "With him, it is always jihad, jihad, jihad," Turabi dismissively told el-Mahdi. Since Turabi is fond of long, lingering conversations that migrate across many topics—especially ones in which the former professor can do most of the talking—Turabi agreed to meet bin Laden only a handful of times, Mahdi recalls. Bin Laden's terrorist attacks could be overlooked by Turabi, but not his lack of conversational charms.

Then, an argument between Turabi and Ijaz began. Turabi mentioned an American "non-paper," the unsigned document on blank letterhead sent by a government to communicate a message, often a threat. "It is designed to be deniable," former U.S. State Department director of East African affairs, David Shinn, told the author. Shinn confirmed that U.S. ambassadors had delivered two such threatening "non-papers" to Sudan, one in 1993 and one in 1995.

Turabi refused to give Ijaz the details of the letter, but Turabi's advisor, Sanousi, did, and he was furious.[8] "Let me tell you what they said to us. That damn ambassador came into our office and he put the letter in front of us and he said 'read this.'"

That "damn ambassador" was Donald Petterson, the U.S. ambassador to Sudan from 1991 to 1995. The text of the non-paper was unambiguously threatening—and the Clinton Administration later denied its existence.

Luftur Khan reminded Ijaz of his conversation at the State Department. "You ought to tell Turabi what he said."

Ijaz was silent.

Turabi leaned forward. "You mean there's another threat?"

"Well it's not exactly a threat, more of an admonition," Ijaz temporized. "My real purpose here as an American is to find a way to reverse this very dangerous trend that has started in my father's home country [Pakistan] and that you apparently are helping to propagate by bringing these guys together" at the annual Popular Arab Islamic Conference.

Turabi grew angry. "Look, your government calls these things terrorist planning sessions. For me these are sessions for them to vent their steam. They get their aggravation out, at least they're not going to go kill somebody somewhere."[9] To believe Turabi on this point, one would have to think that terrorists are driven by anger and frustration, instead of cold, ideological calculation.

And then Sanousi interrupted with a threat of his own. "If you come to the Sudan, welcome. We will make Vietnam look like a picnic for you," he said.

Turabi continued. "See, now, this is why we have so many problems with your government. We try to send a message and it gets blocked at the lowest level. We send a message at a higher level and it falls back down to the lower level. People are not willing to read, or even listen, to what we have to say, much less analyze it."

Ijaz and Turabi would meet five times over the next seven days. Ijaz urged the Sudanese parliamentary leader to write a letter to President Clinton proposing full cooperation with America's efforts to stop global terrorism. Turabi agreed. The financier and the parliamentarian spent hours writing and rewriting drafts.

NAIROBI, KENYA—A few days later, a fax machine in the U.S. embassy in Nairobi, Kenya, grumbled to life. The U.S. ambassador to Sudan, Tim Carney, had been working out of Kenya ever since the U.S. embassy in Khartoum had been "vacated" in February 1996. Relations with the Sudanese had soured. Carney's regular flights to Sudan yielded little but frustration on both sides. A courtly man and a career diplomat, Carney spoke Arabic and practiced patience.

Then the fax appeared. It was sent on Turabi's personal letterhead and seemed to offer warmer relations with the United States. "It was the most extraordinary thing," Carney said.[10]

This was the breakthrough he had been hoping for. Carney said he sent it simultaneously to three different places: the State Department, the CIA, and the National Security Council at the

White House. The ambassador might as well have sent it to the dead letter office.

THE WHITE HOUSE—Deputy National Security Advisor Sandy Berger was not happy. He summoned "Citizen Ijaz" to his White House office. On August 21, 1996, Berger and Susan Rice, then in charge of African Affairs at the National Security Council, were loaded for bear. Berger says that he doesn't recall the specifics of the meeting. Rice says she was just the note-taker, not a participant. Ijaz recounts the conversation this way:

"So what were you doing there?" Berger thundered. "And why did you feel compelled to get this letter written?"

Berger had evidently forgotten that he had been briefed about Ijaz's planned trip to Sudan and that, only weeks earlier, he had set up a meeting for Ijaz at the State Department.

Ijaz explained what had happened in Khartoum.

Berger became cool and analytical. "What does this letter really mean? What is it trying to say? What is he really trying to say to us?"

Ijaz explained that the Sudanese wanted a new relationship with the U.S. and offered to share their intelligence on Osama bin Laden. Neither Berger nor Rice said anything. Not a word. "He was seeing me not as a resource to unwind a difficult problem. He was seeing me as a political favor to the president," Ijaz told the author.

Then Ijaz had questions of his own. "I understand that we delivered some sort of a non-paper threat to the government in Sudan. How is it, Sandy, that the U.S. government gets away with making those types of threats?" Ijaz asked. "When you trample the ego of a nation, that nation is going to react. And these are all people that would love to go to Allah tomorrow if they can."

Berger stared back at him. "Mansoor, I don't believe that incident ever took place."

In this case, either Berger was lying or Berger's boss, National Security Advisor Tony Lake, hadn't told his deputy about it.

Ijaz decided to up the stakes. "Sandy, what are you going to do if I go back to the Sudan and I get that piece of paper and bring it back to you?"

Berger laughed as he rose from his chair, signaling the end of the meeting. "Go get it and then we'll talk about it."

KHARTOUM, SUDAN—Ijaz returned to Sudan a few days later. He was taken into the office of Gutbi el-Mahdi, the great-grandson of the famous Mahdi who in Khartoum in 1885 had led the massacre of British General Charles George "Chinese" Gordon as well as the British and the Egyptians under his command.

Gutbi el-Mahdi is a soft-spoken man. He is thoughtful and believes that deep currents of institutional history drive current events. When Ijaz met him, he ran Sudan's intelligence services. (Today he is a diplomat with an office in the presidential palace. That office, he told the author, was once General Gordon's bedroom.)

As Ijaz arrived, he was offered tea. Then he was shown a single slip of paper, the original "non-paper." Ijaz asked for, and was given, a copy.

NEW YORK—On September 13, 1996, Ijaz sent Berger a confidential memo. He attached a copy of the threatening letter that Berger had said did not exist. U.S. ambassador Petterson later publicly acknowledged that he had personally delivered the letter. And, astonishingly, the next U.S. ambassador to Sudan, Tim Carney, had been asked to deliver a virtually identical letter to Khartoum. (Why does the U.S. government issue such threats? The State Department's former Director of East Africa Affairs told the author, "Sometimes some senior official gets frustrated by the lack of progress and wants to shake things up. It is almost never a good idea.")

Several days later, Berger phoned Ijaz's office in New York. Ijaz remembers it as a short conversation. The deputy national security advisor said, according to Ijaz, "Let's look at all of this after the election."

The 1996 presidential election was less than three months away. The administration apparently believed that any opening toward Sudan would trigger political counterattacks on the president from Christian conservatives who sided with the poor, black, predominantly Christian Southern Sudanese in their war against the aggressive Muslim government in the north.

Meanwhile, the consummate "friend of Bill" had a more important task to do, at least in the eyes of the White House. In a few days, Ijaz was hosting a fundraiser for Vice President Al Gore at his Manhattan penthouse. That September 1996 event raised some $200,000 for the Clinton-Gore reelection effort.

KHARTOUM, SUDAN—The afternoon sun in this desert city can be scorchingly hot. But the real heat was in the voice of the president of Sudan. Nothing seemed to placate the Americans or lead them to deal with us, the president thundered. Bin Laden was expelled from Sudan at America's request, but the sanctions were not lifted. And, he added, we have extensive intelligence on bin Laden and his vast terrorist network. That's information that your government should want.

Mansoor Ijaz and Sudanese President Omar Hassan al-Bashir were sitting in the shade, in Bashir's private residence. Ijaz tried a bold move. He proposed that the Sudanese make an unconditional offer to share intelligence with Washington.

Bashir insisted that he could never get such an open-ended initiative through his nation's parliament, which was then largely controlled by hard-line Islamic clerics. And he doubted it would work anyway. (Months later, Sudan would make a plain, no-strings-attached offer to share its intelligence. It didn't work.)

"Look, you are a well-intentioned young man," Bashir said. "But this is not the first time" that Sudan has tried to re-establish friendly ties with the United States.

Then came the bombshell. "Are you aware that I sent General Fatih Erwa to Washington to discuss bin Laden's extradition to

Saudi Arabia?"[11] Then, Bashir explained, Sudan made an offer to send bin Laden to the United States. Neither offer was accepted.[12] Ijaz was shocked. No one at the White House had mentioned these diplomatic moves to him.

"We tried it your way because you had access in a different layer of your government. But don't take us for fools," the Sudanese president warned.

"Is there a way that I can see some of the intelligence data?" Ijaz asked.

President Bashir waved his big hand. "No," he said.

Eventually, the president changed his mind.

Within days, Ijaz said, he was ushered into a low-slung brick building encircled by a steel fence. It was the headquarters of Sudan's Mukhabarat, its intelligence service.

Gutbi el-Mahdi, the intelligence chief, had a small pile of file folders sitting on the corner of his desk. These were carefully redacted extracts from Sudan's intelligence reports.

It was clear that Sudanese intelligence had been watching bin Laden and his men closely for the past five years. The Sudanese Mukhabarat was watching bin Laden not because of his terrorist operations, but, as el-Mahdi told the author in 2002, because of his many meetings with leaders of Egyptian Islamic Jihad, a terror group committed to the violent overthrow of the Egyptian government. Egypt and Sudan had eyed each other suspiciously for centuries—and bin Laden's meetings threatened to worsen that relationship.

Ijaz says that he was shown complete copies of the passports of bin Laden's top operatives. He saw passport numbers, copies of photographs, visas, dates of travel, plane tickets. He was also shown extensive Arabic-language reports about the movements of bin Laden's men, the assessment of their characters, and their role in al Qaeda. (The author was later shown and received copies of similar documents in Khartoum.)

With this intelligence, the CIA and the FBI would have had the names and travel histories of hundreds of al Qaeda members. Many of these same names would turn up after terrorist explosions killed a score of American diplomats and embassy staffers in the 1998 bombings in Kenya and Tanzania.

NEW YORK—Upon his return to New York, Ijaz sent the Deputy National Security Advisor another memo on October 27, 1996—detailing what he had seen inside those Sudanese intelligence files.

> *...As you recall, during our August meeting, I told you I thought this data could be invaluable in genuinely assessing terrorism risk from Sudan and neighboring countries... His [el-Mahdi's] central contention is that Sudan is prepared to share data on those people attending the conferences and belonging to banned groups, such as Hamas, Hezbollah, Egyptian Islamic Jihad, Jamaah Islamiyah, and others, if we are prepared to genuinely engage and incentivize the Sudan away from its present course. He complained bitterly about repeated efforts to communicate with the administration, which are as I understand it, being blocked at very low levels because of what he called 'blind spots.' He showed me some files in which the data seemed pretty compelling—names, bio data like dates and places of birth, passport copies to show nationality, recent travel itineraries in some cases, and a brief description of each individual to delineate which groups they claim loyalties to. In short, it seemed to me everything we discussed in August was available. Strongly suggest we test the Sudanese on the data, perhaps even try to get at the data on an unconditional basis...*

Berger's response was the same. "Very interesting, we'll deal with this after the [1996] elections are over."[13]

Yet nothing changed after President Clinton's victory in the 1996 election.

At Ijaz's urging, the president of Sudan sent President Clinton a long letter on February 16, 1997, offering another olive branch. But there was no specific offer on counterterrorism efforts.

On April 5, 1997, Sudan's president wrote another letter, this time making an unconditional, no-strings-attached offer of counterterrorism assistance to Democratic Congressman Lee Hamilton of Indiana, who had long been an influential voice on foreign policy. The letter was hand-delivered by Ijaz on April 16, 1997. On April 19, 1997, Ijaz sent Berger a copy of the Bashir letter. Another copy was sent to Berger from Hamilton's office. The offer presented in the letter to Hamilton was unconditional and unambiguous. It invited the FBI's counterterrorism unit, and other official delegations, to visit Sudan and probe its intelligence files. There was no official response from the Clinton Administration.

Ijaz believed that President Clinton needed to take action against bin Laden and that the president could not succeed in thwarting the terrorist's murderous plots without the help of these Sudanese intelligence files. It was time to see his friend, the president.

In a never-before reported meeting, Ijaz met Clinton at a political fundraising dinner on May 21, 1997. While Ijaz shook hands with the president, he told Clinton about Sudan's letter to Congressman Hamilton. "This is a letter that contains an offer of unconditional assistance on terrorism," he says he told the president.

"Bill Clinton cannot say, under any circumstances, that he did not know that the offer was there, that the [Sudan] offer was unconditional, and what the offer purported to make," Ijaz said. "I personally told him that on May 21, 1997."

The president looked him in the eye, the way he always did. Ijaz remembers Clinton's response: "I appreciate the efforts that you have tried to make. I'll make sure that Sandy gives me a report on this."

Yet these extraordinary offers were ignored. What if President Clinton had accepted any one of these variant offers and America's intelligence services had received the Sudanese intelligence files in 1997?

Ijaz speculates that Clinton and his senior officials spurned Sudan's many offers because of a campaign fundraising scandal raging at the time. "Clinton knew how hard I had worked on the Sudanese problem and that if he responded...given the fundraising scandal that had broken out," Ijaz said. "I would then be seen as having tried to influence the president with my money, to be able to get a policy changed."

The Clinton Administration was reeling from a campaign fundraising scandal in which impoverished Buddhist monks, many of whom were not citizens of the United States, had allegedly contributed thousands of dollars to Clinton's 1996 reelection effort. Under U.S. election law, non-citizens cannot contribute to candidates for federal office. That led reporters into the file rooms of the Federal Election Commission, a government agency that records all donations to presidential campaigns. There they discovered that a list of major Clinton donors and the list of guests invited to spend the night in the Lincoln bedroom in the White House overlapped. Pundits soon drew the conclusion that Clinton was selling sleepovers in the White House for campaign cash. One Clinton donor famously compared getting a meeting with the president to riding the subway; in both cases, you have to pay a toll first.

In the political climate established by the Clinton scandals, though, it is very likely that the press and the Republicans who ran Congress would have pilloried the president for changing U.S. policy to please a campaign donor, Mansoor Ijaz.

Of course, a different kind of president might have taken the political risks and made the national-security case to the nation. But Clinton was on the defensive from a plethora of scandals; he couldn't stomach one more.

Interestingly, career federal bureaucrats almost saved the Clinton Administration from itself. The U.S. ambassador to Sudan, Tim Carney, never gave up on trying to improve relations with Sudan. He wanted to accept the Sudanese offer as a way to test Sudan and perhaps learn some valuable things about bin Laden.

Inside the State Department an age-old argument raged: Is it better to engage or isolate rogue regimes? Many counterterrorism hawks favored isolation, while failing to appreciate that defeating bin Laden required intelligence—and some of the best intelligence regarding him was held by Sudan. Admittedly, given that Sudan was a haven for terrorists, dealing with that regime was unappealing—but the alternative was worse.

A systematic interagency review of government policy toward Sudan, which included the CIA, the FBI, the State Department, the Defense Department, and the National Security Council, began. That interagency process lumbered forward in the spring and summer of 1997.

By September, every major executive-branch office involved in national security had agreed to send an intelligence team to Khartoum. Those who favored limited engagement had won. America would send to Khartoum eight diplomats, some of whom were actually CIA and FBI counterterrorism officers. In time, even Ambassador Carney would return. Secretary of State Madeleine Albright unveiled the plan on September 24, 1997.[14]

But the quicksand of the Clinton White House swallowed up the promising policy change. According to one former State Department official, in the first two weeks of October 1997, the head of the Africa Bureau at the National Security Council, Susan Rice went to see Richard Clarke, Clinton's counterterrorism czar. Clarke confirmed to the author that Rice came to see him in October 1997 to overturn the State Department's initiative toward Sudan. They agreed to go around Madeleine Albright. But they had to move quickly. Rice had been nominated to be Assistant Secretary of State for East Africa and Albright would soon be her boss.

Whatever the cause, within six days, the State Department announced that it was scrapping its own initiative to re-engage Sudan in the hopes of combating terrorism.[15] American intelligence agents would not see Sudan's treasure trove of information on bin Laden until July 2001.

Bureaucratic infighting had saved bin Laden again.

NAIROBI, KENYA—In a shabby apartment on the outskirts of Nairobi in September 1997, three al Qaeda operatives met with Mohammed Atef, the head of al Qaeda's military wing. The Sudanese had detailed dossiers on every one of the terrorists meeting that night in Nairobi—but the Americans did not. Atef wanted a progress report on their scouting and bomb-making missions. A year later, their effort would affect thousands and destroy two towering symbols of American power abroad.

CHAPTER SEVEN

KILLING THE
MESSENGER

WASHINGTON, D.C.—The Chinese embassy was celebrating its national holiday on September 29, 1996—and Janet McElligott was running late. Wearing a Chinese *chepal*, a long embroidered red silk dress with a high Mandarin collar, McElligott quickly threaded her way through the crowd. Then she collided with a tall, dark-skinned man in white robes and a turban.[1]

Little did she know that her chance encounter was about to open the way for a unique partnership that would present President Clinton with his last chance to break up al Qaeda before the 1998 embassy bombings that killed hundreds and to stop the September 11 attacks that exterminated thousands. In a series of never-before-reported meetings, she would become the FBI's sole link to Sudan's vast repository of intelligence on bin Laden's growing global terror network. It is a story of missed opportunities and squandered chances.

McElligott, as is her style, didn't apologize for nearly knocking over the man wearing the turban. "I have no idea where you're from, but now I know where Baltazar came from."

"Baltazar?"

"Yeah, he was one of the three wise men on his way to see Jesus, and I bet you're not going there."

"Jesus?" He was incredulous.

"Yeah, I'm on my way to get a drink. I bet you don't want one of those either."

He just started laughing. "And who are you?"

"Janet McElligott, lobbyist and consultant. Nice to meet you."

He announced that he was Mohammed Ibrahim, Sudan's ambassador to the United States. They exchanged cards.

The next day, the Sudanese ambassador invited her to lunch. Sudan was desperate to persuade the U.S. to lift its sanctions and still hoped to change the Clinton Administration's policy by providing reams of intelligence on bin Laden. But National Security Advisor Sandy Berger and incoming Assistant Secretary of State for East Africa Susan Rice, had no interest in improving relations with Sudan and little interest in its bin Laden files.

As a result, the Sudanese could not even secure a meeting with any senior Clinton official. "I'm the only one in the administration [at a senior level] who would meet with the Sudanese," Ambassador Joseph Wilson, who served in both the Clinton National Security Council and at the State Department's Africa desk, told the author.[2]

So Sudan was desperate. The Islamic republic had tried working with the Clinton Administration through formal channels (using its ambassadors and special envoys, as explained in Chapter 5), informal channels (via a Friend of Bill known as Mansoor Ijaz, as detailed in Chapter 6), and now was about to try a wild card named Janet McElligott.

Ambassador Ibrahim peppered her with questions about the inner workings of Washington.[3] McElligott, who had worked in the U.S. Senate and in the White House under President George H. W. Bush, was happy to oblige. Up to a point. She wanted a lobbying contract. At the time, she had never heard of Osama bin Laden.

Before McElligott and Ibrahim could talk again, the United States found itself in a hostage crisis in Sudan.

LOKICHOGGIO, KENYA—Pilot John Early had made runs like this all the time. The New Mexico native worked out of a staging area for United Nations relief efforts, on a high desert plateau in western Kenya. His job was to fly over and through the civil war in southern Sudan, land in its deserts, and deliver food and medicine to some of the poorest people on earth. The risks were great and Early and other pilots were paid well. Today, he would earn it.

"Loki," as the pilots called it, was a good place to make a small fortune but it wasn't glamorous.[4] Dozens of antique cargo planes baked under the hot sun. A windsock flapped as a gust of wind blew trash and dust over the settlement: a pile of spent shipping containers the size of small trucks; a thatch-roof bar where pilots drank Tusker beer, and a Kenyan Customs shack where the occupant also drank Tusker beer; and orderly rows of huts, tents, and outdoor showers for diplomats, administrators, journalists, aid workers, and assorted do-gooders.[5] Here the United Nations runs Operation Lifeline Sudan.

As Early knew, each flight over Sudan had to be approved by both the rebels, encamped in a cluster of run-down buildings in Nairobi, and the government of Sudan, based in a string of office blocks built at the peak of the British empire in Khartoum. This administrative procedure was supposed to keep relief flights from being shot down. The day before, his employer had received approval from both sides for Early's mission: to return some rebels, who had been hospitalized by the International Committee of the Red Cross, to their home region. On that day, it meant that Early had to fly to a cluster of mud huts known as Wunrock.[6]

Early strapped himself into a twin-engine plane. He and his copilot, Moshen Raz, an Indian native of Kenya, boarded six passengers: a nurse from Australia named Mary Worthington and five rebels carrying AK-47s—typical carry-on baggage in Loki.[7]

After two hours over the sunburned country of south Sudan, Early brought the plane down near a scattering of huts, cows, and goats. As the dust settled and crowds surrounded the plane—the usual routine—Early must have noticed that something was amiss.

Wunrock was rebel-held territory. The Sudanese People's Liberation Army, the main rebel group, had held the village...until the night before. Now it was held by a different rebel faction, which did not respect the rights of noncombatants. Kerubino Kwanyin Bol, the commander of that faction, was infamous for rapes, murders, and mutilations.[8] Faustino Atem Galdual, Kerubino's deputy, was equally fearsome. Kerubino's men were cutthroats and brigands; they fought rebels and government troops alike. They would willingly fight the whole world, if it came to the dry wastes of south-central Sudan.

Within moments of Early's landing, Kerubino's men discovered that the plane contained their worst enemies: other rebels. Then they found the guns. Kerubino seized them all, including Early, as prisoners of war. They would be held hostage until someone paid $2.5 million—or Kerubino got bored and killed them.

WASHINGTON, D.C.—Ambassador Ibrahim came right to the point.

He told McElligott about the hostages and Kerubino. To make matters worse, he said, the new Assistant Secretary of State for East Africa, Susan Rice, claimed that his government had control of the hostages. Her reasoning was perfectly logical and completely wrong: Sudan is divided into rebels and government loyalists. Since the hostage-takers held rebels and aid workers, they had to be government allies.

Of course, the reality was that the rebels were subdivided into factions, none of whom, as Ambassador Ibrahim pleadingly explained to the low-level State Department employee who phoned him, were controlled by the government. Indeed, the salient fact about rebels is that they're beyond government control.

McElligott listened for a while. She had no idea who any of these people were. Finally, she asked, "And what do you want *me* to do about this?"

"Do you know Congressman Bill Richardson?" He made it sound like three names "Rich-ard-son." He wanted her to come to a meeting with the congressman who represented the pilot John Early's hometown.

She said she would wait in the ambassador's car while he attended to a few other details.

An hour and half later, the Sudanese ambassador peered into the rear window of his black Lincoln Town Car to find McElligott sprawled on the back seat, asleep, overcome by jet lag.

"We have decided that you will be a secret liaison between the two of us," the ambassador explained.

"Excuse me. What are you talking about?"

"We've decided that you will pass messages back and forth between us to help free these hostages."

Over the next thirty-eight days she shuttled between Congressman Richardson's office and the embassy of Sudan. She and Richardson became fast friends. (Richardson, now governor of New Mexico, did not speak with the author despite repeated written and phone requests.)

A few weeks before the 1996 presidential election, Richardson went to see President Clinton.[9] The congressman was earning a reputation for freeing hostages and he was passionate about it. He also hoped to win a cabinet post in the second Clinton Administration, which might be secured by a high-profile rescue. But, in October 1996, Clinton was friendly, concerned—and unhelpful. He didn't want to do anything until after the 1996 election, Richardson told McElligott.

Days after the election—in which Clinton won forty-nine percent of the popular vote—Richardson went to see Clinton again about the American held hostage in Sudan.

Clinton was still hesitant. His advisors didn't want any change in the relationship with the Sudanese government. Then Richardson told him that John Early was dying.[10]

A few days later, McElligott had a first-class seat on a Lufthansa flight bound for Khartoum, Sudan, by way of Frankfurt, Germany.

It was not until she was airborne and seated beside Ambassador

Ibrahim that the panic set in. What do I think I'm doing? I'm not a congressman, she thought. I'm not an ambassador. I have never been to Africa or the Middle East. I don't speak the language. So she shook the sleeping ambassador. "You need to help me do something."

"What is it?"

"You need to teach me some Arabic."

Patiently, he taught her the standard salutations in Arabic.

"No, no, that's pointless. I need something that's going to be useful."

"What could be more useful than saying 'God be with you?'"

It is a standard greeting in the Arab world.

"I want you to teach me to say, 'Help I am a hostage' and 'my father will pay twice the amount you paid for me.' And you need to teach me how to write it, too, in case they gag me."

He laughed. "That is entirely possible."

KHARTOUM, SUDAN—"It is so cool to see a U.S. Air Force jet land in Khartoum, isn't it?"[11] These were Richardson's first words when he met McElligott. (Her Lufthansa flight had arrived a day before his government plane.) With the president's approval, Richardson had use of a plane from Ramstein Air Force Base in western Germany, although Richardson was not acting on behalf of the U.S. government. With luck, he could use it to bring the hostages out to freedom. But the plane also assured Richardson's rapid escape—at the time, Sudan then had only three outgoing flights per week—so he could be back in Washington before Clinton announced his new cabinet lineup. Richardson hoped to become Commerce Secretary or, failing that, ambassador to the United Nations.[12]

GOGRIOL, SUDAN—The next morning, Richardson, McElligott, Sudan ambassador Tim Carney, and two other State Department employees boarded a cargo plane for the long flight to Gogriol.

The negotiations were held under a banyan tree. After five hours, Richardson, Carney, and the other Americans realized that they were deadlocked. The rebels wanted $2.5 million in cash. But Americans don't pay ransom.

The military delegation from the government of Sudan was also at a loss. As the Americans broke off negotiations, Richardson got an idea. "Janet, I need you to go talk to the Sudanese. Tell them I have to leave here in an hour and a half."[13]

"Can I be liberal when I deliver your message?"

He said yes.

She walked over to the large canvas tent where Ambassador Mahdi and General Dabi of Sudan's military intelligence sat. She pulled back the tent flap and told them about Richardson's imminent departure.

"I am well aware of this," Ambassador Mahdi said.

"But you don't understand that if he goes back without these hostages and he spends the rest of his career as a congressman instead of the Secretary of Commerce or ambassador to the United Nations, he'll have a lot of time to think about why that is. And if you think there's onerous sanctions against Sudan now, you just wait."

"Sanctions? We aren't talking about sanctions. That's not fair."

McElligott was blunt. "You know what—life isn't fair. This is a political game and the political stakes have just changed."

"You can go back and tell him we understand," said the general. "Tell him we understand and we will do what we must."

The cash-strapped government of Sudan seemed prepared to pay its mortal enemies $2.5 million—in order to ensure better relations with the U.S.

If this point had been fully appreciated at the time, the Clinton Administration would not have so easily dismissed Sudan's repeated offers to turn over its intelligence files on bin Laden. The civil war in Sudan had raged, with one significant interruption, since 1955. Tens of thousands of Sudanese had been killed by war and perhaps two million more had been left starving, sick, or homeless. The landscape of the south, as the author has seen, is littered with the shattered remains of armored vehicles. The government of Sudan would not have agreed to pay off the rebels unless it was extremely serious about improving diplomatic relations with the U.S.

A deal was cut. Richardson left with all of the hostages. McElligott would be held in the Khartoum Hilton under a lone rebel guard until the rebels received $2.5 million worth of generators, trucks, and other items. The government paid the rebels within a week.[14]

WASHINGTON, D.C.—By February 1997, McElligott was a registered lobbyist for the government of Sudan. Her job was to build a normal, diplomatic relationship between Khartoum and Washington by resolving the Clinton Administration's concerns about Sudan's links to terrorists. But no senior national-security official would even meet with her. So she went to see Raphael Perl, the lead counterterrorism researcher at the Congressional Research Service.

Perl went through the history of the U.S.-Sudan relationship. Then, he added, "Janet, see what they know about bin Laden."[15]

She had no idea who bin Laden was, but she thought that he might be a Jewish businessman imprisoned by Sudan. She promised to find out.

KHARTOUM, SUDAN—"Bakri Hassan Salih wants to meet you. He's our Minister of Interior," Ibrahim told McElligott, who had flown into Khartoum only days before. It was February 1997. "I assumed he was director of parks, just like in America," McElligott told the author. In reality, the Interior Minister dealt with all threats to the regime from inside the country—from rebels to terrorists.

The Minister of Interior was dressed in camouflage knee-high combat boots, carried a riding crop, sported a red beret, and wore dark sunglasses that hid his eyes.[16]

They talked for a few minutes about American attitudes toward Sudan. They were speaking through a translator. Finally, McElligott decided to ask her question. "Who is Benjamin Laudon?"

The translator was confused. "Benjamin Laudon? Who? Who did they ask about *exactly*?"

"They just said Ben Laudon."

"You mean Osama bin Laden?"

McElligott looked around the room. She could see the surprised looks on the faces of the staff. "Yeah, that's the one."

"You don't need to know about that," Salih said, through his translator.

"Actually, I do."

"I told you, you don't need to know that."

Now McElligott was determined. "You pay me a lot of money to work for you in Washington and when a senator or congressman asks me about something, I can't tell them 'you don't need to know that.' So, I suggest that you tell me who this gentleman is."

"This is over," Salih said, waving her away.

McElligott stood up and yelled at him. "Don't you use that tone of voice with me. And another thing. You know, why are you speaking to me in Arabic? You speak English perfectly well because every time I say something, he [the translator] doesn't say a thing. You just use him so you can yell at me twice and I won't have it. Do you understand me? So I want you to sit down. I want you to tell me who this Osama bin Laden character is. Do you understand me? No wonder you have problems. No wonder you're on the terrorist list."

He took his sunglasses off and stared at her. Wearily, he asked Ambassador Ibrahim, "Are all Americans like this one?"

He then proceeded to talk about bin Laden for two and a half hours, mentioning that Khartoum kept meticulous files on bin Laden, which they would be happy to share with Washington. Sudan had become concerned when bin Laden met with Amin al-Hazari, a Cairo-based member of Egyptian Islamic Jihad, in 1991.

McElligott's lobbying role was transformed. She had contacts with the FBI, which the Sudanese asked her to use on their behalf. By May 1998, she was a regular courier, bringing tips and information to FBI Special Agent-in-Charge David Williams, a key counterterrorism official. (Williams was unavailable for an interview.)

Sudan's Interior Minister Salih and the head of the Sudanese intelligence service began warning the FBI that al Qaeda appeared to be planning a major terrorist attack on Americans somewhere in the Horn of Africa.

While the intelligence chatter provided no specific targets, the information was voluminous and continuous. Bin Laden's former tannery factory and his other business properties were bugged and subject to active surveillance. Sudan believed that the arch-terrorist had left behind dozens of "sleeper cells" amounting to several hundred operatives. Bin Laden seemed to have left them behind to coordinate funds and secret messages to cells in Somalia, Kenya, and elsewhere. In the spring of 1998, travel and long-distance phone calls among these operatives picked up markedly. To long-time bin Laden watchers, it seemed suspicious and ominous. "They [Sudanese officials] just knew there was trouble brewing in Africa," McElligott told the author.

In a few months, the suspicions of the Sudanese would turn out to be devastatingly correct. She regularly passed the Sudanese warnings onto the FFBI. For her pains, McElligott received a letter from the U.S. Treasury Department's Office of Foreign Asset Control. She had applied for a waiver from American sanctions against Sudan in order to continue transmitting messages between Sudan and the FBI. FBI officials had told McElligott not to worry about getting a waiver; it was in the works. But they were wrong. The May 1998 letter ordered her to immediately "cease and desist."

The Clinton Administration simply did not want her help—or her warnings.

In the next few months, two U.S. embassies would explode and McElligott would play a vital role in trying to capture two al Qaeda ringleaders.

CHAPTER EIGHT

BIN LADEN DECLARES
WAR, AGAIN AND AGAIN

NEAR KHOST, AFGHANISTAN—When Osama bin Laden decided to publicly declare war on the Western world for the *fifth* time in the Clinton presidency, he called a press conference that began with gunshots.[1] It was May 1998.

Each of bin Laden's previous declarations of war had essentially been ignored by the Clinton Administration. The arch-terrorist *first* publicly declared war on America on October 12, 1996. "It is the duty of every tribe in the Arabian peninsula to fight jihad and cleanse the land from these Crusader occupiers. Their wealth is booty to those who kill them."

Amazingly, the Clinton Administration largely ignored bin Laden's plain threat. One reason might have been timing. With less than three weeks to go before the 1996 presidential election, Clinton was thinking about re-election, not national security.

Meanwhile, bin Laden upped the ante. In a February 1997 Arabic-language television interview, bin Laden declared, "If someone can kill an American soldier, it is better than wasting time on other matters."[2] He thought it was his duty, his moral obligation, to kill American soldiers—and again, the Clinton did not respond.

Bin Laden turned up the volume. On February 23, 1998, the "World Islamic Front for Jihad against Jews and Crusaders" issued a *fatwa*, a declaration of war, signed by bin Laden. (Bin Laden had taken control of the group only weeks before, according to *Al-Sharq al-Awsat*, a London-based Arabic-language newspaper that serves as a bulletin board for militant Muslims.[3]) The Front announced its desire to kill *all* Americans, even civilians. The edict was explicit. "The ruling to kill the Americans and their allies—civilian and military—is an individual duty for every Muslim who can do it."[4] This marked the first time that bin Laden had publicly declared war on American civilians, although it was his third declaration of war. Again Clinton said nothing and did nothing.

A few months later bin Laden appeared on al-Jazeera television and said, "Our enemy is every American male, whether he is directly fighting us or paying taxes." It amounted to bin Laden's fourth declaration of war.

The May 1998 press conference held in the hills near Khost, Afghanistan, was to be bin Laden's last declaration of war before his most devastating attacks on Americans yet.

Several Pakistani journalists and, curiously, a Chinese reporter were contacted by al Qaeda and offered a chance to meet bin Laden. They were smuggled across the Pakistan-Afghanistan border and driven up and down switchback roads for two days. This was, according to one of the reporters invited, an attempt to disguise the location of bin Laden's base.

Finally, the journalists arrived at a high-altitude camp somewhere near Khost in southeastern Afghanistan, roughly ninety miles southwest of Kabul. They were told to wait. Hours passed. Then came wild bursts of gunfire. "All of a sudden there was shooting and firing," said Ismail Khan, a Pakistani reporter who was invited to meet bin Laden that day. "I thought the camp had come under attack from the U.S."[5]

The camouflaged men, firing their automatic weapons into the air, were simply signaling the arrival of "Sheikh Osama."

A collection of dust-coated trucks rolled to a stop. Two dozen armed men emerged. Many wore masks. Then, improbably, came an al Qaeda camera crew.[6]

Dressed in white robes with his beard combed straight, bin Laden emerged and slowly moved forward. He seemed serene and serious. Without any introductions, he began speaking in Arabic and paused only for al Qaeda interpreters to render his words into local languages. It was a long-winded speech. From the beginning, it was clear he was declaring war on the West, principally America.

> *By God's grace, we have formed with many other Islamic groups and organizations in the Islamic world a front, called the International Islamic Front, to do jihad against the Crusaders and Jews.*
>
> *And by God's grace, the men reacted to this call and they are going on this path and they are doing a good job. By God's will, their actions are going to have a successful result in killing Americans and getting rid of them.*[7]

Bin Laden was working himself into a frenzy. Tears rolled down his cheeks and his voice broke as he talked about the presence of American troops in Saudi Arabia.[8] To him, it was an unbearable abomination. A personal affront. The Americans were infidels and their garrisons propped up a corrupt, insufficiently Islamic Saudi elite. His jihad would humiliate the American interlopers, crush them, drive them out, and stain them with defeat.

What drove bin Laden to issue his fifth declaration of war on America in May 1998? Aside from his stated ideological reasons, some longtime observers of bin Laden suspect a psychological motivation. In Paris, one senior French intelligence analyst told the author he believed that bin Laden was hoping to provoke a showdown between his forces and American troops in the wastes of Afghanistan.[9] His theory is interesting, though unverifiable: A war in Afghanistan would allow bin Laden to relive the anti-Soviet jihad of the 1980s and, after a long Vietnam-like conflict, he would defeat America, the world's sole remaining superpower. After such a historic victory, he would be a Muslim hero on par with Saladin, who drove the Crusaders from Jerusalem in the twelfth century. In this new Afghan jihad, unlike the last, he would be a commander, not a quartermaster. (The September 11 attacks would have the same motivation, according to this theory: to lure America into a war in Afghanistan, which bin Laden was sure he could win.) The idea that he, bin Laden, could lose never seems to have occurred to him.

In 1998, bin Laden wanted a provocation that even Clinton could not ignore. He had already selected the martyrs for the operation. One of them was a short, bearded man named Mohammed Rasheed Daoud al-Owhali. Unknown to the journalists gathered to listen to bin Laden in May 1998, al-Owhali was among the crowd of gunmen that day.[10] Soon he would be on his way to Nairobi to murder and mangle thousands.

LANGLEY, VIRGINIA—Instead of fighting bin Laden, President Clinton spent 1998 fighting for his own political survival, as he faced a series of devastating scandals that involved accusations of witness tampering, obstruction of justice, perjury, sexual harassment, and illegal campaign contributions. By May, Clinton's lawyers were filing endless, futile motions to stop an array of government officials from testifying before a federal grand jury. The Monica Lewinsky scandal began when the former White House intern filed a false affidavit, claiming she never had a sexual relationship with Clinton, on January 7, 1998. A few days later, Linda Tripp turned over tapes of phone calls with Lewinsky revealing that the former intern had knowingly filed a false affidavit—and appeared to have done so at the behest of the president. Witness tampering and obstruction of justice are both serious crimes, if proven. But Clinton did not stop there. On January 17, Clinton denied under oath that he accepted sexual favors from any employee. This would later prove to be false, adding another serious crime—perjury—to the charges against him. On January 26, Clinton had famously said that he "never had sexual relations with that woman, Miss Lewinsky." This was no crime, merely an expedient lie. Politics as usual.

Other scandals would quickly follow. On February 3, a Democratic campaign contributor was taken into custody by the FBI. Another Clinton-Gore campaign donor, Maria Hsia, was indicted on February 18, on charges stemming from illegal contributions raised at a Buddhist temple in California. More questionable campaign contributors would come to light when Johnny Chung struck a plea bargain in March. On March 15, Kathleen Willey appeared on *60 Minutes*, saying that Clinton groped her in a room near the Oval Office. This would appear to demonstrate a pattern of sexual harassment—the very pattern that former Arkansas state employee Paula Jones was trying to establish in court.

While Clinton was consumed by scandal, the CIA and the FBI tried to fight bin Laden. Referring to bin Laden and other terror masters, the Director of Central Intelligence, George Tenet, had testified before a closed-door session of the Senate Appropriations Committee in May 1997. "I think we are already at war," he said. "We have been on a war footing for a number of years now."[11]

What this "war footing" amounted to was a series of vital, but small, bureaucratic steps. The CIA's Counter-Terrorism Center (CTC) had established a special bin Laden unit in January 1996. By 1998, more than one hundred case officers and intelligence analysts were serving on the bin Laden station. With the help of the CTC, forty terrorists from the former Yugoslavia were captured and turned over to Arab governments,[12] usually Egypt. Egyptian security is believed to have tortured, tried, and executed many of them. In this way, al Qaeda cells were quickly smashed in Albania, Bosnia, and elsewhere.[13]

But these small successes were not followed by broader and stronger measures. These would have required presidential decisions and Clinton was too sapped by scandal to make them. Instead, American intelligence agencies spent their time gathering data, information that would never drive Clinton to act.

Throughout 1998, the intelligence effort widened. The CIA's covert operations teams recruited informants in Pakistan, Afghanistan, and Uzbekistan to gather intelligence on bin Laden's movements, sources of funding, and future plans. The FBI and the CIA shared most of their overseas cables with each other (though intelligence gathered by the FBI in the course of criminal investigations *inside* the United States remained off limits). Such cooperation and coordination meant that by January 1998, the CTC had an in-depth understanding of al Qaeda's structure across some fifty countries. That knowledge was represented by a giant chart mounted on the wall of the Counter-Terrorism Center. The chart, with operatives' names and criss-crossing reporting lines, was said by one observer to be the length of a highway billboard.[14] Now that vast store of intelligence would have to be put to productive use, if Clinton would approve a covert strike. But, apparently, he was thinking about Lewinsky, not bin Laden.

Still, many officials inside the Clinton Administration were developing a serious battle plan. One was Richard Clarke.

Clarke officially became America's first "counterterrorism czar" in May 22, 1998. For the first time, the U.S. government's counterterrorism effort—sprawled over forty agencies—would be coordinated by one man. In theory, Clarke's appointment could have been the beginning of the end of al Qaeda.

But the lack of presidential leadership, government inertia, and bureaucratic squabbling often got in the way. Clarke publicly complained that he had too little power to get the job done. He didn't have the authority to command the various agencies that he had to coordinate and had little control over the more than $7 billion per year that those agencies spent on counterterrorism. His only power was "persuasion," he told *USA Today* in 1998.[15]

The price of Clarke's powerlessness soon became clear.

KABUL, AFGHANISTAN—The CIA utterly failed to make use of anti-Taliban forces in Afghanistan during the Clinton years. Northern Alliance offers to infiltrate al Qaeda required money and other assistance, which the CIA didn't provide. At the time, the Northern Alliance's annual budget hovered around $10 to $12 million a year. A small amount of money could have weakened bin Laden's hold in Afghanistan and kept the Taliban off balance, Northern Alliance officials told the author.

The Northern Alliance supplied regular information about bin Laden's movements. They tracked his convoys of sport-utility vehicles moving from Kandahar, Oruzgan, Kabul, and Jalalabad, and once to Mazar-i-Sharif. Yet the U.S. refused to act and kept demanding "absolute proof." What if we hit the wrong truck? they asked. "It was impossible," Haroun Amin, the Northern Alliance representative in Washington, told the author.

Meanwhile the Northern Alliance kept up its own efforts to kill al Qaeda leaders. Using inside informants, the Alliance would place bombs under trucks or in buildings where the targets were expected to pass by. Dozens of al Qaeda leaders were killed. But bin Laden eluded them.

Other opportunities were missed.

Roughly thirty miles north of Kabul, Northern Alliance forces found an al Qaeda training manual after a brutal battle on the Shomali plains in 1999, but, a Northern Alliance representative told the author, the CIA had "no interest" in it. "There was no sense of urgency" to get bin Laden, Amin said.

Several weeks before the legendary Afghan fighter Ahmad Shah Massoud died on September 9, 2001, he talked to Haron Amin about the CIA's operations in Massoud's territory. When Amin asked about its progress, Massoud first grinned, then laughed. "There is no way to achieve the objective in such a way," he said. There were too many bureaucratic restrictions and too little executive zeal, an utter lack of leadership.

Still, Clarke hoped to change that. He helped develop a daring covert-operation plan. Helicopters launched from an aircraft carrier in the Indian Ocean would deposit Special Forces near a bin Laden camp. Hours before dawn, using night-vision scopes, the commandos would surprise bin Laden's guards and kill or capture the arch-terrorist. But the plan had to run a bureaucratic obstacle course.

The first hurdle was cleared in the spring of 1998. In the middle of "Monica-gate," Clinton signed a secret memorandum of notification—informally called a "finding"—that explicitly allowed the CIA and other U.S. armed forces to take actions that might lead to bin Laden's death. Before the finding was signed, the military and the CIA were supposed to avoid any action that might, conceivably, result in the death of bin Laden or other targeted persons. Unfortunately, the finding was not a death warrant. Clinton's order did not overturn a long-standing ban on political assassinations.[16] The legal distinction was Clintonesque: bin Laden could be killed accidentally, but not on purpose. So a covert team could accidentally shoot bin Laden in the crossfire, but not aim at him. At least inside America's increasingly rule-laden intelligence services, this was seen as a major bureaucratic step forward. Operatives no longer had to avoid actions that might set off a chain of events that might possibly result in bin Laden's death. If bin Laden was killed, the covert team would have little to fear from military or Justice Department lawyers. Ordinarily, if a covert operation turned lethal, a federal criminal investigation could be launched.

The next bureaucratic hurdle was bigger: What if bin Laden was taken alive? CIA analysts considered that possibility remote—they believed that bin Laden would "martyr" himself rather than be taken a prisoner. But if bin Laden was captured, the policy that was he would be put on trial. Moving along a parallel track, the FBI and a New York U.S. Attorney had been preparing charges against bin Laden since January 1998. Bin Laden was accused of murdering Americans in Somalia in 1993 and in Riyadh in 1995, among other offenses. The secret charges were formally handed up by a grand jury sometime in the spring of 1998.[17] The indictment was sealed and remained secret for months. But it was in force. Now, by summer 1998, the second hurdle was cleared. The Justice Department had a plan for putting bin Laden on trial.

Meanwhile, the U.S. Special Forces Command and CIA planners continued to draft a detailed operations plan. All of the elements were in place for a bold covert operation to take bin Laden, dead or alive. But it was the plan, not bin Laden, that was soon killed.

The problem was the CIA, Clarke told the author. Director of Central Intelligence George Tenet asked that the plan be extensively revised, touching off another months-long cycle of meetings, drafts, and consultations. Tenet's stated reasons sounded as if he was either repeating or anticipating White House objections. Bin Laden and his band often traveled with their wives and children, raising the risk of unintended civilian deaths. That would be unacceptable to the president. (Of course, bin Laden had no qualms about civilian deaths.) Tenet wanted better safeguards for non-combatants.

Yet another concern came from the Pentagon: U.S. military casualties. Once a firefight began, it would be very difficult to extract wounded or trapped soldiers. If the mission went sour, dozens of Americans would be dead and bin Laden might escape. The military wanted a war without casualties or risks. The planners went back to the drawing board.

The Chairman of the Joint Chiefs of Staff, General Henry H. Shelton, opposed a small special-forces operation.[18] Rather than oppose the operation directly, the general fell back on a favorite Pentagon tactic: counteroffer with a proposed operation so large that the president and his senior staff would back down. This is a time-honored technique for killing ideas that the Pentagon opposes. Without giving away his motivation, Shelton explained his reasoning to Barton Gellman of the *Washington Post*. "The greatest risk is that you would have a helicopter or a [special-operations] aircraft that would encounter mechanical problems over those great distances, or you have an accident. You want to have the capability if that happens to go in and get them, which means a combat search-and-rescue capability, and if you want to send those people in, you have to have an air refueling operation."[19] At that point, thousands of soldiers, sailors, and airmen would be involved, as well as several ships and dozens of aircraft. That was far from the small, surgical operation Clarke and others had in mind.

So, in the spring and summer of 1998, the Clinton Administration was deadlocked. Tenet had essentially vetoed covert operations to seize bin Laden. Clinton might have wanted to get bin Laden, but he didn't want to overrule the Pentagon to do it. Neither could the president stomach sending thousands of troops into harm's way, as General Shelton proposed.

America was at war with bin Laden. But on America's side it was a phony war, while America's adversaries were waging a real one.

NAIROBI, KENYA—On the morning of August 7, 1998, Mohammed Rasheed Daoud al-Owhali fully expected to become a martyr.[20]

The Saudi had come to the Kenyan capital to die and had spent months preparing for his last moments on earth. He had flown in from Lahore, Pakistan, eight days earlier. He seems to have purchased a round-trip ticket simply to avoid suspicion, a classic al Qaeda technique. On August 4, three days before his appointment with death, he and his accomplices had gone to inspect the attack site: a busy street, off a traffic circle, beside the U.S. embassy.

Al-Owhali had nothing to lose and paradise to gain. He was unemployed, unmarried, and, ostensibly, homeless. His only assets in the world were a 1992 Chevrolet Caprice and some $12,000 that his father had loaned him.[21]

One of the few known early pictures of al-Owhali shows a young man with curly black hair and a long mustache. His face is half-turned to the camera, smiling. It is a remarkable picture for a terrorist in training; usually they glower at the photographer or stare straight ahead as if already dead, with wide-open eyes. By contrast, al-Owhali seems happy, maybe confident or benignly mischievous.

Since the days of that photograph, he had changed. He grew a beard. Al Qaeda had become his life. He had taken a *bayat* (loyalty oath) to bin Laden. Though a low-level member of the terror group, he had met bin Laden many times in management meetings and planning conferences. He had learned to make bombs and to shoot to kill. Bin Laden had given him permission to fight along-side the Taliban in Afghanistan in the mid-1990s and he had done so gratefully. Al Qaeda supplied him with the only skills he ever had, housed him, fed him, and gave his life direction and purpose.

He had met the other cell members at the Hilltop Lodge (sometimes erroneously referred to as the Hilltop Hilton in news accounts), a rundown hotel favored by Arab small-business owners. Later meetings were held in unit 43 at the New Runda Estates, a Nairobi apartment complex. That's where he learned that he would be in the passenger seat of the van that delivered the bomb. That's how he was supposed to die.

Shortly before 10 A.M. on August 7, 1998, al-Owhali climbed into a Toyota truck at the New Runda Estates parking lot. The vehicle had been purchased by two other al Qaeda terrorists, Mohammed Ali Msalam and Sheik Ahmed Salim Swedan, in June 1998. (The author has seen Sudan's intelligence dossiers on both Msalam and Swedan.) The driver was another young Saudi recruit, known only as Assam. In the only known photograph of Assam, he is clean-shaven, with a red-and-white checkered *keffiyeh* (head covering) billowing in all directions. His eyes look faraway and lost. He was a sheep abandoning himself to slaughter.

They drove toward the U.S. embassy. Ever the murderous engineer, bin Laden himself had specified the exact placement of the bomb-laden truck.[22]

Al Qaeda had been planning to attack the embassy in Nairobi since 1993. Ali Mohammed, the double agent who worked for both the FBI and al Qaeda, confessed to taking surveillance pictures of the U.S. embassy during a visit to Nairobi in 1993 and providing them to bin Laden in that year. Mohammed also trained many of the terrorists involved in the August 1998 attacks.

On their drive toward the target, Al-Owhali and Assam sang religious songs to keep up their morale.[23]

The van glided around the corner of the embassy and headed to the rear parking lot.

Now came al-Owhali's task. He opened the passenger door, stepped out, and threw a hand grenade at the Kenyan guards. The defective grenade did not explode, but the guards fled anyway.

Al-Owhali was supposed to get back in the van and die, but, instinctively, he started to run away instead.

Assam, the driver, drove on toward martyrdom.

Seconds later, the van exploded. The blast reached out in all directions. It punched upward into the embassy's chancery building, tearing it apart from the bottom up. It smashed the face of a seven-story bank building near the embassy and shattered windows for blocks. The crowds on the sidewalks were smacked to the ground or buried under tons of concrete rubble.

In an instant, 256 people were dead and another 4,500 were wounded.[24]

Strangely, al-Owhali was not among them. Hot flying rubble and glass had cut his face, hands, and back. But he was able to get up and walk away. Miraculously, the martyr had lived.

DAR ES SALAAM, TANZANIA—Not even ten minutes later, in the dirty capital city of Tanzania, the guard at the gate of the U.S. embassy watched a Nissan Atlas truck pull up. Another water delivery for the embassy compound. Strangely, it wasn't the usual driver but an Egyptian he had never met before. But his paperwork was in order.

The guard waved him in.

Then the truck bomb exploded. In seconds, eleven people lay dead. Another U.S. embassy attacked.

NAIROBI, KENYA—U.S. ambassador to Kenya Prudence Bushnell was in one of those boring but necessary meetings around a conference table covered with binders and water glasses.[25] If she swiveled her chair a bit and walked to the window, she could see the U.S. embassy from the conference room's seventh-floor window.

Then the room shook. The building rocked. The windows shattered. A wave of jagged glass and pulverized concrete rushed toward her. Her face was bleeding, her eyes stung, and she was choking on dust.

Someone helped her off the floor. "Ambassador, we have to leave," someone else said.[26]

She began the agonizing climb down the emergency stairs amidst a throng of worried, bleeding, crying people.

On the street at last, she looked over at the chancery of the embassy through the smoke and haze. She saw the bent steel skeleton of the building. Here and there, clumps of concrete still stuck to the structure's steel ribs. All order and symmetry was lost. It was a smoldering mound of metal, concrete, and broken glass. Police and passersby were trying to dig out the wounded and the dead.

With the American embassy in rubble, there should have been no doubt now that bin Laden had declared war on the United States.

THE WHITE HOUSE—President Clinton cut short a political fundraising trip to California. Within hours, he had flown back to the White House, landing before dawn.

Clinton faced two big questions: *Who did this?* and *What should we do?* It would be days before he privately answered the first question and almost two weeks before the president would publicly answer the second.

The day before, August 6, Monica Lewinsky testified before a federal grand jury. She recanted her January affidavit—admitting she had lied to the court. Of course that meant Clinton had lied too. Now, in the wake of the embassy bombings, Clinton would have to fight a two-front war: one for his own political survival, the other for his country's security. Unfortunately, it was the former that seemed more pressing.

LANGLEY, VIRGINIA—On "bin Laden Boulevard," in the Counter-Terrorism Center at CIA headquarters, the hunt was on. Bin Laden's organization had sent faxes to newspapers and broadcast outlets in France, Qatar, and the United Arab Emirates.[27] While those faxes took responsibility for the embassy attacks, they did not directly name al Qaeda or bin Laden.

Still, American intelligence was soon able to establish bin Laden's involvement. Through the CTC's bin Laden unit, National Security Agency satellites were used to trace bin Laden phone calls. At the time, bin Laden's satellite phone number was 873-682-505-331. He placed more than 2,200 minutes of calls from November 1996 to August 1998.[28] An analysis of the faxes themselves also connected bin Laden to the attacks. Indeed, these faxes were probably written before the attacks: the faxes mentioned the death of the Egyptian driver in Dar es Salaam and two Saudis in Nairobi.

In fact, al-Owhali had survived—but bin Laden's men did not know that until hours after the faxes were sent. Al-Owhali called an "emergency number" in Yemen, and someone at that number phoned bin Laden. Al-Owhali wanted money to make his escape. He was apparently told to wait.

NEW YORK—The FBI was in the midst of the largest overseas investigation in its history. Some three hundred special agents arrived in Nairobi within days. Forensics experts from the FBI crime lab examined the rubble for bomb residue. Ultimately, they shipped back to the FBI lab in Quantico, Virginia, more than one ton of debris and other physical evidence. Expert interviewers, working alongside their Kenyan counterparts, questioned hundreds of witnesses, many in their beds in Nairobi hospitals.

That's where they found al-Owhali. At first, he claimed to be just another hapless pedestrian who inadvertently became an eyewitness to the greatest terror attack ever carried out on Kenyan soil. But his story didn't add up. His description of the event was unusually vague; most observers had a fairly sharp recollection of the blast and its aftermath. More telling, al-Owhali had open wounds on his back and wrists, but the clothes he wore to the hospital had no trace of his own blood on them.[29] Unlike other victims, he had decided to change clothes before seeking treatment. That was suspicious. Finally, his Yemeni passport turned out to be false, although the Kenyan visa stamp—which showed he had arrived in the country only a week before the blast—proved to be genuine.

Kenyan police quickly turned up another important lead about al-Owhali: while interviewing a hospital janitor, they learned that he had found truck keys and several bullets in a bathroom near al-Owhali's bed.[30] His fingerprints were on both, and the keys matched a padlock recovered from the rubble. That padlock, FBI lab analysis later learned, had been on the rear gate of the bomb truck.

Within days, FBI and Kenyan investigators were convinced that al-Owhali was directly connected to the Nairobi bomb plot.

Al-Owhali was soon flown to New York. He was later convicted of twelve counts of murder and sentenced to life in prison.

ISLAMABAD, PAKISTAN—Days after the embassy bombings, Clinton was searching for nonviolent solutions to the bin Laden threat. He would try a final, secret diplomatic offer. It is reported here in full for the first time.

He sent U.S. ambassador to the United Nations Bill Richardson to the capital of Pakistan in the second week of August 1998. Richardson's most important meeting was the one *not* listed on his official schedule—a secret meeting with the Taliban.

The Taliban representative, Mullah Mohammed Rabbani, was one of the few Taliban leaders who spoke English and one of the many who wanted better relations with the United States. It wasn't that the Taliban had warmed to the "great Satan." The Taliban's radical Islamism was as fevered and intense as ever. But economic sanctions and the Taliban's diplomatic isolation were taking their toll. Only three nations on earth recognized the Taliban government as legitimate.[31] United Nations relief convoys had stopped rolling, and private humanitarian groups had fled. Hunger grew and hospitals began reusing bandages. Even the Taliban realized that as the displeasure of the ordinary Afghans swelled, an anarchic tide threatened to sweep them from office.

Richardson had met with Rabbani months earlier in April 1998, and that meeting had gone reasonably well. The mullah made some encouraging remarks about improving girls' access to schooling and ending the harassment of non-Muslim nonprofit groups. Later, Maulvi Abdul Wakil Mutawakil, a member of the Taliban's ruling council, publicly announced that the Taliban would turn over bin Laden if it received "conclusive proof" that bin Laden was a terrorist.[32]

Days after the embassy bombings, Richardson came armed with definitive proof of bin Laden's link to the attacks.[33] Following Clinton's instructions, Richardson asked Afghanistan to expel bin Laden, just as Sudan did two years before.

This demand seems to illustrate how distracted Clinton had become by scandals. Clinton had long been seen as a "policy wonk's policy wonk," a man who was in command of even the most minute details about government policy. But somewhere Clinton the über-policy wonk failed to recognize that expelling bin Laden had been tried in the Sudan. A relocated bin Laden had now blown up two American embassies and murdered some two dozen Americans along with hundreds of luckless Africans. It was one of the largest attacks on American civilians since World War II. Why would repeating this failed expulsion policy work any better this time? Wouldn't it simply provoke another attack?

Rabbani politely declined to expel bin Laden. Apparently, the Taliban's earlier pledge to turn over bin Laden if given conclusive proof of terrorism proved to be so much hot air. The Taliban had adopted a Saudi Arabian notion of hospitality—bin Laden was a good Muslim, a guest of the regime, and therefore could not be expelled. In reality bin Laden had other attributes the Taliban valued. He supplied weapons, ammunition, and military training to the Taliban. In some cases, al Qaeda troops even fought alongside the Taliban's militias against the Northern Alliance. And bin Laden had shrewdly married off one of his teenage daughters to a son of Mullah Omar, the Taliban's one-eyed leader. They were family now. Asking the Taliban to remove bin Laden was mission impossible. Again, something he should have known before ordering Richardson to Islamabad.

Within an hour, Richardson called Clinton on a secure telephone line. No deal. No surprise.

A gregarious southern politician, Clinton had assumed he could cut a deal with anyone. Just like LBJ. And, like LBJ, he refused to see that Communists and Islamists were unappeasable.

KHARTOUM, SUDAN—Sudanese intelligence had been trailing two Arab Afghans since their Kenyan Airways flight arrived in Sudan's dusty, decrepit airport on the afternoon of August 4, 1998.

In the gloomy shadows of the airport hangar that housed Sudan's customs and immigrations desks, they waited for the men to present their passports and consent to search of their luggage. Customs was looking for illegal alcohol (Sudan is a dry country), but the men in fact carried far more dangerous baggage. What happened next has never been reported before and will go down as perhaps the biggest squandered opportunity in Clinton's counterterrorism legacy.

Nossair Sayed Abbas (Pakistan passport number 553540) and Skander Said Suliman (Pakistan passport number 61482) carried Pakistani passports with valid entry visas to Sudan. The visas required the name of a local Sudanese contact. Both of the men had written down the name of the manager of Osama bin Laden's former leather tannery in Khartoum. The manager had been acting suspiciously for weeks and Sudan's Mukhabarat never believed his claims that he had cut all ties to bin Laden. And the two Pakistani men hailed from and had received their visas in Quetta, Pakistan, an area long known for its jihadi activity. They had purchased their Kenyan Airways tickets with cash the day before their flight.

Finally, the pages of their passports—which were covertly photocopied by the Sudanese—revealed a strange pattern of travel to countries known for suffering Islamist terrorism. (A copy of their passports and tickets, made available to the author by Sudan's intelligence service, is reprinted in Appendix B.) They said they planned to return to Nairobi and then travel on to Libya. All of this seemed suspicious.

Finally, Sudan checked with Pakistan's intelligence service. Abbas and Suliman were believed to be financial couriers for bin Laden, the Sudanese were told. They usually arrived with money and departed days before large attacks. Both men had been trained in bin Laden's Afghanistan camps to make explosives and to fire rocket-propelled grenades and 14.2-mm artillery pieces. So the mysterious visitors were trailed from the airport to the Badr Tourist Hotel, a favorite of traveling terrorists when bin Laden lived in Khartoum. The hotel's seafood-themed restaurant, on its top floor, offers a panoramic view of Khartoum, an ideal place from which to select targets.

Three days later, two U.S. embassies exploded.

On the morning of August 9, as senior Sudanese intelligence officials were debating whether or not to take Abbas and Suliman into custody, when a report from one of the agents shadowing the two men came in. It seemed that Abbas was negotiating to rent an apartment—directly across the street from the U.S. embassy. From the apartment's third-floor balcony, one could watch all of the activity inside the American embassy's courtyards and potentially use long-range listening devices to overhear phone calls. It was the perfect vantage point from which to plan an attack. Gutbi el-Mahdi told the author that he didn't need to hear any more. "Take them in," he ordered.

Abbas and Suliman were arrested and taken to Kober Prison, a

British-built fortress-like structure in North Khartoum. The interrogations began almost immediately. Sudan knew that these men would be interesting to American investigators, so some seven hours of the interrogations were recorded on videotape and a full transcript was made by a Mukhabarat transcriber. As it happened, the U.S. government never saw the footage or the transcript, because of the Clinton Administration's intransigence.

Separated and threatened, the two suspects soon broke down. Under hard questioning, they admitted that they had served together in the Afghan jihad, regularly met bin Laden, and were in Sudan on his business. They admitted that they had come to deliver money to several al Qaeda sleeper cells that planned to use the apartment as a staging area to attack the U.S. embassy in Khartoum, which was technically not closed but "vacated." Non-American embassy personnel continued to work there. But the last revelation was the most shocking: there was going to be a second wave of attacks on U.S. embassies in Africa and Central Asia. Bin Laden meant what he said when he had declared war.

Gutbi el-Mahdi telephoned Janet McElligott, Sudan's erstwhile lobbyist in Washington, D.C. Standing in the kitchen of her Georgetown townhouse, McElligott was surprised. She was no longer a paid lobbyist for Sudan—and el-Mahdi had never called her before. He asked her to contact "the boys"—an agreed-upon code for the counterterrorism agents at the FBI.

Always cagey on an unsecure telephone line, el-Mahdi wouldn't say exactly what he wanted. This is how McElligott remembers his message: "You go tell your boys that I have something for them but they have to come here to Khartoum to get it."

El-Mahdi was hoping for a face-to-face meeting with FBI officials to improve the relationship between the two intelligence services—and to take the two embassy bombers off his hands.

She phoned FBI special agent Glenn Posto, who worked for David Williams at the FBI counterterrorism office.[34] "Look, Gutbi doesn't call me every day. This is Gutbi. Pay attention. I don't know what he has but he says he has something for you. You need to go to Khartoum to get it."

Nearly a week later, McElligott phoned Posto again. Khartoum was getting impatient. Hanging on to terrorists can be dangerous. Posto told her that the request had been approved all the way up the chain of command at the FBI. "We've been stopped by the State Department," he told her.[35]

As a bureaucratic technicality, the FBI needed "country clearance"—a kind of internal federal visa—to travel to Sudan. This is an archaic custom designed to ensure that the U.S. ambassador's relationship with the host government is not confused with mixed messages from visiting federal officials with little knowledge of local politics. It is a bureaucratic power that the State Department has been known to misuse.

Over at the FBI, David Williams, as well as two special agents working for him, told McElligott that the State Department was blocking their request to go to Sudan. Williams faulted Assistant Secretary of State for East Africa Affairs Susan Rice, a Clinton appointee and a protégé of Madeleine Albright. The excuse was that the U.S. government doesn't do business with terrorists, and Sudan was considered a terrorist state. An FBI trip to Sudan would be considered a concession, a slight warming in a purposely ice-cold relationship. Rice hotly denied that she blocked any counter-terrorism request. She told the author that she would have never blocked any such counterterrorism request, and furthermore that she had never heard of special agent David Williams.[36]

What actually happened next is a mystery. No one at the State Department in the chain of command for issuing country clearance for Sudan acknowledges that country clearance was in fact denied, and the author spoke to almost everyone, including Rice, Carney, and the Sudan desk officer. (The charge d'affaires for Sudan, who is now on assignment in Kampala, Uganda, told the author that he "doesn't speak to members of the press that he doesn't know.") Several FBI officials with knowledge of the case insist that it was denied.

The State Department's coordinator for counterterrorism, Michael Sheehan, told the author that he investigated the charges that two al Qaeda suspects slipped away because of a State Department intransigence. "I was mad enough to hang someone," he said, even though he was not in his State Department post when the bombers got away. Sheehan launched a full investigation. He could not find a single piece of paper relating to the FBI's request or anyone at State who had heard of it. So he phoned his colleagues at the FBI. No one, Sheehan told the author, at a senior level of the FBI knew of the Sudanese offer or the suspects it had in custody. The press reports are wrong, Sheehan said; the Sudanese offer "died at the FBI.

Whatever the cause, the two ringleaders of the embassy bombings sat in a jail cell in Khartoum and the FBI was unable to take them into custody. Another Clinton Administration failure.

KHARTOUM, SUDAN—By September 2, 1998, Sudan could not wait any longer for the Clinton Administration to come to its senses and take custody of Abbas and Suliman.

Khartoum had no legal basis to hold the terrorists. They had committed no crime in their country and were traveling on illegal Pakistani passports, not illegal Sudanese passports.

Sudanese intelligence was in contact with its Pakistani counterpart, known as the Inter-Services Institute (ISI). On September 2, two Sudanese intelligence officers, with Abbas and Suliman in tow, boarded a flight for Karachi, Pakistan. There they were met by a number of armed ISI agents.

What happened next is a matter of dispute. When the CIA chief of station in Islamabad learned that the ISI had two ringleaders of the embassy attacks, he asked the government of Pakistan to turn them over or at least allow the men to be questioned by American intelligence officials. Here accounts diverge. Some say that the CIA was told that the men had escaped while being taken from the Karachi airport. This is unlikely. More likely is the second account. Pakistan's then–Prime Minister Nawaz Sharif is believed to have traded Abbas and Suliman to bin Laden in exchange for fundamentalist and Islamist support that kept Sharif in power for another year.[37] Whatever the reason, the Clinton Administration's bureaucratic blunders and Pakistan's shady dealings allowed the two embassy bombers to get away. They are still at large today.

KHOST, AFGHANISTAN—Clinton dubbed it Operation Infinite Reach. "Impotent Gesture" would have been more honest.

Clinton hoped that the missile strike would demonstrate that bin Laden would find no refuge anywhere on the globe, not even in the wilds of Afghanistan. A hail of some eighty cruise missiles would strike several bin Laden camps, killing the arch-terrorist and some three hundred of his lethal disciples.

The reality was far different. Clinton decided to surrender the element of surprise. Pakistan would be told about the attack, because Clinton feared that missiles crossing its airspace could be misinterpreted as an attack from India—possibly touching off an atomic exchange on the subcontinent. Unfortunately, Pakistan's intelligence service was known to have many links to jihadi organizations and in all likelihood to bin Laden himself. Certainly Pakistan's ISI had been recruiting informants and contacts with bin Laden's operation since 1989, when bin Laden lived in Pakistan. The risk? A pro-Islamist within the ISI could tip off bin Laden, allowing him to escape.

So, Clinton crafted one of his famous compromises. An American Joint Chiefs of Staff Vice Chairman, Joe Ralston, would meet with Pakistan's Army Chief of Staff (now Prime Minister) Musharif, on August 20. At a pre-arranged time, minutes after the Tomahawk cruise missiles crossed into Pakistan's airspace, Ralston would calmly inform the Muslim leader about the strike.

According to one account, the chief of staff was surprised by the general's remarks and excused himself for a few minutes.[38] When Sharif returned, the conversation returned to its earlier course: U.S.-Pakistani military cooperation. In the meantime, bin Laden was alerted and had just enough time to escape. He abruptly canceled a visit to the Harkatul Jihad al-Islami camp in Khost. The cruise missiles fly at the speed of commercial airlines, about 350 miles per hour. According to one account, bin Laden escaped in a truck driven by Khalid Shaikh Mohammed (with an identical truck acting as a decoy) with only minutes to spare.[39]

Perhaps one could argue that Clinton did the best he could given the constraints. But these constraints were self-imposed. If the president had chosen a different missile flight path—say through eastern Pakistan (Baluchistan), where military radars are sparse, or over Iran—or used Stealth bombers, which are virtually invisible to radar, he would have risked neither nuclear war nor bin Laden's escape.

If Clinton was not distracted by his own political troubles, he might well have made better decisions. Clinton appears to have approved the missile strike on the morning of August 14, 1998. That following Monday, August 17, Clinton testified before a federal grand jury, via closed-circuit television. The examination, led by independent prosecutor Kenneth Starr, lasted for four hours.

KHARTOUM, SUDAN—The second missile strike was even less successful. The cruise missiles landed precisely on target, but the strike backfired.

Touring the bombed-out factory in 2002, the author could still see the impressive effects of long-range precision weapons. The central office—a two-story concrete tower—had taken a dead-center hit and collapsed inward. The bottling plant was hit several times, blasting away the corrugated metal room and leaving deep craters now well filled with water and Nile rushes. Everywhere lay small brown bottles, their labels still readable in English and Arabic. All appear to be animal vaccines.

A Sudanese military officer still marvels at the attack. "I wish we could do this," he told the author.

Half a world away, in 1998, Janet McElligott was planning to give the Clinton Administration a well-deserved black eye. She knew that the pharmaceutical plant that the U.S had bombed was operating under a UN license and had been extensively inspected by a UN task force only months before. Such inspections, designed to ensure quality control, were routine. She knew the plant was not heavily guarded, the way one might expect a chemical-weapons plant to be.[40] She also seriously doubted that the Sudanese were capable of making chemical weapons.

Then she received a call from a friend at NBC News, Bob Arnot. No reporters were being allowed into Sudan after the missile strike and he wanted to know if McElligott could pull some strings. From a vacation property in the South of France, where he and his wife Courtney were celebrating her birthday, Arnot asked McElligott, "So, queen of the Nile, can you take me in?"[41]

She saw it as a golden opportunity to set the record straight. "Yep."

Within hours, she had persuaded the Sudanese government to issue visas to Arnot and an NBC camera crew. They arrived in Sudan a day later.

The factory was still smoking when the NBC camera crew arrived. The Sudanese Army had set up camp in a vacant lot across the dirt road from the plant. McElligott approached one of the guards, who refused to look at her. By now, her Arabic was good enough to haggle. She demanded that the guard run a message to the Minister of Interior, who was sitting in a tent under armed guard in the distance. He hesitated. Go now or I'll go to the palace, she threatened. By now, McElligott's contacts were good enough to make good on her threat—even if she had long since ceased working for the Sudanese. In fact, she was under contract with NBC News.

When the Interior Minister arrived, McElligott persuaded him to unlock the bombed factory's gates and to give an on-camera tour of the wrecked plant—live on NBC's *Today Show*. Arnot and the Interior Minister walked through the plant. There they found the stamped aluminum remains of one of the Tomahawk cruise missiles. (It is still there.) And everywhere lay small bottles with burnt labels. Arnot picked up one at random and twisted off the cap. As McElligott recalls, both the reporter and the minister dipped their fingers into the whitish contents off camera. It tasted slightly bitter. "I don't know what this is," the minister said.

Arnot, a medical doctor, thought for a minute. "I think it tastes like aspirin. Yeah, I think it is aspirin."

Forevermore, the pharmaceutical plant became known as "the aspirin factory" in press accounts.

After a series of NBC News stories, other reporters began flooding into Khartoum. What they discovered did not burnish the image of the Clinton Administration. The plant was targeted based on a soil sample gathered by a CIA source several months earlier. That sample allegedly showed traces of EMPTA, a precursor for the making of VX nerve gas. EMPTA has no known commercial uses. But the test results were never verified by an independent laboratory and it turned out that the CIA had mistaken Roundup, a common legal herbicide, for EMPTA. What's more, the CIA informant who gathered the sample was a Tunisian who had links to the rebel movement and had been caught lying to the CIA in the past. Nor does it appear that the Clinton Administration ever checked the United Nations records on the plant. These records, which the author has seen, include extensive blueprints of the plant and the results of numerous UN technical inspections of the facilities. Finally, the records reveal the plant was not owned by the government of Sudan or bin Laden, but by a Saudi businessman with a clean record. It was one of the biggest intelligence failures of the Clinton years.

How did it happen? One participant in high-level White House discussions following the embassy bombings says that Clinton wanted two targets in two different countries—as a kind of symmetrical answer to bin Laden's attack on two American embassies. But outside of Afghanistan, the Joint Chiefs of Staff had few solid bin Laden targets. So the CIA was asked to find one—quickly. The result was the aspirin factory—a blunder that would have the tragic result of persuading Clinton and his top officials that retaliation against bin Laden was politically hazardous and best avoided.

KHOST, AFGHANISTAN—The attack in Afghanistan, however, was even more frustrating. The missiles had exploded over the camp, right on target. But bin Laden, who had been there earlier, was gone. Among the dead were two Pakistani intelligence officers.

Ayman al-Zawahiri triumphantly telephoned a Pakistani reporter to crow: Bin Laden was still alive.

The attacks misfired. Not only did bin Laden triumphantly proclaim his survival, and only did the Clinton Administration's desire to use force against bin Laden evaporate, but the missile strike might have helped the Communist Chinese. Two of the missiles launched as part of Operation Infinite Reach did not explode. These duds were sold to Chinese operatives, who shipped them overland back to China, according to Northern Alliance intelligence reports. No doubt the advanced guidance programs were helpful to China's missile research efforts.

NEW YORK—In a public room in Manhattan's Waldorf-Astoria hotel, in September 1998, Richard Clarke stepped up to the podium. It was a rare public appearance by the ultimate insider.

He wanted to talk about America's Achilles heel. "Where is that?" he asked. "It's here. It's in Manhattan and Washington, D.C. It's where we are weakest, where we don't have two thousand troops and tanks and bombers to protect the U.S. It's where our national brain trust is."[42]

He did not know just how prophetic his warnings would be.

CHAPTER NINE

THE MILLENNIUM PLOT

THE WHITE HOUSE—Early in the morning of December 2, 1999, in the office of America's counterterrorism czar, Richard Clarke, the phone rang. The CIA's head of antiterrorism, Cofer Black, was on the line.[1] He was characteristically blunt: "We're in deep trouble."[2]

The night before, in the capital city of Jordan, Black explained, Jordanian agents had detained thirteen men believed to be part of the bin Laden cell. In the homes of some of the men, the security service had seized several computers. At a farmhouse[3] near Amman, Jordan's Mukhabarat—its external intelligence service—discovered seventy-one barrels of chemicals used for making bombs, a cache of automatic rifles, ammunition, and maps. Jordanian intelligence believed that the cell was planning multiple attacks on Americans designed to coincide with the millennium, the night of December 31, 1999.[4]

Had the Jordanians captured the entire cell? Were there more cells with the same mission? Was bin Laden planning to attack America? The CIA only had questions, not answers.

The FBI had received several boxes of computer diskettes, which Jordanian intelligence had copied from the captured computers.[5] Those disks held copies of every file on the computers, but they were

187

in Arabic and, ominously, encrypted. Indeed, the high level of encryption surprised the FBI investigators—it was military-grade.

The more the FBI and the CIA learned about the Jordan cell, the worse it looked. A Jordanian intelligence operative found a rough sketch of a building with a flag on top. Was bin Laden plotting to destroy another American embassy? And, if so, where? By December 3, U.S. embassies around the world were put on "high alert."[6]

Days later, the CIA had decrypted and translated the disks. The outlines of a massive terror spree appeared. The plot involved machine gun attacks and bomb blasts. Like the 1997 attack in Luxor, Egypt, in which AK-47-wielding Egyptian fundamentalists (unrelated to al Qaeda) methodically hunted and killed dozens of Western European tourists, who died crouching behind ancient ruins, valiantly trying to shelter their children, bin Laden's men planned to ambush tourists at a historic site.

But this time the target would be Americans and the site would be holy. They planned to strike near Mount Nebo in Jordan, a place of Christian pilgrimage for some fifteen centuries. Terrorists with automatic weapons would charge along the Jordan River—near the spot where John the Baptist is believed to have baptized Jesus—and Christians would be murdered as they prayed.

Another cell was preparing to place a massive bomb on the grounds of the SAS Radisson Hotel in Amman, a favorite oasis of traveling American executives and diplomats. If successful, it could have been the deadliest attack on Americans in the Middle East since the truck bomb assault on sleeping U.S. Marines in Beirut in 1983 that killed more than 240 Americans and more than fifty French servicemen.

Deep in the White House basement, in the Situation Room, Clarke and Director of Central Intelligence George Tenet briefed President Clinton on December 8, 1999. "We have to assume there's more," Tenet said. "And possibly a lot more."[7] The CIA believed that as many as fifteen plots against Americans were in progress, all timed around the millennium.[8]

Clarke passed out loose-leaf binders labeled "Millennium Threats Plan." He and other staffers had spent the weekend drafting the covert plan, which now needed the president's approval.[9] A key part of the still-secret plan: foreign intelligence agencies would arrest and deport people believed to be connected to bin Laden. This time there would be no talk of indictment-proof evidence or formal extraditions. These would be covert raids to capture some of the world's most dangerous men and turn them over to the tender mercies of some of the Middle East's most hardened intelligence services, including Egypt's.[10]

The plan was not immediately accepted. State Department Chief of Diplomatic Security David Carpenter opposed even issuing a warning to travelers about planned terrorist attacks. "What specifics do we have? We need to know more," Carpenter said.[11]

Those words could have been the anthem of the early Clinton years. But, by December 1999, President Clinton and National Security Advisor Sandy Berger had seen enough murder and mayhem to know that strong measures were needed. This was war.

By December 14, the plan was approved and in force. The CIA, the FBI, and the intelligence services of at least eight nations were now hunting bin Laden.

PESHAWAR, PAKISTAN—Pakistan's ISI struck first. They moved in on a shabby two-story building in Peshawar, a crowded, poor city near the Afghan border, on December 14. Their target was Khalil Deek, a short man with a long list of al Qaeda connections.

The ISI had received Deek's name from the CIA, which found it on one of the encrypted disks from the Amman cell. Deek's home was believed to be a way station for those moving in and out of al Qaeda terrorist camps in Afghanistan. Now, they would have to make Deek talk. What was bin Laden planning? When and where?

PORT ANGELES, WASHINGTON—Later that day, December 14, Diana Dean, a uniformed U.S. Customs agent, had a funny feeling.[12]

Alongside the longest unguarded border in the world, which divides the United States from Canada, Dean was watching cars with Canadian plates roll off the ferry from Victoria, and drive to the sales-tax-free shopping district in Port Angeles, Washington.

But she had suspicions about the driver of one car. When she asked the usual questions—"business or pleasure?"—the driver of the rented Chrysler was evasive. His papers said he was from Vancouver, Canada, a predominantly English-speaking region, but his English was poor.

So Dean and other Customs officials told him to open the trunk. The man fumbled with the keys, got out of the car, and walked around to the trunk. He put the keys in the lock and stepped back.

As the trunk lid sprang open, Dean saw two canisters of nitroglycerine, 118 pounds of urea, and four Casio watches wired to batteries and circuit boards. Even to the untrained eye, it looked like bombs and timers.[13]

As the Customs agents were staring in disbelief, the driver bolted. Two officers chased him. After a six-block pursuit snaking through pedestrians and parked cars, they caught him. He was handcuffed, read his rights, and arrested.

The U.S. government later learned the mysterious stranger was an Algerian terrorist known as Ahmed Ressam. He had been part of a "sleeper cell" in Montreal waiting close to six years for his chance at murder and martyrdom.[14] His apparent mission: destroy Los Angeles International Airport on the night of the millennium, while the whole world watched.

THE WHITE HOUSE—Clarke immediately suspected a wider conspiracy. "He's connected to someone," he said. "People don't just walk around with that stuff in their kit bag."[15]

The Ressam file quickly thickened as reports came in from all over the world. Ressam had ties to the GIA, an Algerian terrorist group behind gruesome bombings in Algeria and France. He had attended bin Laden's terrorist training camps in Afghanistan. He had been recruited and trained by bin Laden's network.

After midnight on the day that Ressam and Deek were arrested, State Department counterterrorism chief Michael Sheehan decided it was time to tell the Taliban that the president knew what bin Laden was planning and to talk about consequences. It was the middle of the afternoon in Afghanistan, but in Sheehan's mind, it was high noon. Using the secure line in the kitchen of his Arlington, Virginia, home, he phoned the Taliban's foreign minister, Wakil Ahmed Muttawakil. Sheehan demanded the Taliban either expel or extradite bin Laden. "It is no longer possible for you to act as if he's not your responsibility. He is your responsibility."[16]

Muttawakil reminded Sheehan that bin Laden was a "guest" in Afghanistan and Islamic law and custom did not permit bin Laden to be turned over to those whose law was not the Koran, to those who were nonbelievers.

Nevertheless, a former Taliban representative in Washington, D.C., told the author that on other occasions Muttawakil and other senior Taliban officials actually wanted to turn bin Laden over to the Americans provided it could be done in a face-saving way. Mullah Omar, the Taliban leader, was determined not to go down in history as the Muslim who had turned bin Laden in, so Muttawakil suggested that if bin Laden were to go on trial, it should be before experts on Islamic law in The Hague, the Netherlands, a recognized center of international law. The offer seemd to be both insincere and a delaying tactic. Sheehan saw it for what it was.

THE WHITE HOUSE—While newspapers were filled with scary scenarios about the "millennium bug"—a computer glitch that some feared would shut down the nation's infrastructure as 1999 became 2000—the Clinton Administration spent the month of December quietly preparing for all-out war.

On December 21, just days before the "Christmas crush" at the nation's airports, the Clinton Administration announced the strengthening of airport security measures. The Federal Aviation Administration and the major airlines were worried about possible terrorist attacks. Baggage and passengers were supposed to be methodically scrutinized as a precaution. But lax airport security rules were not rewritten—and would not be until well after September 11, 2001. Also put on high alert—by presidential order—were all worldwide American military bases, though base commanders were not specifically told to expect terrorist attacks.

Counterterrorism czar Richard Clarke strongly championed a plan to raise the reward for information leading to the arrest of bin Laden from $2.5 million to $5 million. At the time, it was the highest monetary amount allowed by federal law for a wanted man. President Clinton agreed to Clarke's plan. By December 1999, bin Laden was officially public enemy number one.

In the beginning, Clinton used a "war room" to win the presidency and later to push Hillary Clinton's health-care plan. In the second administration, the war room was revived to defend the president from impeachment charges in the House of Representatives and removal from office in the Senate. Now a war room was convened to fight a real war, albeit a secret one.

Days after Christmas, Clarke met with FBI Director Louis Freeh. Freeh was openly dismayed by the president's headline-making ethical and legal lapses. And many in the Clinton White House were suspicious of Freeh. But Clarke needed every soldier on the front line against terrorism. And, as always, Clarke came armed with a detailed, secret plan.

On the eve of the millennium, December 31, 1999, the Clarke-Freeh plan quietly swung into action. Freeh mobilized all fifty-six FBI field offices and directed that they stay open all night. FBI agents had to be ready to arrest terrorists, secure attack sites for evidence, and chase down any fleeing suspects. Even off-duty special agents were required to bear a gun, carry a beeper or cell phone, and be ready to roll at a moment's notice. Clarke had called out the "minutemen."

NEW YORK—On the last night of 1999, FBI counterterrorism chief John O'Neill sought out perhaps the most dangerous place on earth: Times Square, New York City.[17]

Tens of thousands of people had crowded the intersection of Broadway and Forty-second Street to watch the fall of a giant crystal ball that was supposed to mark the start of a new millennium. It was believed to be the most tempting terrorist target in the world—offering the possibility of a large number of deaths and simultaneous global television coverage. Moments before midnight, in the thick of the throng, O'Neill tapped a long, memorized number into his cell phone.

The telephone rang at the FBI's Strategic Information Operations Center in Washington, D.C. Ever the daredevil, O'Neill boasted that he was standing smack dab in the middle of the bull's eye, daring bin Laden to come and get him.[18] O'Neill believed that bin Laden wanted to target him personally[19] and he wasn't going to cower in the face of evil.

WASHINGTON, D.C.—Dressed in a tuxedo, Richard Clarke presided over a group of casually dressed CIA and National Security Council staffers at a secret command center located at 1800 G Street, N.W., a few blocks from the White House.[20] They anxiously monitored television sets, computer screens, and foreign news wires, trying to detect any sign that the millennium plots were in motion. CNN droned in the background, gradually announcing the celebrations in Australia, the Middle East, and Europe. As the world spun, the millennium hour crept closer to the East Coast of the United States.

Still, the hours crawled by. *Did we catch them all?* Clarke wondered. *What was bin Laden planning?*

Just before midnight, Clarke climbed the stairs to the command center's rooftop. From his cold, windswept perch, he watched the fireworks explode on schedule over the Washington Monument and heard the bundled-up crowds roar and applaud. They had no idea what they had just been spared.

A few minutes later, Clarke's cell phone rang. It was Sandy Berger, who was standing beside President Clinton near the Lincoln Memorial. As the fireworks display built toward its finale, Berger congratulated him on a job well done.

"It is still too early to celebrate," Clarke said soberly.[21] Unlike O'Neill and the others, he was yet to have his first sip of champagne. The millennium, Clarke explained, won't even happen on the West Coast for another three hours.

Three hours later, Berger phoned again. This time, the national security advisor was more cautious. "How's everything been?"

"We won this battle," Clarke said, "but the war definitely isn't over."[22]

Still, Clarke had poured himself a little champagne in a plastic cup. It was a moment to be quietly savored. The Clinton Administration believed it had beaten bin Laden, at least for now. And no one knew it.

ADEN, YEMEN—A few days later, it became clear that American officials were expecting an attack according to the Western calendar. But bin Laden followed the lunar calendar of traditional Islam.

January 3, a date of religious significance during that year's Ramadan holiday, was bin Laden's target date. It was known in traditionalist circles as "the night of power"[23]—when the angel Gabriel is said to have visited the prophet Mohammed. It was seen as an auspicious time to attack.

Like most al Qaeda attacks, it had been planned for years. Yemeni intelligence would later learn that bin Laden began preparations for the attack in 1997.[24]

On that night, in the far-reaching arm of Aden's harbor, a few men in a small fiberglass skiff pushed off from a deserted dock. The skiff was loaded with explosives.

The moon hung in a starry night sky, illuminating their target: an American destroyer, anchored a few miles away. The USS *The Sullivans*, a warship named to commemorate the five Sullivan brothers who had died simultaneously when their U.S. navy cruiser was surprised by the Japanese during World War II, was about to face a surprise attack of its own.

But, as the men approached through the cool water, their boat began to sink. The explosives were too heavy and the cheap craft too flimsy to float the load.[25]

As always, bin Laden's men would learn from their mistakes. The next time they targeted an American naval vessel in Aden harbor, it would not escape unscathed.

American intelligence would not learn about the attempted attack on the night of January 3 for almost a year.[26] And by that time it would be too late to do any good.

THE WHITE HOUSE—Over the next few months, Clarke became increasingly convinced that al Qaeda had sleeper cells inside the United States.

He had no specific intelligence to support that supposition, but it seemed to fit an emerging pattern. The 1993 World Trade Center attack, the 1998 embassy bombings in East Africa, and the millennium plots each involved minor penetrations of America's security apparatus. And, given bin Laden's goals, developing long-term secret cells among Muslim immigrants or fellow travelers inside America was a logical move.

Clarke formed the Millennium After-Action Review, a task force designed to detect and defeat al Qaeda operations on American soil. Sometimes the task force and other antiterrorism bodies that Clarke ran met three times a week. As a group, they were looking intensely for threats that the FBI's counterterrorism units had missed.

No bureaucratic power was left dormant. The Internal Revenue Service was instructed to track and crack down on the movements of terrorist-related funds. While terror groups could no longer open bank accounts in their own names—without the fear that their funds would be confiscated—charitable groups affiliated with radical Islam in Texas, Virginia, and Michigan were safe. This was a political decision made inside the Treasury Department—it didn't want to be accused of shutting down "innocent" charities or being anti-Muslim. Indeed, the Holy Land Foundation—an Islamic front group—was spared an FBI raid at the insistence of the Treasury Department, Clarke told the author. As a result, of the Treasury Department's reluctance, relatively few terrorist bank accounts in the United States were seized. After September 11, president Bush directed Treasury agents to swiftly shut down these bogus charities.

Outside the United States, Clarke won some minor operational victories. America disrupted some al Qaeda cells in Albania, Bosnia, Italy, and the Middle East. That spelled the end of at least six al Qaeda cells. But how many more were there?

A major terror cell, affiliated with bin Laden, in Brussels, the capital of Belgium, was left untouched. Two members of this cell, carrying Belgian passports, would later assassinate Northern Alliance military chief Ahmed Shah Massoud in the mountains of Afghanistan on September 9, 2001, as a precursor to the September 11 attacks.

CHAPTER TEN

CLINTON'S RUMOR OF WAR

NORTHERN ALLIANCE TERRITORY, AFGHANISTAN—In the wake of the devastating 1998 attacks on the U.S. embassies in East Africa, Clinton secretly approved a series of covert operations against bin Laden. The secret war would slowly escalate in 2000, the last full year of the Clinton Administration. It was a series of heartbreaking half-measures.

A covert four-man team landed in territory held by the Northern Alliance in Afghanistan in the winter of 1999.[1] Two of the men were part of the CIA's Special Collection Service, and the other two worked for the National Security Agency.[2] Haroun Amin, a Northern Alliance official, describes the four-man team as "purely technical."[3] They were interested only in setting up their equipment and training the Northern Alliance to use and repair it. They were not coming to help the Northern Alliance or to fight the Taliban and bin Laden. They came only to help Washington listen.

All the team did was establish a listening post for the interception of al Qaeda communications, to be manned and monitored by the Northern Alliance specialists.[4] Two days later, the specialists left the snow-covered mountains. They never returned. Washington made little use of the intercepts from this remote, essential post. The Northern Alliance's commander, Massoud,

197

quickly surmised that Clinton "was not serious" about defeating bin Laden.[5]

Even four years later, when the author met him in his basement office near Nineteenth Street in Washington, Haroun Amin seemed visibly disappointed. Amin and other Northern Alliance officers were hoping for money, training, and guns. Even a small sum of money—say $3 million—would have energized the Northern Alliance and put bin Laden's forces in Afghanistan on the defensive. (Clinton's counterterrorism czar told the author that in fact the Alliance had secretly received several hundred thousand dollars in 1999 and 2000, but conceded that it wasn't enough.[6] Much more could have been done.) Of course, the Bush Administration later succeeded in disrupting bin Laden's operations using this very strategy.

Instead, the Alliance was forced to rely mostly on funds from Iran, which opposed Pakistan's interests in Afghanistan. As a result, the Alliance was chronically short of funds and ammunition. Amin ruefully told the author, "We could have done much more than listen to the radio."[7] Unlike Clinton, they were eager for action.

Much to the annoyance of American intelligence officials, the Northern Alliance was actively plotting to kill bin Laden. Amin told the author of three never-before-reported attacks on bin Laden in 1999 and 2000. The first attack was a bomb placed in the wall of a building which bin Laden's convoy was expected to pass in Kandahar, Afghanistan. The bomb had a cheap detonator and exploded seconds too late—destroying the vehicle *behind* bin Laden's—in 1999.[8] When American intelligence officials learned about the assassination attempt, they were not happy. At the time, the Northern Alliance intelligence liaison was a Tajik named Amrullah Saleh, known for his charming manner and American accent.[9] He briefed CIA officials in Washington, D.C., in December 1999. Saleh received a lecture on the laws of war—and was sternly told not to do it again.[10]

Despite American pressure, Northern Alliance commanders kept trying to kill bin Laden. It would have been reckless for them not to go after the arch-terrorist, whose arms, money, and legions of men were an essential strategic asset to their enemy, the Taliban. Simply assassinating bin Laden could win the war for the Alliance. It's a pity that the Clinton Administration did not seem to take the same view.[11]

The next two Northern Alliance attempts to take out bin Laden were simply not reported to the Americans. Why bother? The first was a daring nighttime assault on bin Laden's convoy in 2000. The second was an ambush in the canyons south of Mari-i-Sharif, also in 2000.[12] "We killed a lot of their officers and men," Amin insists, acknowledging that with American arms and training they would likely have been still more successful. Indeed, with a little help from Uncle Sam, they might even have nabbed bin Laden before September 11.

The Clinton Administration also spurned the Northern Alliance's non-lethal opportunities to defeat bin Laden. By 2000, the Alliance had accumulated well over one thousand al Qaeda prisoners. With the exception of one brave female analyst from the Defense Intelligence Agency, who donned a burka and smuggled herself into Afghanistan twice, these prisoners were never interrogated by American intelligence officials before September 11. The Clinton Administration later ordered the Defense Intelligence analyst to cease all travel to Afghanistan, even during her vacations. They just didn't want to know.

As usual, an intelligence backchannel opened up. An American civilian had the opportunity to interview the al Qaeda prisoners in 2000. Ottilie English, the sister of Congressman Phil English, is a veteran observer of Afghan politics who worked as a Washington representative of the Northern Alliance in 2000 and 2001. She had traveled deep inside Afghanistan since the late 1980s and knew the people and the politicians there fairly well. English returned with more than seven hours of videotapes of conversations with the al Qaeda prisoners held in Northern Afghanistan in 2000. Some of these tapes were made available to the author. Filmed at a camp in the Pansjir Valley, the prisoners are defiant. "We are coming to the U.S.," one threatened repeatedly.

In March 2000, English met with a CIA officer in Tajikistan, who was in charge of monitoring Afghanistan. She told him everything she had gleaned from the al Qaeda prisoners. He was interested, but did not think Washington would be. "Good luck. I've been writing that in reports for years now and nothing happens. Maybe *you* can get them to listen."[13]

THE INDIAN OCEAN—Two nuclear-powered Los Angeles class submarines navigated in a carefully defined arc between the mouth of the Persian Gulf and the coast of Pakistan in the summer of 1999.[14] Their sole mission: to launch cruise missiles to kill bin Laden. But Clinton kept the submarine commanders waiting for targeting coordinates—endlessly.

Three times in 1999, warning klaxons rang and the crew assumed battle stations. They waited for the final order from the White House to launch cruise missiles on bin Laden's bases in Afghanistan. These cruise missiles, fired from a submarine, are extraordinarily accurate. With the proper Global Positioning System (GPS) coordinates, they can strike within feet of their targets.

But the final orders never came. Each time, Director of Central Intelligence George Tenet decided that the evidence was simply not strong enough.[15] According to a knowledgeable participant, Tenet insisted that the intelligence was "single threaded," i.e., based on one source. Ideally, he wanted more than one source, a very high standard of proof. That meant that at least two sources— satellite surveillance, telephone intercepts, or human sources—had to simultaneously confirm the exact same set of facts. In practice, this standard is unrealistically high. What if the target's communications could not be intercepted? Or could not be decrypted in time? Or an informant can not safely contact headquarters? Tenet kept insisting that, at a minimum, he wanted a second source before any strike. Clinton did not overrule his objections.

Intelligence is an art of shadows and inferences. Often, the CIA supplied single source information. An intriguing satellite photo. A cell phone call intercepted from a secret listening post in central Asia. A tip from the Northern Alliance. But it was never enough.

To be sure, sometimes Tenet's caution made eminent sense. Perhaps the closest of close calls was in the winter of 1999. Tenet phoned Berger[16] to tell him a National Security Agency spy satellite had revealed a large entourage camped out in the desert. Armed bodyguards ringed a commanding figure in Saudi-style robes. The news was passed to Clinton. He demanded that the CIA confirm the information as quickly as possible.[17]

It can take up to six hours for a U.S. Navy submarine to prepare its cruise missiles and put them on target. Clinton ordered that the crew begin preparations. The countdown began.

Hours later, the target proved to be a wealthy Arab sheikh hunting with his prized falcons.[18]

Later in 2000, as we shall see, the CIA would receive unambiguous intelligence, including live videotaped images of bin Laden, and still Tenet would not put aside his caution.

The search continued. The CIA's Directorate of Operations' Special Activities Division, composed of selected members of U.S. Army Special Forces, secretly flew in and reconnoitered a desert airstrip near the Taliban stronghold of Kandahar. It was remote and long unused. The special activities team surveyed the field, mapped it, and took notes. If a major covert operation were launched to capture bin Laden, this would be the forward air base. Bin Laden's last glimpse of Afghanistan would be from the open door of a helicopter lifting off from this icy field.

The Administration wanted the preparations to be perfect. No one wanted another "Desert One," a covert operation in Iran that went horribly wrong in 1980. In that instance, as the covert team transferred from an Air Force transport plane to U.S. Army helicopters at a remote airstrip code-named "Desert One," a local Iranian bus passed nearby—blowing the cover of the covert team sent to rescue American diplomats held hostage in Tehran. Then, in a hurried evacuation, a helicopter collided with an Air Force plane, killing eight soldiers. The mission was scrubbed, the bodies flown home, and the Carter Administration humiliated. Poor preparation and training had made the American superpower seem bumbling and impotent. The Carter presidency, already reeling from high unemployment, rampant inflation, rising interest rates, and the Iranian hostage crises, never recovered. The Clinton Administration did not want to suffer the same fate.

Meanwhile, the administration was laying the groundwork for a major assault. Would Clinton commit troops?

The problem was the Pentagon. When asked repeatedly to consider the use of special forces on the ground, the Chairman of the Joint Chiefs of Staff, General Henry H. Shelton, stubbornly opposed the idea.[19] At Berger's insistence, Shelton's staff did prepare a series of options for Clinton involving raids on al Qaeda encampments. Each of these options involved "boots on the ground."[20] Some plans involved low-altitude parachute drops of Delta Force and U.S. Army Rangers into the mountain strongholds of bin Laden. But Shelton stressed that the Army would need thousands of troops and tons of equipment. The president and his senior advisors had little military experience and could not judge whether Shelton was simply highballing his estimates to forestall military action that the Pentagon chiefs opposed.

If the military operation failed, Clinton's advisors feared that disgruntled officers would tell congressional staff that Clinton had not given them the troops and equipment they said they needed—and they would have the memos to prove it. It would be another Mogadishu, another "Black Hawk Down." No one in the White House wanted to risk that.

In the spring of 2000, Clinton insisted on yet another plan of attack on bin Laden. The Navy was tired of maintaining a strike force in the Indian Ocean—the pointless patrol was expensive and its sailors were far from friendly ports for months on end, which hurt morale. Meanwhile, the Army was not any more enthusiastic about waging open war on bin Laden than it was in 1998 or 1999.

Clinton summoned Berger into the Oval Office. "What else can we do to get bin Laden?" he said. "We've got to think of something new."[21]

Berger passed the message on to Clarke, who soon organized a meeting in his office to find a new approach.[22] Michael Sheehan, the State Department's counterterrorism coordinator, senior military officers, and others gathered in Clarke's office in the Old Executive Office Building to come up with a new plan to get bin Laden. Charlie Allen, an assistant Director of Central Intelligence, mentioned the Predator, a small, unmanned plane that could take extremely clear moving pictures from high altitudes.[23] It was the first time that Clarke had heard of the secret spy-drone plane—but he would spend the remainder of the Clinton years championing it against its many bureaucratic enemies within the Clinton Administration.

In Clarke's office a bold plan was born. The idea: launch the plane from a secret airstrip in Central Asia and let it roam the skies of Afghanistan, hunting for bin Laden. Its real-time video would provide perfect targeting information for the Navy warships waiting nearby.

The Predator was a proven technology. It had been widely used, and with great success, by the U.S. Air Force in Kosovo. But given the ease with which it could be shot down or crash, its use had been confined to military tactical support, not as a covert intelligence asset. According to one former counterterrorism official, "The Predator itself was not new, but what was coming together... was an incredible improvement in video technology. You could see with incredible precision what was happening on the ground while the Predator itself could, with luck, remain completely unnoticed."[24]

The Predator also had a tremendous bureaucratic advantage. It would be the "second source" that Tenet had always insisted on when vetoing attacks on bin Laden.

Now a base to launch it from was needed. General Anthony Zinni ran the U.S. Army's Central Command, also known as CENTCOM, based in Tampa, Florida, and was responsible for operations in the Middle East and Central Asia. Zinni had forged strong ties with senior military officials in Uzbekistan. That nation agreed to host a secret base for two of America's Predators. The first of the unmanned drones took off in September 2000.

At the time, the Predator was limited to daytime missions in fair weather. Half a world away, in the middle of the night in McLean, Virginia, Clarke and others could watch the live video streaming in from Afghanistan. It was exhilarating.

The next morning, with the Predator safely back at its Uzbekistan base, Clarke would sometimes screen the black-and-white videos for Berger.[25]

The digital video images were remarkably clear. "I am sure that I saw bin Laden at least three times" on Predator tapes, Clarke told the author.

But there were no U.S. military "assets" in place to strike him. All they could do in August 2000 was watch.

Then Tenet came up with another objection against using the Predator. The agency had heard that the U.S. Air Force was developing a plan to arm the Predator with Hellfire missiles. Tenet wanted to wait until that project was completed. Clarke phoned an Air Force official responsible for the Predator program. This is how Clarke described the phone call to the author. How long will it take to arm the Predator? The officer talked about engineering, test flights, procedure. How long? Three years. Clarke suspected that the CIA's position was another bureaucratic delay tactic. Okay, he told the officer, if you throw out all the rules, how long will it take?

The officer thought a minute. "About a month," he told Clarke. "Do it," Clarke said.

A month later, on a secret test range, the drone successfully took off and landed carrying a single Hellfire missile—which was more than half its weight. It was now a bird of prey.

Increasingly, Clarke and the counterterrorism experts he worked with were gripped by the same dream of high-tech warfare; they expected to watch bin Laden's final fiery moments on video in McLean, Virginia, after submarine-launched missiles had raced across the deserts to attack him.

The armed Predator flew over Afghanistan eleven times in September and October 2000, Clarke told the author. It supplied hours of clear video, showing bin Laden in various compounds.

In October 2000, the Predator crashed in Afghanistan. Whether it was brought down by high winds or machine gunfire, no one involved in the project could say. But what is clear is that within the Clinton Administration, the bottom dropped out for supporting the Predator program.

In the first days of October, Clarke convened a meeting to save the Predator project. Cofer Black, the CIA's anti-terrorism chief, and Clarke shared a similar predilection for action and blunt talk. But now Black turned on his old friend. He said that Clarke was too demanding and that the CIA did not have the funds to endlessly subsidize his pet project. An intelligence source said, "Black was under pressure back at Langley and Clarke saw this as Black was becoming unnecessarily bureaucratic and failing to support an unconventional approach. But Clarke's real beef was Jim Pavitt [the CIA's director of operations and Black's boss], who Clarke thought was the one blocking things."[26]

Clarke's gruff manner with colleagues who failed to live up to his demanding expectations only made things worse. Letting the Predator project fail would be the bureaucrats' revenge.

The Air Force soon joined the CIA in opposition to the Predator project. Air Force generals never liked the idea of pilotless aircraft—at least those that the USAF had to fuel and maintain for the benefit of the CIA. Now the Air Force began raising technical objections to drone planes, claiming that the small, light bird could be smashed by strong winter winds. The U.S. Air Force didn't want to take the blame for what it believed was a looming disaster.

Never a diplomat, Clarke exploded. He shouted at Air Force generals and intelligence officials gathered in his office. "You're telling me it won't work. The real reason is that you don't want to do it!"[27]

"The reality was that the Predator program was shut down because of a petty budget dispute and because certain people resented being bossed around by Clarke," one State Department source told the author. Those "certain people" are believed to be senior officers of the U.S. Air Force and the CIA.

Whatever the cause, the Clinton Administration's most powerful weapon deployed against bin Laden was now grounded. The Predator would not fly over Afghanistan again until September 2001.

UNITED ARAB EMIRATES—Clarke had been building relationships with key intelligence, military, and political leaders in the Emirates since 1990. He put them to work in the fight against bin Laden.

Under the guidance of the UAE's chief of army staff (who was a son of Sheikh Zayed), the Emirate had made the full resources of its military and intelligence directorates available to U.S. counterterrorism officials.

Until now, the full extent of the UAE's secret efforts to defeat bin Laden have not been revealed. Clarke told the author that he twice carried confidential letters written by Clinton to Sheikh Zayed, ruler of the UAE. "We asked them to help. They helped. People disappeared. More people were interrogated. Lots of helpful things went on," Clarke said, without offering any specifics.[28]

The UAE's efforts made its rulers a target for bin Laden. Increasingly specific, credible threats to the royal family poured in from bin Laden's operatives in the Persian Gulf region.

Then a bold plan to capture the arch-terrorist emerged. Sheikh Zayed is one of the Arab world's most respected rulers and his government was one of only three in the world to recognize the Taliban. (Pakistan and Saudi Arabia were the other two.) UAE officials knew that bin Laden was wearing out his welcome in Afghanistan by involving himself in Taliban feuds and attempting to turn the country into an al Qaeda proxy-state. In 2000, Mullah Omar tried to resolve the dispute between bin Laden and himself in the age-old Muslim manner: One of his daughters was offered to one of bin Laden's sons as a wife. But after the marriage, the infighting intensified. Bin Laden was not looking for a safe haven, but a state he could run by proxy. The Taliban were not about to give up the power they had won at the point of an AK-47.

The UAE encouraged Taliban officials to meet with their American counterparts. As a result, the Taliban's intelligence chief was instructed by Mullah Omar to meet with the U.S. Consul General in Karachi, Pakistan, in the spring of 2000. In that meeting, the Taliban official offered to turn over bin Laden under certain conditions. The Taliban later made a second offer to turn over bin Laden, provided he would not be subject to the death penalty. These offers were rejected out of hand by the Clinton Administration. The Taliban offer, Clarke said, "was not serious."

Then a bold plan emerged from UAE officials. Sheikh Zayed would raise and contribute several billion dollars to help the Taliban rebuild their war-torn land and to lessen their dependence on bin Laden's funding. In return, the Taliban would extradite bin Laden to the UAE, where he would temporarily be held at a secure facility subject to Islamic law. Later he would be transferred to the United States or to a third country. The UAE's offer to hold bin Laden and to later transfer the arch-terrorist never left the "talking stage," according to one knowledgeable source.

Perhaps bin Laden would be ill enough that he would die in legal limbo in the UAE. At the time, bin Laden was believed by some to have had serious liver and kidney problems, for which he had supposedly received surgery in Pakistan in 1999.[29] Those reports were probably untrue—at least, an al Qaeda spokesman has repeatedly denied them—but it offered the hope of a politically easy outcome for both the U.S. and the UAE.

But the plan soon fell apart. The Taliban apparently considered the offer in a council of its senior staff—and rejected it. The UAE notified Clarke. Another plan to capture bin Laden fell apart.

Then, in July 2000, the plan seemed to make a comeback.

Mansoor Ijaz, the New York financier, landed in Dubai to meet some of his business partners on June 1, 2000. Ijaz met with a member of a prominent UAE family, whom we will call "Ahmed."

Ijaz described the secret effort he was making for a cease-fire in Kashmir. Fascinated that the Manhattan financier was constructing a backchannel between Pakistan and India, Ahmed decided to share a secret idea of his own—on capturing Osama bin Laden. Unbeknownst to Ijaz, it was remarkably similar to the plan that had been tried and had failed months earlier.

If Ijaz could present the idea directly to the president of the United States and get an informal nod of approval, Ahmed, as a senior official of the UAE, might be able to enlist the resources of his government to present Clinton with a formal, final, viable option for capturing bin Laden.

Ijaz took notes, realizing that he might have found a way to help his friend Bill Clinton get that long sought-after victory against bin Laden. He told Ahmed he had a meeting with White House Chief of Staff John Podesta scheduled for early July.

THE WHITE HOUSE—In the Clinton Administration, as in most Administrations, power was calibrated not by the size of one's office, but by its proximity to the Oval Office. The chief of staff, John Podesta, worked a few feet away from the president in an office with a view of the Rose Garden.

Ijaz was ushered in and seated at Podesta's conference table, where the chief of staff joined him. He carried a thick yellow legal pad. The principal American Muslim financier of Clinton's 1996 campaign had sent along a detailed agenda for the meeting beforehand, a copy of which the author has seen. It was the third of such meetings Ijaz had had with Podesta over the previous seven months to discuss Kashmir, terrorism, and other issues.[30]

Ijaz raised the plan that his business partner Ahmed had proposed. Podesta took careful notes.

And there's one more thing, Ijaz said. The UAE wanted President Clinton to either visit their country or make a personal phone call to ask for Sheikh Zayed's help in seizing bin Laden. It was a curious condition, but one that demonstrated the emphasis Arab societies place on who goes first, who takes the initiative, and whether help is coming because it is asked for or because it is offered. For Sheikh Zayed, a Clinton visit was a matter of prestige.

Podesta thought that a state visit might be difficult. Clinton had a full fundraising schedule for the 2000 Gore presidential campaign and the Middle East peace process made any presidential contact with Arab leaders difficult. Visiting one Arab state might look like favoritism and impede the peace process.

"Well, why don't you let Al Gore carry a letter from President Clinton to Sheikh Zayed, since he may be the next president of the United States?" Ijaz asked. Podesta thought that idea was also a non-starter. Gore's staff later rejected the idea; Ijaz said he was told, "we need him [Gore] here every day to do fundraising."

WASHINGTON, D.C.—In the last week of July 2000, Podesta presented the idea to President Clinton. Clinton asked few questions. He asked Podesta to brief Berger and to talk to Richard Clarke, as the man in the U.S. government with the closest ties to the UAE.

Berger himself did not like the idea and he didn't like Ijaz. He suspected Ijaz was back to his old habits of private diplomacy. Still, Berger confirmed to the author that he asked Clarke to check the offer out with his contacts in the UAE.[31]

Clarke made many phone calls to his contacts in the UAE, asking detailed questions about Ijaz and his well-placed business partner. Was the UAE trying to revive the plan to pay off the Taliban in exchange for handing over bin Laden? Apparently not. His old friend, the head of the UAE intelligence service, put it plainly. "We don't need another backchannel. You and I are the backchannel."

The last bloodless plan to capture bin Laden was dead. Long dead.

THE WHITE HOUSE—Pakistan's Prime Minister Nawaz Sharif met President Clinton on the morning of July 5, 1999, in the upstairs residence of the White House. Sharif and his wife had breakfast with the president, Hillary Clinton, and their daughter, Chelsea, according to a Pakistani source present at the meeting. It was a wide-ranging discussion. They discussed contributions from a Pakistani-American shipping magnate to the Clinton presidential library and financial assistance from the Pakistani-American community to aid Hillary Clinton's senatorial campaign. Sharif also came armed with a bold plan to neutralize bin Laden.

Sharif offered to create a special unit of Pakistani commandos who would remain isolated and secret from his own army and intelligence services, including Pakistan's version of the CIA, Inter-Services Intelligence, which was known to have close links with the Taliban. [32] The team would require American funding and training. Once trained, the commandos would be secretly inserted deep inside Afghanistan to kill bin Laden.

Since the spring of 1999, Clarke—at the president's direction—had convened a Counter-Terrorism Strategy Group, known as the CSG. The meetings were held around Clarke's oval wooden table. The members included Michael Sheehan, the State Department's counterterrorism coordinator, Dale Watson, head of counterterrorism at the FBI, and Cofer Black, who ran counterterrorism efforts at the CIA. The Pakistani plan was presented to the CSG—a few days after Prime Minister Sharif flew home.

Clarke and Sheehan were highly skeptical. They knew how difficult it would be for Sharif to keep the plan secret from his own military and intelligence establishment. But the risks were seen as small, even if the probability of success was small as well. So Clarke and Sheehan cautiously backed the venture.

Shortly thereafter, the Pakistani commando trainees were quietly flown to Andrews Air Force base in Maryland and driven two hours south to Quantico, Virginia. They practiced live-fire exercises and trained to fire accurately at distant, small targets. The commando team returned to Pakistan.

But before they could be put into action, Sharif was toppled in a coup on October 12, 1999. The commando team was swiftly disbanded.

Once again, President Clinton would have to fight bin Laden on his own.

CHAPTER ELEVEN

THE ATTACK ON THE USS *COLE*

ADEN, YEMEN—Jamal Al-Badawi had been waiting to kill and to die for almost two years. Now, in June 1999, his moment had come.

The Yemen native had given his *bayat*—his solemn oath of loyalty—to bin Laden at a training camp in eastern Afghanistan in 1997.[1] Badawi admired the mujihideen, the larger-than-life jihadis who humbled the Soviet Union. His own role in the Afghan war had been minor. Serving bin Laden was a way to capture some reflected glory.

In Afghanistan, Badawi grew close to Tawfiq al-Attash, a veteran of the anti-Soviet jihad. Attash was a hardened man who had seen blood and bombs in the frontiers of Islam, from Afghanistan to Chechnya to Bosnia. Badawi's friendship with Attash may not have been as accidental as it seemed to Badawi. Al Qaeda's camps are divided along ethnic lines; Saudis train Saudis, Yemenis train Yemenis, and so on. And each ethnic camp has its own talent spotter. Attash was the spotter for the Yemeni unit and he would have a use for this ambitious, naïve young man.

Badawi was sent home to Aden, Yemen, and told to wait. He waited and waited, all but giving up hope. But his mission would come.

In June 1999, two men visited Badawi's home. They carried a letter from Attash asking Badawi to go to Saudi Arabia and buy a

213

boat.[2] Later, another letter—this one from bin Laden—was delivered by courier. In flowery Arabic, the arch-terrorist provided detailed advice on how to sink American warships along the Yemen coastline.[3] The plot to sink the USS *Cole* was underway.

It soon grew to include some sixty people, many of whom had little idea about the ultimate objective. A welder made the housing for the bomb; a carpenter built a false bottom in the white fiberglass boat to conceal it. Another cell, composed of corrupt policemen in Lajeh, Yemen, created or purchased false identity cards and other documents.[4] The terror infrastructure included five safe houses, a late-model four-wheel-drive truck, a boat trailer, and a collection of cell phones.[5]

It was planned along classic bin Laden lines. The attack group was organized into cells of no more than three men each. Many of the terrorists were Arab Afghans, who had been trained in bin Laden's Afghanistan camps.[6] The bomb was sophisticated and designed to kill many people. And the plan had been patiently prepared. Indeed, in September 2000, weeks before the attack, two of the bombers took their boat on a test run, according to a Yemeni security service interrogation of a fisherman who had helped the men put their craft into the water.[7]

In a classified report, the FBI later described Attash as "the intermediary between bin Laden himself and the attack planners."[8] Like Ramzi Yousef in the 1993 World Trade Center bombing, Attash would be the mastermind who would assemble the team and get away. By contrast, Badawi would be treated as a "disposable"— and was easily arrested within days of the Cole attack.[9]

Aden harbor was an ideal place for bin Laden's organization to attempt a seaborne attack. The harbor is essentially U-shaped, making it easy to watch the movements of ships from almost any point in the city. No inside information about shipping schedules was necessary; an apartment window would supply all the intelligence any terror cell needed.

Nor would port security pose a problem. The port makes up but a small fraction of the harbor. Beyond the port area, a broad, rocky arm of land offers many coves, inlets, and docks to launch boats for fishermen. Any one of these would be ideal for launching a covert attack.

Even the small craft, powered by a whining outboard motor, would not attract attention. Every day a swarm of nearly identical boats emerged from the far rocky shore, sliced through the port's sea-lanes, and skirted oil tankers and naval cruisers on their way to the fishing grounds. It was a perfect cover.

So once the explosives and the boat were prepared, the cell simply had to wait. A target would soon steam in.

WASHINGTON, D.C.—Throughout the summer of 2000, counter-terrorism czar Richard Clarke became increasingly concerned about bin Laden's next strike on American targets. Intelligence chatter had picked up. Something was happening, but what?

In July 2000, a CIA informant revealed that a terror group based in Sidon, Lebanon, and long affiliated with bin Laden was planning to attack a U.S. naval vessel somewhere in the eastern Mediterranean. Most likely the attack would occur off the Lebanese coast. Clarke confirmed to the author this never-before-reported information.[10]

Bin Laden had never plotted to attack a hardened military target, let alone an American warship. Clarke was alarmed.

But the CIA and Defense Department officials discounted the threat, Clarke told the author. Clarke was told that the U.S. Navy had no ships in the area and no plans to deploy ships to the eastern Mediterranean. It was just another piece of "intelligence chatter."

What Clarke and apparently no one in the White House knew at the time was that bin Laden's operatives had tried and failed to attack the USS *The Sullivans* in Aden, Yemen, in January 2000. And, Clarke said, no one in the upper echelons of the Clinton Administration knew that CENTCOM, which supervised the deployment of Navy ships across the Middle East, had begun monthly refueling operations in Aden.

ADEN, YEMEN—The USS *Cole*, a 505-foot-long Arleigh Burke-class guided-missile destroyer with a complement of 249 men and 44 women, had left Norfolk Naval Station on August 8, 2000. Proudly painted on its hull was its Navy ship number: DDG-67. It was on its way to a six-month deployment[11] with the U.S. Fifth Fleet, currently on station in the Persian Gulf.

The $1 billion ship boasted an impressive array of armaments: anti-aircraft and anti-ship missiles, including Tomahawk cruise missiles, torpedoes, guns that fire five-inch-wide shells, and a 20-mm Phalanx Close-In Weapons System, which fires multi-barrel cannons that will rip a man or a small boat to pieces at a distance of almost one mile in a matter of seconds. But all that weaponry would turn out to be of little use. Even the sentries standing "fore and aft held unloaded shotguns," *Newsweek* noted, "the shells still in ammo belts slung around their waists."[12]

As the *Cole* passed through the Suez Canal and into the Red Sea in October 2000, Lieutenant Commander Chris Peterschmidt, the ship's second-in-command, (known as the "XO" or executive officer) radioed the U.S. embassy in Sana'a, the capital of Yemen. Following standard procedure, the warship was planning to refuel in Yemen in ten days.

Peterschmidt and the senior officers saw it as a routine operation. U.S. Navy ships had been regularly refueling in Aden for the past two years.

The bomb had been carefully prepared for weeks. It was made from C-4, a plastic explosive long used by the U.S. military. The bomb was the equivalent of seven hundred pounds of TNT. The C-4 was packed in heavy steel to direct the blast and magnify its force.[13] The use of C-4 shows sophistication and suggests the involvement of a hostile government. The U.S. sold large amounts of C-4 to Iran in the days of the Shah, and Iraq is believed to have captured some of the plastic explosive during the Iran-Iraq war in the 1980s.

One of the lessons apparently learned by the terrorists from the previous aborted attack on the USS *The Sullivans* was that the bomb needed to be a "shaped charge,"[14] which would cause more damage per pound of explosive and allow the attackers to carry a lighter-weight, more effective bomb. This time, the bomb would not sink the boat.

The USS *Cole* was in Aden harbor, 1,800 feet off shore in a body of water known as the Bandar al-Tawahi, attached to a floating refueling station. The fueling station was owned by Arab Investment and Trading, a private company controlled by a wealthy Yemeni living in London along with some Saudi investors.[15] It wouldn't take long; at 2,200 gallons per minute, the entire fuelling would take less than six hours. The fuelling began at 10:30 A.M.

Forty-seven minutes later, at 11:18 A.M. local time, disaster struck.

A small craft gunned its motor toward the *Cole*. The two men aboard seemed to be aiming dead center between the two towers that rose from the deck of the destroyer. On board the speeding boat was Abd al-Muhsin al-Taifi, a Yemeni man wanted in connection with the 1998 bombing of the U.S. embassy in Nairobi, Kenya.

As the outboard raced toward the *Cole*, telephone records later revealed that the suicide bombers repeatedly phoned Jamal Ba Khorsh, a cell member who was recruited to videotape the attack on the unsuspecting warship. The bombers repeatedly called Khorsh from their cell phones—right up until seconds before the attack. But Khorsh apparently slept through their calls. The suicide bombers desperately tried to get their final moments memorialized on videotape. They were frustrated—they kept getting voicemail.

In the last moments, one American sailor recalls, the two suicide bombers stood stiffly and saluted. It was their bid at a legacy.

Then, the bomb exploded. The explosion smashed its way through the half-inch reinforced steel plating and ripped a forty-by-forty-foot hole in the hull. Within minutes, seventeen sailors were dead or mortally wounded and another thirty-nine severely injured. The *Cole* was taking on water. It was the most devastating attack on an American warship since World War II.

Moments before the blast, Lieutenant Commander Peterschmidt was running a meeting to discuss the crew's morale. The idea on the table was to buy a new thirty-two-inch television set. Then the explosion rocked the ship, snatching the crew's breakroom television out of its wall brackets and smashing it on the floor.[16]

In the cramped corridors, Peterschmidt stepped over men and women moaning for help, their legs broken, their jaws bleeding. If he tarried to help the wounded, the whole ship might be consumed by fire and flooding, and then sink—possibly killing the entire crew.[17] It was the cruel triage of battle, a grim utilitarianism that Navy officers must learn to live with. Navy corpsmen raced to treat the wounded as Peterschmidt rushed to save the ship.

The stench of the high-test fuel, now pooling on the decks and floating on the water, was overwhelming.[18] The number-one engine room was flooded. The pumps worked overtime, but the seals kept springing leaks.

The ship's power was out. For the next three days, there was little fresh water, no hot food, and no rest. Only one flush toilet remained in operation and at least seventy of the crew soon developed diarrhea. The heat was overpowering: 113 degrees in the open and as much as 130 degrees below decks.[19]

The first night after the attack, a senior officer from the headquarters of the Navy's Fifth Fleet phoned Peterschmidt on his mobile phone. (The ship's communications were out.) The staff officer didn't waste words. "You're sinking, aren't you?"

"Yes, sir."[20]

Peterschmidt went to Commander Kirk Lippold, and told his calm commanding officer that he wanted to cut another hole in the hull—to save the ship.

The commander listened silently as Peterschmidt explained the problem. Water was roaring in faster than the pumps could push it up and out. The ship's pumps were straining to force the water up three stories out of the number-one engine room. Cutting another hole, slightly above the waterline, might do the trick. But high-test fuel floated on the water in the engine room—one spark from a welder's cutting torch could touch off an inferno.[21]

It was a risk they would have to take. A seaman carefully cut the hole. The hoses were moved lower. The pumps resumed their vital work. By midnight on October 15, after three days of struggle, the USS *Cole* was saved.

Impressed by the dogged determination of the crew, Peterschmidt told the *Navy Times*, "Their performance answers critics who say that modern sailors don't measure up to those of yesteryear."[22]

NEW YORK—Within hours of the attack on the USS *Cole*, FBI agents from the New York field office boarded commercial flights bound for Yemen.[23] Soon after they landed, the FBI declared war—on the State Department.

FBI counterterrorism chief John O'Neill arrived two days later. He pulled up to the Movenpick Hotel; it was the same hotel that bin Laden's men had bombed eight years earlier. Still wearing his suit and tie in the 100-degree heat, O'Neill marched down the hotel hall to the room that the U.S. ambassador to Yemen was using as an office.

Barbara K. Bodine was worldly and tough. She had served in Baghdad during the run-up to the 1991 Gulf War and had served as counterterrorism coordinator at the State Department. She had worked in Yemen—perhaps the most terrorist-infested place in the Middle East—for three years.

For O'Neill and Bodine, it was hate at first sight. She was barefoot, in a polo shirt and blue jeans.[24] "You'd better get rid of that suit," she told O'Neill. "You'll die from the heat."

O'Neill told Bodine that he believed that bin Laden was behind the bombing of the USS *Cole*. "He's out to get me," he added.

"Who's out to get you?" she asked.

"Bin Laden. He wants to kill me," he said.

"Excuse me," Bodine said. "He's after all of us. He wants to kill any American. Besides, I have a slightly higher profile here than you."

It was the first of many daily confrontations. Every day brought another showdown over a small issue. Bodine and O'Neill argued over the kind of guns his men could carry. He wanted to issue submachine guns to every one of his men. She thought that would eliminate any hope of help from the government of Yemen. Eventually Bodine struck a compromise: A contingent of twenty-four FBI agents would carry guns to protect 150 other agents, who would bear concealed pistols.

After the Nairobi embassy bombing, O'Neill had been in charge of the investigation. The Kenyans were eager for American help. They had lost hundreds in the embassy bombings. Kenyan investigators were impressed by the FBI's scientific methods, technologies, and demeanor.

But Aden was not Nairobi. Years of Soviet and militant Muslim propaganda had made Yemen's police and internal security services skeptical of America. They were not about to allow the FBI to run a criminal investigation on their turf.

Still, the Yemenis were making some progress. On October 16, Yemeni police made a breakthrough. They located an apartment overlooking the harbor that had been rented by two Arabs who had disappeared on the morning of the attack. The landlord recalled seeing a fiberglass boat stored in the backyard, which also disappeared on the morning of October 12.[25]

At another apartment, police found a corrugated metal wall constructed by some of the bombing suspects to shield these boat-building efforts from view. Neighbors complained about incessant banging and work on a boat. On the morning of the bombing, one neighbor saw the boat towed away on a trailer pulled by a truck.

But from the FBI's point of view, the investigation soon stalled. The Yemeni security services refused to allow the FBI to interview the suspects they had taken into custody. Instead, the Americans could submit written questions and receive briefings on the answers. O'Neill did not hide his anger or frustration.

About the only place where the FBI made headway was in the small piece of the "crime scene" that they controlled—the USS *Cole* itself. Inside the *Cole*, the crew found pieces of evidence, including a propeller from the outboard motor of the attack craft and some of the terrorists' teeth.[26] These molars later enabled the FBI to positively identify the suicide bombers.

After three weeks, Ambassador Bodine asked the State Department to have O'Neill recalled. Deputy Secretary of State Thomas Pickering delivered the message to Attorney General Janet Reno, a strong O'Neill supporter. Reno considered the request for two weeks. Then, after just five weeks in Yemen, O'Neill was ordered home. He would never be able to return.

O'Neill tried to run the investigation from New York, but the time difference and the distance only made his diplomatic banishment feel worse. For a veteran investigator who liked to be on the streets with his men, it was humiliating. When the ambassador eventually signed a protocol with the Yemenis that would allow the FBI to directly interview the suspects, O'Neill was desperate to get back to Yemen. But Bodine refused to give O'Neill "country clearance"—a kind of permission that any federal employee must receive from the resident U.S. ambassador before traveling overseas. She had barred him from Yemen and there wasn't a damn thing he could do about it.

"In my view, Bodine may have been too protective of the Yemenis," said one former State Department official, who knew both of them well. "And O'Neill probably was over the top in pushing."

Whatever the cause, the investigation dragged on inconclusively until the end of the Clinton Administration.[27]

THE WHITE HOUSE—Hours after the attack on the USS *Cole*, Clarke chaired a meeting in the Situation Room in the White House. Around the table were Michael Sheehan, the State Department's coordinator for counterterrorism, Cofer Black, the CIA's point man on counterterrorism; Brian Sheridan, assistant secretary of defense for special operations; and Dale Watson, head of counterterrorism at the FBI. Over a late lunch,[28] these four men debated what action to recommend to the principals, who would in turn recommend a policy to the president.

Both Clarke and Sheehan told the author that they had little doubt that bin Laden was behind the attack on the USS *Cole*. Within minutes of the attack, Clarke had ordered his staff to review existing intelligence to see if there were any clues about possible attackers. While the evidence was fragmentary, as it usually is, it seemed to point to bin Laden. The arch-terrorist had at least once before launched attacks on U.S. military targets in Yemen, in December 1992. And the threat to a Navy ship from a bin Laden-affiliated group in Lebanon took on new importance. Other intelligence also seemed to link bin Laden to the attack. (Al Qaeda's failed attack on the USS *The Sullivans* on January 3, 2000, was not yet known inside the White House in October 2000.)

But Black and Watson, representing the CIA and the FBI, wanted to reserve judgment until more evidence came in. America has many terrorist enemies. Their respective agencies wanted to investigate before drawing any conclusions.

Clarke reminded the participants that the Pentagon had drawn up "target decks"—on-the-shelf, regularly updated and detailed strike plans that specified aim points throughout specific target buildings—for both bin Laden's training camps and strongholds in Afghanistan as well as key Taliban buildings in Kandahar and Kabul. The plans, based on satellite photographs, included GPS coordinates and preferred attack mode (cruise missile type, bomber type, bomb type, and so on). They were designed to be put immediately into action, at the president's command. But Clarke's small group could not agree on a course of action. "At the CSG that day, my staff and I were convinced that the attack was from al Qaeda. CIA and FBI deferred judgment pending their investigation," Clarke told the author.[29] They were deadlocked.

Later, Clarke attended a meeting with Secretary of Defense William Cohen, Director of Central Intelligence George Tenet, Secretary of State Madeleine Albright, Attorney General Janet Reno, and others. Several others were in the room, including Leon Fuerth, Gore's national security advisor; Jim Steinberg, the deputy National Security Advisor; and Michael Sheehan, the State Department's coordinator for counterterrorism. An American warship had been attacked without warning in a "friendly" harbor—and, at the time, no one knew if the ship's pumps could keep it afloat for the night. Now they had to decide what to do about it.

Clarke had no doubts about whom to punish. The Joint Chiefs of Staff had compiled thick binders of bin Laden and Taliban targets in Afghanistan, complete with satellite photographs and GPS bomb coordinates—the Pentagon's "target decks." The detailed plan was "to level" every bin Laden training camp and compound in Afghanistan as well as key Taliban buildings in Kabul and Kandahar. "Let's blow them up," Clarke said.[30]

There was some policy basis for Clarke's position. The Clinton Administration had publicly announced a new policy, months before, to hold the Taliban accountable for any future bin Laden attack. This was similar to the Bush post-September 11 policy of punishing nations that harbor terrorists as if they were terrorists themselves.

But to many of the participants Clarke's plan for a retaliatory strike was old hat. He had been recommending such a strike for months. Clarke wanted to attack the training camps, in his words, as a "bolt out of blue,"[31] without waiting for another bin Laden attack. Now that there had been another terrorist attack, it seemed that Clarke was pushing his policy with a new justification.

Around the table, Clarke heard only objections—not a mandate for action. "All of the principals wanted to do something about bin Laden," Clarke insists.[32] "They had signed off on findings to use covert lethal force against him [in 1998]. They were ready to approve an additional cruise missile attack if he could be located. They were pressuring the Taliban and Pakistan diplomatically." But their conditions of the use of force were numerous and difficult to meet.

This is how Clarke remembers the meeting, which has never before been described in the press. Attorney General Janet Reno insisted that they had no clear idea who had actually carried out the attack. The "Justice [Department] also noted, as always, that any use of force had to be consistent with international law, i.e. not retaliation but self protection from future attack," Clarke told the author.[33] Reno could not be reached for comment.

Director of Central Intelligence George Tenet[34] joined Reno in insisting on an investigation before launching a retaliatory strike. Tenet "did not want a months-long investigation," CIA spokesman Bill Harlow said. "He simply believed that before the United States attacked, it ought to know for sure who was behind the *Cole* bombing." While Tenet noted that the CIA had not reached a conclusion about what terror group was behind the surprise attack on the USS *Cole*, "he said personally he thought that it would turn out to be al Qaeda," Clarke recalls.

Secretary of State Madeleine Albright was also against a counterstrike—but for diplomatic reasons. "We're desperately trying to halt the fighting that has broken out between Israel and the Palestinians," Albright said.[35] Clarke recalls her saying, "bombing Muslims wouldn't be helpful at this time." Some two weeks earlier, Ariel Sharon had visited the Temple Mount in Jerusalem, which touched off a wave of violence known as the "second Intifada" and threatened to completely destroy the Clinton Administration's hopes for Middle East peace settlement.

Clarke remembers other objections from the State Department. "State noted that we had been bombing Iraq and Serbia and were getting the reputation internationally as a mad bomber nation that could only address its problems that way."[36] "It would be irresponsible," a spokeswoman for Albright told the author, for the Secretary of State, as America's chief diplomat, not to consider the diplomatic impact of a missile strike that might try but would quite likely fail to kill bin Laden.

Albright urged continued diplomatic efforts to persuade the Taliban to turn over bin Laden. Those efforts had been going on for more than two years and had gone nowhere. It was unlikely that the Taliban would ever voluntarily turn over its strongest internal ally. Clarke summed up the diplomatic efforts in a conversation with the author as amounting to "lots of cups of tea."

Secretary Albright remembers the principals' meeting somewhat differently. Albright wrote the following to the author:

Between the time of the Africa embassy bombings on August 7, 1998, and the day I left office, the administration was actively considering military strikes directed at Osama bin Laden and al Qaeda. Following the initial strikes against a terrorist training camp in Afghanistan and a facility linked to bin Laden in Sudan, the president directed the Pentagon and our intelligence community to stay alert for opportunities to kill or capture bin Laden. The State Department fully supported this effort and signed off on several planned strikes that were ultimately aborted due to the shortage of reliable real-time intelligence. After the bombing of the Cole, our law enforcement authorities required approximately four months, until after the new [Bush] administration was in office, to definitively link al Qaeda to the attack. The logical time to strike militarily would have been after that connection had been established, and a public explanation justifying the attacks could have been made. To strike without evidence or any expectation of hitting bin Laden would have turned world opinion against the United States at the very moment we were seeking maximum cooperation in tracking down the terrorist network responsible for the murders. I certainly do not recall the Pentagon or CIA confirming that we had reliable information concerning the whereabouts of bin Laden in the days after the Cole tragedy.

Albright later added that if there was "definitive" proof that bin Laden was behind the USS *Cole* blast and if there was reliable intelligence about his current whereabouts, she would have taken a different view at the meeting.

Secretary of Defense Cohen also did not favor a retaliatory strike, according to Clarke. The attack "was not sufficient provocation," Clarke remembers Cohen saying, or words to that effect. Cohen thought that any military strike needed a "clear and compelling justification," Clarke recalls. (Cohen, despite repeated phone calls over more than one week, failed to respond to interview requests.) Cohen also noted that General Anthony Zinni, then head of CENTCOM, was concerned that a major bombing campaign would cause domestic unrest in Pakistan (where bin Laden enjoyed strong support among extremists) and hurt the U.S. military's relationship with that nation.

Cohen's views were perfectly in accord with those of the top uniformed officers and Clinton's political appointees at the Pentagon, Sheehan told the author. "It was the entire Pentagon," he added. The chief lesson that the Defense Department seemed to draw from the assault on the USS *Cole* was the need for better security for its ships, what was invariably called "force protection." Listening to Cohen and later talking to top military officers, Sheehan, a former member of special forces before joining the State Department, told the author that he was "stunned" and "taken aback" by their views. "This phenomenon I cannot explain," he said. Why didn't they want to go hit back at those who had just murdered American servicemen without warning or provocation?

The issue was hotly debated. Some of the principals were concerned that bin Laden might somehow survive the cruise-missile attack and appear in another triumphant press conference. Clarke countered by saying that they could say that they were only targeting terrorist infrastructure. If they got bin Laden, they could take that as a bonus. Others worried about target information. At the time, Clarke said that he had very reliable and specific information about bin Laden's location. And so on. Each objection was countered and answered with a yet another objection.

In the end, for a variety of reasons, the principals were against Clarke's retaliation plan by a margin of seven to one against. Clarke was the sole one in favor. Bin Laden would get away—again.

After the meeting, Sheehan told the author that he sought out Clarke. He could not believe the Pentagon's weak response to the attack on the USS *Cole*. He was incredulous and frustrated. "What's it going to take to get them to hit al Qaeda in Afghanistan? Does al Qaeda have to attack the Pentagon?"[37]

Instead, the Clinton Administration focused on the investigation and improving the cooperation with Yemen. Clinton phoned the president of Yemen twice, demanding better cooperation between the FBI and the security services of Yemen to determine who was behind the attack on the *Cole*. To some senior Clinton officials, the president's forceful phone calls to Yemen were a positive sign. "The calls were about as forceful as you could expect from one head of state to another," one official, who was in the Oval Office for both Clinton calls, told the author. But, in the end, his calls did little good.

The president did even less to clear the roadblocks inside his own government. Less than one month after the attack, in November 2000, CIA analysts had fingered bin Laden as the culprit—even if senior CIA officials had not yet made up their minds. While John

O'Neill immediately (and correctly) suspected that bin Laden was behind the attack, the FBI team in Yemen continued to believe that the arch-terrorist had nothing to do with the bombing. That curious belief may have been driven by the frustrations of their investigation in Aden. What little the FBI knew came from sixty suspects arrested or questioned by Yemeni police. These suspects were minor figures: a corrupt policeman who supplied false papers, a man who sold the bombers a boat. All were Yemeni nationals. Still, the FBI didn't appear to have read all of the translated transcripts that the Yemeni police provided. These interview transcripts included hundreds of pages of the interrogation of Jamal al-Badawi, a key player in the Cole attack. Badawi, according to *Veterans of Foreign Wars* magazine, said "he was led to believe—but never directly told—that bin Laden was giving the orders."[38]

Some CIA officials were apoplectic. Bin Laden had all but claimed credit. Standing beside members of the Taliban elite, bin Laden rose to read a poem that he had composed in January 2001.[39] It was no love sonnet. Even the opening verses, translated from Arabic, read like a boast:

> *A destroyer: even the brave fear its might.*
> *It inspires horror in the harbor and in the open sea.*
> *She sails into the waves.*
> *Flanked by arrogance, haughtiness and false power.*
> *To her doom she moves slowly.*
> *A dinghy awaits her, riding the waves.*[40]

A few months later, an al Qaeda recruiting videotape was obtained by a Middle Eastern intelligence service. A copy was given to the CIA and another copy was obtained by a Kuwait City newspaper. The tape included news footage of the *Cole* attack and called on Muslim men to wage jihad against the Jews and the "Crusaders," Americans and Europeans. The voiceover includes a boisterous song with the lyrics, "We thank god for granting us victory the day we destroyed the Cole in the sea."[41]

Finally, the CIA was able to trace the $5,000 sent by bin Laden to the cell in Yemen that carried out the attack on the *Cole.* Bin Laden "specifically allocated funds to videotape the attack, a task that could not be accomplished."[42]

But with Clinton trying to broker a peace settlement in Israel, a presidential election imminent, and the two-term Clinton administration ending, serious plans to retaliate went nowhere.

In the last days of his administration, Clinton decided not to fire a parting shot at bin Laden. The terrorists of the world were left with another lesson: even American warships could now be attacked with impunity. The world's sole superpower would not dare to strike them.

During the Clinton Administration, fifty-nine Americans were killed by bin Laden's operations. And while almost fifty terrorists had been tracked and captured, and dozens of plots had been foiled and six terror cells smashed, the administration had waged no real war against its overt enemy. Instead, the administration reacted in fits and starts—half-measures that frustrated those who knew what needed to be done.

What was needed was a full-fledged war on terror to kill bin Laden and destroy al Qaeda. But that would be left for the next administration, the administration of George W. Bush, which took on an overt war against the terrorists.

As the Clinton Administration wound down, its challenge to defeat al Qaeda and bin Laden unmet, the planning for bin Laden's most spectacular attack was already well underway.

In his last night in office as president of the United States, Clinton was at his desk past midnight. He wasn't issuing last-minute orders to smash al Qaeda or capture bin Laden. He was signing pardons for dozens of well-connected friends. He and the world did not know that September 11, 2001, was less than nine months away.

APPENDIX A

THE IRAQ–AL QAEDA CONNECTION

Even after the liberation of Iraq, debate rages about the relationship between Saddam Hussein and Osama bin Laden, between a secular dictatorship that had persecuted Islamists for decades and an Islamist terrorist organization bent on bringing Allah's will to Earth.

Unless Iraqi intelligence archives are made available to the public, we may never know the full extent of the relationship between the Iraqi strongman and the arch-terrorist. But there can be little doubt that there *was* a working relationship between Iraq and al Qaeda, beginning in 1993.

Indeed, the case that Iraq and al Qaeda forged an alliance is far stronger than the conventional wisdom would suggest—and the case against it far weaker.

A Saddam-bin Laden partnership offered each side significant advantages. The Iraqi dictator gained an energized terrorist network, whose actions he could plausibly deny. Bin Laden gained expertise and the logistical support that only a client state can offer. Certainly, bin Laden had need of Saddam's skills—developed with the aid of the Soviets and East Germans—for planning covert operations, forging documents, and coordinating large campaigns over vast areas.

231

Even during the Clinton years, counterterrorism officials began noting the advantages of a strategic relationship between Iraq and al Qaeda. "It's clear that the Iraqis would like to have bin Laden in Iraq," Vincent Cannistraro, who had run the CIA's counterintelligence operations, told Knight Ridder in 1999.[1] "The Iraqis have all the technological elements, the tradecraft that bin Laden lacks, and they have Abu Nidal," the notorious Palestinian bomb expert.

The most compelling reason for bin Laden to work with Iraq was money. Al Qaeda operates in some fifty countries. Its fighters must be trained, housed, armed, and fed—as must their families, who often live with them in safe houses or camps. In addition, al Qaeda buys and maintains computers—for tracking its extensive databases and posting covert messages on online bulletin boards—as well as heavy equipment ranging from bulldozers to airplanes. Operating in Yemen, Afghanistan, and other hellholes also means that bribes must constantly be paid to bandits and government officials. Finally, because al Qaeda seems to send most of its important messages by courier, air travel is a major expense. None of this comes cheap.

Al Qaeda operatives have testified that the organization has always been desperate for cash. Senior employees fought bitterly about the $100 difference in pay between Egyptian and Saudi workers (the Egyptians made more). Jaif Al-Fadl, who was connected to the 1998 embassy bombings, described his bitterness when he was told that al Qaeda could not pay for his pregnant wife to see a doctor.

Virtually all of bin Laden's businesses, according to the trial testimony of some captured former employees, lose money. Bin Laden told an Arab reporter that he lost $150 million in his Sudanese investments. What's left of his fortune is tied up in real estate in Sudan, Yemen, and elsewhere or has been seized or frozen by various governments in the last few years.

Bin Laden's personal wealth alone is simply not enough to support a profligate global organization for years on end. Besides, his fortune is probably not as large as some imagine. Informed estimates put bin Laden's personal wealth at perhaps $30 million—not the $300 million usually cited in the press. $30 million is the budget of a small school district, not a global terror conglomerate.

So bin Laden needed money. And Saddam, who ran one of the most oil-rich nations on Earth, was far richer. Forbes estimated his personal fortune at $2 billion.[2] The Iraqi state treasury, despite sanctions, also had vast reserves. American soldiers in Baghdad have stumbled onto some caches of cash. One series of boxes yielded more than $650 million.

Would Saddam give money to bin Laden? Iraq certainly didn't shrink from financing international terrorism. Indeed, throughout the Clinton years, the U.S. State Department routinely listed Iraq as one of the world's largest funders of terrorism. Saddam paid the families of suicide bombers in Israel $25,000 each for the loss of their sons. Later, he upped the reward to $50,000. And Baghdad had a long history of funding terrorist campaigns, beginning in 1969 in the Beluchistan region that straddles Iran and Pakistan.

Saddam even had a history of financing Islamist terrorists with links to bin Laden. Secret documents found among the debris of the Iraqi Intelligence Center in Baghdad in April 2003 prove that Baghdad funded the Allied Democratic Forces, a Ugandan terror group led by an Islamist cleric linked to bin Laden since the mid-1990s.[3] The terror organization volunteered to send recruits to the "headquarters for [the] international holy warrior network" in Baghdad.[4]

Saddam funded other openly jihadi groups linked to bin Laden. Melan Krekar, the leader of the Iraqi Kurdish Group, which is explicitly modeled on the Taliban, admitted that he met bin Laden and other senior al Qaeda figures in Afghanistan.[5] After September 2001, hundreds of al Qaeda fighters are believed to have holed up in the strongholds of the Iraqi Kurdish group in northern Iraq. The Iraqi Kurdish group was based on Iraqi soil, near the border with Iran, and was both encouraged and funded by Saddam to war with Iran and independent Kurds in the northern no-fly zone.

There is no reason to believe that Saddam would be willing to fund the allies and associates of bin Laden, but not the arch-terrorist himself. In fact, there is a wealth of evidence attesting to such an alliance.

Starting in 1997, bin Laden's fighters attended training camps in Iraq.[6] The Director of Central Intelligence, George Tenet, recently told the Senate Intelligence Committee, "Iraq has in the past provided training in document forgery and bomb making to al Qaeda. It also provided training in poisons and gasses to two al Qaeda associates; one of these [al Qaeda] associates characterized *the relationship* [emphasis the author's] as successful. Mr. Chairman, this information is based on a solid foundation of intelligence. It comes to us from credible and reliable sources. Much of it is corroborated by multiple sources."[7]

Perhaps the most infamous training facility used by al Qaeda lies southeast of Baghdad in a place called Salman Pak. At a vast compound run by Iraqi intelligence, Muslim militants trained to hijack planes with knives. They practiced on a full-size Boeing 707. Secretary of State Colin Powell later provided satellite photos of this training camp in the buildup to the Iraq war.

The chief of the intelligence arm of the Iraqi National Congress, an Iraqi opposition group, told the author there is a long history of contact between Iraq and the arch-terrorist. This claim is all the more credible, given the INC's successful record of smuggling scores of defectors out of Iraq to be debriefed by America's Defense Intelligence Agency and Britain's MI-6.

Iraq reportedly delivered small arms and money to bin Laden's organization, and Iraqi intelligence agents allegedly met repeatedly with bin Laden or his operatives in Sudan, Turkey, Afghanistan, and Prague.

Bin Laden is believed to have met several times with officers of Iraq's Special Security Organization, a secret police agency run by Saddam's son Qusay. Bin Laden also seems to have had ties to Iraq's Mukhabarat, another one of its intelligence services.

Perhaps the most dramatic meeting occurred in December 1998, when Farouk Hijazi, a senior officer in the Mukhabarat who later became ambassador to Turkey, journeyed deep into the icy Hindu Kush mountains near Kandahar, Afghanistan. Mr. Hijazi is "thought to have offered bin Laden asylum in Iraq," according to a 1999 report in the *Guardian Weekly*, a British newspaper.[8]

Later, another Iraqi intelligence operative, Salah Suleiman, was arrested near the Afghan border by Pakistani authorities in October 2000.[9] He was apparently returning from a visit to bin Laden.

Some skeptics dismiss the emerging evidence of a long-standing link between Iraq and al Qaeda by contending that Saddam ran a non-Islamic dictatorship hated by Islamists like bin Laden. Secular states and Islamic radicals don't work together.

In fact, there are plenty of "Stalin-Roosevelt" partnerships between international terrorists and Arab dictators. Documents discovered in Baghdad prove beyond any reasonable doubt that Iraq has financed militant Islamist terror groups and that those groups are indisputably connected to bin Laden.

The idea that Iraq would not work with al Qaeda on purely ideological grounds is simply a prejudice of a handful of analysts, most of whom are hostile to waging a war on terror. American intelligence services have "finally realized that there is no distinction between terrorist organizations," Rita Katz, recently told *National Review Online*. Katz is the author of *Terrorist Hunter: The Extraordinary Story of a Woman Who Went Undercover to Infiltrate the Radical Islamic Groups Operating in America*. "I give, for instance, several examples in the book of how al Qaeda, Hamas, and Palestinian Islamic Jihad all work together and share operatives, training, and financing," she said.[10]

Besides, the religious aspect of bin Laden's killers is overplayed. Even overlooking the Koran's injunctions against murder and killing of women and children in war, the lifestyles of the al Qaeda terrorists don't reflect orthodox Islam. Mohammed Atta, for example, reportedly "slugged down vodka like a sailor."[11] The night before the September 11 attacks, several of the plotters were reported to have had a drunken party at a Florida strip club—two major violations of Islamic law. Many of the captured al Qaeda terrorists lacked full beards, which fundamentalists believe the Koran instructs cannot be shaved. One disco-loving hijacker has been traced to another al Qaeda terrorist plot in the Philippines, where a fellow terrorist lived with a non-Muslim girlfriend. A third terrorist boasted of his sexual conquests on a phone tapped by the Philippine police. Audio files on the computer used by the 1993 World Trade Center bombers contain numerous obscenities. And so on. Bin Laden's men are political extremists in religious garb—not Islamic zealots—who probably felt right at home with Saddam's thugs.

It is unclear how long Iraq and al Qaeda were working together in a joint project of terror against America and the Western world. One former Clinton campaign national security advisor believes Iraq's secret war against America may have begun with the 1993 World Trade Center bombing. Iraq became involved, author Laurie Mylorie believes, after learning of the bomb plot from a terrorist holed up in Iraq who was an uncle of one of the ringleaders. One of the perpetrators placed forty-six calls—some more than an hour long—to that uncle in a single month before the bombing, according to phone records collected by the FBI.[12]

The two ringleaders both had connections to Iraq. The mastermind, Ramzi Ahmed Yousef, entered the U.S. on an Iraqi passport and was known to his associates as "Rashid the Iraqi." It was he who persuaded the bombers to make their target the World Trade Center. (Yousef is also the nephew of Khalid Shaikh Mohammed, who was the third-ranking al Qaeda commander until his capture in 2003.) The other man, Abdul Rahman Yasin, fled to Baghdad, where, ABC News reported in 1994, he had been put on Iraq's government payroll.

Iraqi agents, Mylroie persuasively argues, also supplied false passports and escape routes. They might have provided bomb-making expertise and money. The hydrogen-cyanide gas that was supposed to be spread by the explosion—luckily it was burned up instead—is an Iraqi specialty. The Iraqis, who had the Third World's largest poison gas operations prior to the first Gulf War, have perfected the technique of making hydrogen-cyanide gas, which the Nazis called Zyklon-B.

The Iraqi terror campaign intensified in the mid-1990s, after bin Laden and Iraqi intelligence became better acquainted, most likely in Khartoum, the capital of Sudan. Iraq ran an extensive intelligence hub in Khartoum until the late 1990s, when Sudanese officials ordered them to leave. Bin Laden was based in Khartoum until 1996, when Sudan kicked him out at the request of the U.S. government. There are documented meetings that occurred between bin Laden and Iraqi agents at the time, beginning in 1994.

After a June 1996 Arab League summit—the first since the Gulf War—issued a communiqué in favor of maintaining sanctions against Iraq, Iraq's government-controlled press seethed with anger. "Before it is too late, the Arabs should rectify the sin they committed against Iraq," one Iraq state-run paper warned.

Saudi Arabia was the prime mover behind the Arab League's bold statement. Two days after the meeting ended, a truck bomb exploded outside the Al Khobar towers complex in Saudi Arabia. The U.S. government never publicly accused Iraq, but General Wafiq Samaraii, an Iraqi defector, did. He said Saddam had asked him to join a secret committee to commit terrorist acts against U.S. forces during the Gulf War. The Al Khobar bombing was strikingly similar to the plans of that committee, Mr. Samaraii said. (That bombing might well be the work of Iran, not Iraq, however.)

Next, Iraq seems to have played a role in bin Laden's plot to bomb two U.S embassies in East Africa.

Bin Laden's February 23, 1998, call for jihad lists three grievances: that U.S. warplanes use bases in Saudi Arabia to patrol the skies of Iraq, that United Nations sanctions have caused grievous suffering in Iraq, and that America's Iraq policy is designed to divert attention from Israel's treatment of Muslims.[13] In short, bin Laden's call to arms reads as if it were issued from Baghdad.

Beginning on May 1, 1998, Iraq warned of "dire consequences" if the United Nations sanctions were not lifted and the weapons-inspection teams removed.[14] Eight days later, bin Laden released another statement calling for jihad against America. Throughout the summer, Iraq's and bin Laden's threatening statements moved in lockstep. Iraq expelled UN weapons inspectors on August 5. Two days later, the bombs went off in Nairobi, Kenya, and Dar-es-Salaam, Tanzania.

Terrorist attacks are often planned on certain anniversaries, to send a message. Two U.S. embassies were bombed on August 7, 1998—eight years to the day after President George H.W. Bush announced that American troops would be deployed to Saudi Arabia to protect the kingdom from Iraq.[15]

Speaking before the United Nations, Secretary of State Colin Powell, citing intelligence gathered from an Iraqi source, said that a bin Laden associate "had been sent to Iraq several times between 1997 and 2000 for help in acquiring poisons and gases."[16]

Iraq provided funds to bin Laden since at least 1994 and training facilities inside Iraq since 1997, if the intelligence gathered by Sudan and the Iraqi resistance groups is correct. It provided travel documents for terrorists (in some cases very high quality fake passports, in other cases legitimate passports with stolen or false identities),[17] access to safe houses, and a means of communicating and moving money for al Qaeda through Iraq's diplomatic channel.

Saddam and bin Laden had common enemies, common purposes, and interlocking needs. They shared a powerful hate for America and the Saudi royal family. They both saw the Gulf War as a turning point. Saddam suffered a crushing defeat that he had repeatedly vowed to avenge. Bin Laden regards the U.S. as guilty of war crimes against Iraqis and believes that non-Muslims shouldn't have military bases on the holy sands of Arabia. Al Qaeda's avowed goal for the past ten years has been the removal of

American and allied forces from Saudi Arabia, where they stood in harm's way solely to contain Saddam.

There might even have been a role for Iraq in the September 11 attacks. Israeli intelligence services reportedly met with CIA and FBI officials in August and warned of an imminent large-scale attack on the U.S. There "were strong grounds for suspecting Iraqi involvement," a senior Israeli official later told London's *Sunday Telegraph*.[18]

In 1999, an Arab intelligence officer who knows Saddam personally predicted in *Newsweek*: "Very soon you will be witnessing large-scale terrorist activity run by the Iraqis." The Arab official said these terror operations would be run under "false flags"—spookspeak for front groups—including bin Laden's organization. And Iraqi government agents were in contact with bin Laden in the days leading up to the September 11 attacks.[19]

Tellingly, Mohamed Atta, believed to be the commander of the hijacking crew that smashed American Airlines Flight 11 into the World Trade Center, met with an Iraqi intelligence agent in Prague several times in 2000 and 2001.[20] While some dispute whether these meetings ever occurred, Czech intelligence and the Czech Prime Minister have publicly and repeatedly insisted that they did. The Iraqi diplomat was later expelled from the Czech republic when he was linked to a plot to bomb Radio Free Europe.

Certainly, Iraq behaved strangely in the wake of the September 11 attacks. Hours after the attacks, Iraqi soldiers moved away from likely military targets. And Iraq alone among the twenty-two members of the Arab League failed to condemn the atrocities of September 11. Indeed, Baghdad celebrated them. Saddam's government issued a statement, quoted widely in *Al-Iraq* and other state-run papers, which said America deserved the attacks.[21]

Perhaps Iraq's official response indicates nothing more than a continuing hatred of America, but Middle Eastern leaders who are no friends of the U.S. acted differently. Iran sent its condolences. Yasser Arafat expressed sorrow and gave blood. Even Libya's

Moammar Gadhafi called for Libyans to aid the American victims, adding that the U.S. had the "right to take revenge."[22]

Vice President Dick Cheney and National Security Advisor Condoleeza Rice have been careful to say that there is no evidence linking Iraq to the September 11 attacks—though they have not ruled it out either. In any case, Cheney, Rice, and other senior Bush Administration officials have steadfastly maintained that Iraq and al Qaeda had a long relationship.

Why didn't the Clinton administration follow up on the Iraqi-al Qaeda connection? Part of the answer is bureaucratic bungling. The New Jersey FBI office released a suspect who was sought by the New York office in connection with the 1993 Twin Towers bomb plot. There was little communication or trust between the FBI and the National Security Agency. And the FBI turned much of its evidence in the 1993 bombings over to the defendants long before America's national security specialists saw it. During the Clinton years, some of America's antiterrorist units suffered from the lowest ebb of morale since the 1970s, according to a recent National Commission on Terrorism report.[23]

Another possibility is that administration officials didn't want to see a connection, that they saw their job as containing Saddam, not confronting him. Sandy Berger, President Clinton's National Security Advisor, told the *Los Angeles Times* in 1996 that dealing with Saddam was "little bit like a Whack-a-Mole game at the circus: They bop up and you whack them down, and if they bop up again, you bop them back down again."[24]

To avoid targeting Iraq, Clinton administration officials blamed the governments of Sudan and Afghanistan or a loose network of Islamic extremists. Both explanations seem incomplete. Sudan and Afghanistan are among the world's poorest nations; their governments cannot control sizeable sections of their own territories.

The idea that loose networks of Islamic hardliners randomly come together to plot attacks is also hard to credit. It takes organization, money, patience, and precision to carry out these attacks—

qualities not usually present in volatile, itinerant extremists. Clinton officials should have noticed that the 1998 U.S. embassy bombs detonated within nine minutes of each other and the perpetrators had false papers and plane tickets for Pakistan.

But the Clinton administration kept talking about a shadowy network of Islamic extremists—not a campaign of terror by a vengeful Saddam Hussein.

APPENDIX B

INTELLIGENCE DOCUMENTS AND PHOTOS

Bin Laden's house in the Rihadyh section of Khartoum.

A close shot of bin Laden's house in Khartoum. In the late afternoon, his wives would sit on the porches watching passersby while bin Laden sat on the ground level talking jihad with the men.

A guest house bin Laden maintained for traveling terrorists. This was also briefly the home of Mohammed Atef, the head of al Qaeda's military wing.

What passes for prosperity in Sudan's industrial park in Khartoum, where bin Laden owned a tannery factory.

The grim interior of bin Laden's tannery factory, where animal hides from south Sudan were cleaned with abrasive chemicals.

The mosque where bin Laden prayed and sometimes preached the Friday sermon.

Another view of bin Laden's neighborhood mosque.

The street view of the entrance to bin Laden's headquarters in Khartoum, from which he ran his global terror operation from 1991 to 1996.

Bin Laden's plane, left smashed on a runway in Khartoum in May 1996.

The cockpit of bin Laden's purposely smashed plane.

Another view of bin Laden's plane.

Sudanese Intelligence Documents

الأسم : صبحي عبد العزيز محمد أبو سته .

الكنية : محمد عاطف .

أبو حفص المصري .

أبو خديجة .

تيسير .

- حضر للسودان في مجموعة بن لادن في العام 1992 وكان من المقربين لبن لادن وكان يرافقه في كل تحركاته .

- كان يمثل القيادة العسكرية لانه كان يلقب وسط جماعته بالقمندان بالأضافة لخلفيته العسكرية .

- كان يسافر الي نيروبي والصومال كثيراً وغالباً ما كان يسافر بعد سفر سيف العدل وأبو عبيدة البنشيري كدلاله علي الاطمئنان علي العمل والمتابعة وكان غالباً ما يعود بعد فترات قصيرة ويقابل بن لادن مباشرةً بعد وصوله .

- كان كل الذين يسافرون الي نيروبي والصومال يقابلونه مباشرةً .

- سافر مع بن لادن الي افغانستان في العام 1996 .

Sobahi abdul aziz
Aliases : Abu Hafs al-[masri]
Abu Kjadiji
Mohamed Atef
He came to the Sudan in bin Laden's group in 1992 and he was one of the close circle of bin Laden. He was with him [bin Laden] in all of his movements. He used to [represent] the [military command] because he was called amongst his group "[the commander]" together with his [military command].

He used to go to [Nairobi] and Somalia a lot. Usually he would go after Seif al-Adel and Abu Obeida al-Bansheery as a sign of that he was checking their work, and following it up.

He would come back after a short period and meet immediately [with] bin Laden after his arrival.

All those who went to [Nairobi] and Somalia would meet him [Atef] after they came back, immediately.

He went to Afghan with bin Laden in 1996.

الأسم : محمد إبراهيم مكاوي .

الكنية : سيف العدل المدني .

ضابط سابق في الجيش المصري .

- غادر مصر 1988 الي السعودية ومنها الي افغانستان .

- حضر للسودان في العام 1992 م مع بن لادن .

- كانت تربطه علاقة قوية مع بعض قيادات جماعة الجهاد مثل أبو عبيده البشيري وابو حفص المصري .

- كان يسافركثيراً الي كل من نيروبي والصومال وكان يستخدم جواز سفر يمني .

- صلته بكل من ابو عبيده البشيري وأبو حفص تؤهله لكي يكون الخليفة في قيادة الجناح العسكري لتنظيم القاعدة لما يتمتع به من خلفية عسكرية والمكانة المقربة من بن لادن .

- غادر السودان مع بن لادن في عام 1996 م .

Mohammed [Rbrahin] Makawi
Aliases: Saif al-adl [al] madani

Previously was an officer in Egyptian Army. He left Egypt in 1988 and went to Saudi Arabia and went from there to Afghanistan.

He came to Sudan in 1992 with bin Laden. He [had strong ties] with some of the leaders of the [Egyptian Jihad] group, such as al-[Bansheery] and Abu [Hafs]

He used to go to [Nairobi] and Somalia and used a [Yemani] passport. His relationship was with al-[Bansheery] and Abu [Hafs], which would [qualify] him to be his successor in the leadership of the [military] of al Qaeda organization because of his [military] background and his relationship to Osama bin Laden.

He left the Sudan with [Laden] in 1996.

السم : شيخ أحمد سالم سويدان .

- كان يتردد اثناء وجود بن لادن بالسودان ولم تكن له مهمة واضحة حيث كان يحضر من كينيا ويمكث فترة في بيت الضيافة ويقابل بن لادن ثم يغادر .
- هنالك عدد من الأفارقة غالباً ما كان يحضرون من كينيا وعدة دول افريقية أخري لم يكن لهم اختلاط مع بقية الوجود العربي ولم تكن اسمائهم معروفة .
- يمكن التعرف عليهم من خلال عرض صور لو وجدت .

[Ahmed Salim Svedan]
no aliases listed

He used to frequent the Sudan while bin Laden was there. He did not have a clear mission. He used to come from [Kenya] and stay for some time in the [bin Laden's] guesthouse, meet bin Laden and then leave. There was a group of Africans that used to come from [Kenya] and several other African countries. Usually they did not [mingle] with other Arabic persons and their names [were] not known [to Sudanese intelligence]. They can be identified from a photo gallery, if one is present. [The Africans were later connected to the embassy bombings.]

الأسم : خالد شيخ محمد .

- من مواليد الكويت 1964 .
- كان يعمل في مجال الاغاثة والمساعدات الانسانية ببشاور وشارك في الجهاد الافغاني .
- تربطه علاقة بكل من ازمراي ويوسف رمزي .
- زار السودان لفترة قصيرة اثناء وجود بن لادن وقابله وعاد الي دولة قطر .

Khalid [Sheikl] Mohammed

Was born in Kuwait, 1964.
He used to work in relief and [humanitarian] aid [in] [Pershewar], and took part in the Afghan Jihad.

He had a relationship with [Ramzi Yousef]. He visited Sudan for a short period while bin Laden was [here] and met him and went to Qatar.

الأسم : هارون فضل .

الكنية : أبو فضل القمري .

- كان ضمن مجموعة بن لادن الموجودة بالخرطوم وقد سبق وان اشترك مع احد زملائه
  في الاعتداء او التعرض لدبلوماسي بالسفارة المريكية في العام 1995 مما استدعي
  ابعاده من البلاد في ذلك الوقت .

- حضر للسودان في العام 1997 دون ان يحصل علي تاشيرة دخول وترتب علي ذلك
  ارجاعه من المطار وكانت وجهته دولة كينيا .

- يحمل جواز سفربالرقم 062185 وزوجته تحمل جواز بالرقم 044371 .

المرفقات : -:

صورة من جواز سفره .

صورة جواز سفر زوجته .

[Harum] Fadl
Aliases: Abu Fadl al-[Qamri]

He was amongst bin Laden's group in [Khartoum] and he had previously
taken part in the attack or the diplomatic intervention on the [American]
diplomat in 1995 which resulted in his being kicked out of the country
(Sudan).

He came to the Sudan in 1997 without getting an entry visa and that
resulted in his being returned from Khartoum airport in Kenya. He carries
passport #062185 and his [wife] carries passport #044371.

[Attachments]: photocopy of his passport and his wife's

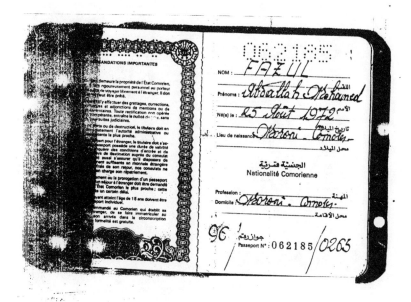

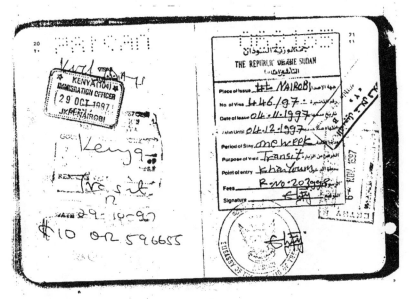

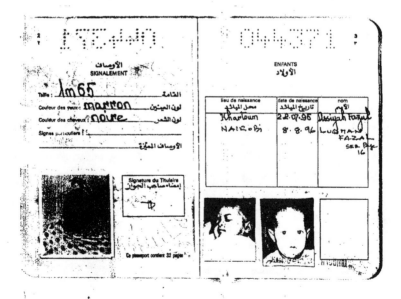

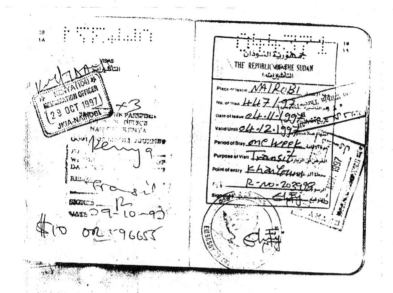

١. الأسم : نظير سيد عباس .

جواز سفر باكستاني رقم 553540 صادر بتاريخ 7/16 / 1996 م كويتا .

٢. يا سنكدر سيد سليمان ، جواز سفر باكستاني رقم 61482 صادر بتاريخ 1997/7/28م (كويتا) .

- وصلا السودان بتاريخ 8/4/ 1998 بالخطوط الكينية من نيروبي اقاما بفندق بدر السياحي بالخرطوم .

- سبق أن تردد السكندر علي نيروبي مرتين شاركوا في الجهاد في افغانستان يجيدوا استعمال السلاح والمتفجرات .

- كانت وجهتهم بعد الوصول الي السودان المغادرة الي الجماهيرية الليبية .

- تم ترحيلهم بتاريخ 1998/9/2 الي باكستان .

مرفقات :-

صورة من الجوازات .

صورة من تذكرة السفر ز

Nossair sayed Abbas
Pakistani passport #553540
Issued on 16 July 96, in [Quetta] (Pakistan)

Skander Said Suliman
Pakistani passport #61482
Issued on 28 July 97 in [Quetta]

He arrived in Sudan on [4] August on Kenya [airways] from Nairobi and he [resided] in the Badr Tourist Hotel in Khartoum. Skander had previously frequented Nairobi twice. They both took part in the Jihad in Afghanistan and they can use weapons and explosives quite well.

Their stated [destination] after arriving in Sudan was to depart to Libya. They departed on 2 September 98 to Pakistan.

Attached photocopies of passports and tickets.

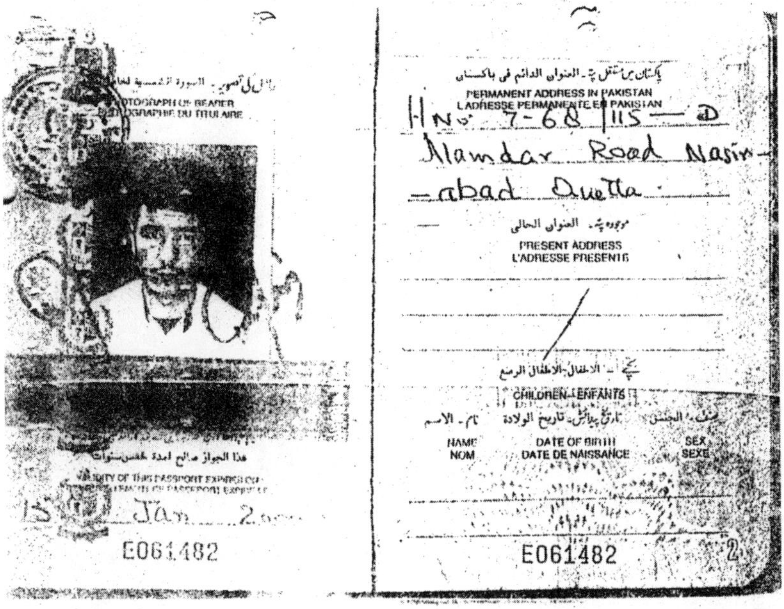
PHOTOGRAPH OF BEARER
PHOTOGRAPHIE DU TITULAIRE
15 Jan 2
E061482
PERMANENT ADDRESS IN PAKISTAN
L'ADRESSE PERMANENTE EN PAKISTAN
H No 7-68 115 — D
Alamdar Road Nasir-
-abad Quetta
PRESENT ADDRESS
L'ADRESSE PRESENTE
CHILDREN—ENFANTS
NAME
NOM
DATE OF BIRTH
DATE DE NAISSANCE
SEX
SEXE
E061482
2

PAKISTAN
E061482
Syed Sikander
Syed Sulfan
NAME OF FATHER/HUSBAND
Business
PROFESSION OF BEARER
PROFESSION
Quetta
1976
PLACE AND DATE OF BIRTH
Muslim
RELIGION
NATIONAL STATUS
NATIONALITE
PASSPORT
QUETTA
SALAH UD DIN RAKANI
ASSISTANT DIRECTOR

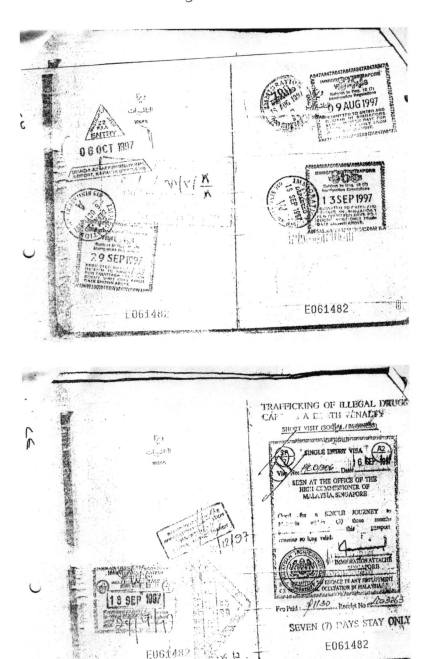

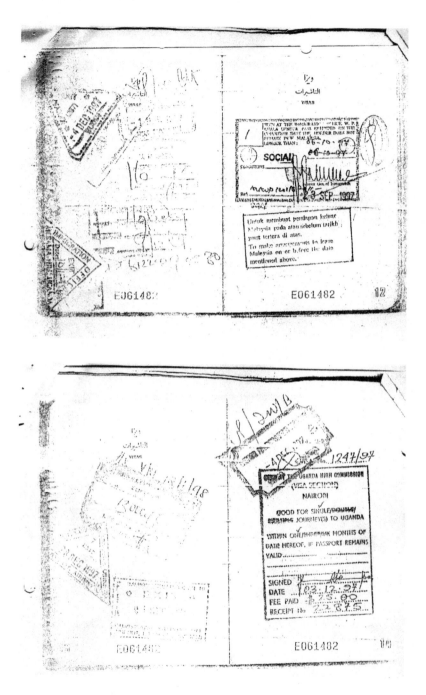

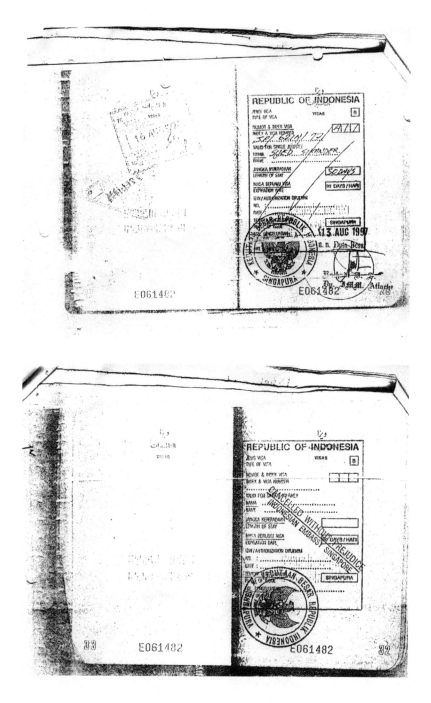

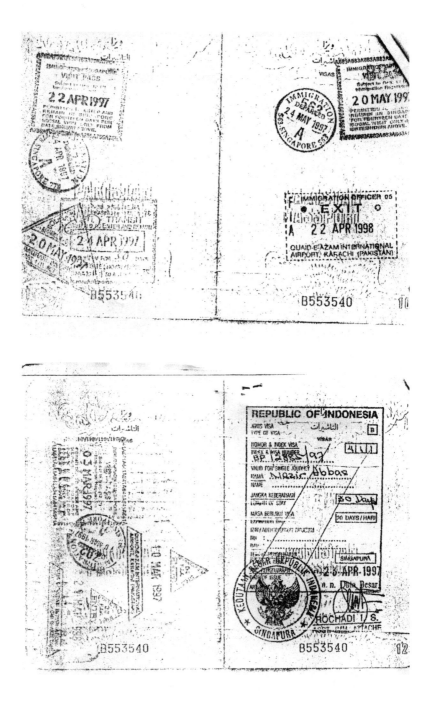

Minister Mahdi Ibrahim Mohammed, Sudan's president, Omar El Bashir, and Janet McElligott at the presidential palace in Khartoum, Sudan, 1977.

McElligott at the camel market in Khartoum. Mahdi Ibrahim is behind her.

Janet McElligott and Northern Sudanese soldiers.

Mansoor Ijaz and President Clinton at a Democratic
senatorial campaign committee fundraiser, fall 1996.

Mansoor Ijaz and his wife, Haifa, with Clinton at Le Cirque in New York City, February 1999.

The Clintons with Haifa and Mansoor Ijaz in the Oval Office on January 1, 2000, before the the president's Millennium Radio Address to the nation.

NOTES

INTRODUCTION

1. "Conversation with Terror," *Time* magazine, January 11, 1999.
2. The author is counting the deaths in the 1993 World Trade Center attack, the assault on U.S. Army Rangers in Somalia in 1993, the bombing of a U.S. company in Saudi Arabia in 1995, the two simultaneous explosions at U.S. embassies in East Africa, and the waterborne terror strike on the USS *Cole* in 2000. The 1996 attack on U.S. Air Force barracks, known as the Khober Towers, is not counted.
3. Even *Newsweek* in a recent cover story interview with former President Clinton said as much. "Life is Fleeting, Man," by Jonathan Alter, Newsweek, April 8, 2002.
4. Of course, all modern presidents use polls. But it how those opinion surveys are used that is important. An effective leader may use polls to measure the effectiveness of his message, but not to decide on a course of action.

CHAPTER ONE

1. According to a news report from Yemen's state-run television, which was cited in French and American reports.
2. For reasons of Islamic law, the sale and consumption of alcohol is illegal in Yemen, except in specially licensed establishments. Most of those establishments are in Aden.
3. The two men were later identified as Wahib Abdessalem and Saber Mahari. It is unclear which of the two men lost his arm.

4. The Aden Hotel is now part of the global Movenpick hotel chain.

5. This account is based on a compilation of wire reports from (in order of importance) Agence France Presse, the Associated Press, Reuters News Service and several Yemen-based web sites.

6. Ibid.

7. Some accounts wrongly suggest that the bomb beneath the car exploded. But those accounts leave out the suitcase bomb. All published accounts agree that there were only two explosions. Apparently, the bomb blast in the parking lot and the eyewitness reports of the terrorists placing something under a car were conflated. The early wire-service reports, especially the ones by the Associated Press, seemed garbled. This is understandable, because they were written from Sana'a, not Aden.

8. Some accounts say the seventh floor.

9. Some accounts, including Reuters News Agency, say 9:40 p.m. local time. A Dow Jones News Service article, which moved on December 29, 1992 at 4:26 p.m., puts the Goldmore hotel bomb blast at 12:30 p.m. (Eastern Standard Time) or 9:30 local time. The exact timing will probably never be known.

10. Some accounts say that one or two Australians perished in the attack. But this seems to be a mistake. All contemporaneous accounts, from Yemeni, American and other reports, limit the victims to Austrian tourists and a local janitor, who was not a citizen of Yemen. The earliest report of an "Australian" appears in 1996 and is apparently a typo.

11. "Fundamentalists Blamed for Hotel Bomb Attacks," (no byline), Agence France Presse December 30, 1992.

12. "Fundamentalists bomb hotels with U.S. soldiers, Austrian killed," (no byline), Agence France Presse December 30, 1992.

13. "Yemen Blast Kills Janitor, Austrian Tourist" by Abbas Ghalib, Associated Press, December 30, 1992

14. This is the first known attack by bin Laden on Americans. Yet it is possible that bin Laden was behind a successful assassination plot on Rabbi Meir Kahane, the leader of the Jewish Defense League in New York City.

15. "U.S. Military Slips out of Bomb-Plagued Yemen," by Nabila Megalli, Associated Press, January 2, 1993

16. "The Road to Ground Zero," *The Sunday Times*, January 6, 2002.

17. Ibid.

18. "The Road to Ground Zero," January 7, 2002. I was part of the world-wide investigative team for this series. This is also mentioned by Simon Reeve, *The New Jackals: Ramzi Yousef, Osama bin Laden and the Future of Terrorism* (Boston: Northeastern University Press, 2002), 185.

19. Simon Reeve, *The New Jackals: Ramzi Yousef, Osama bin Laden and the Future of Terrorism* (Boston: Northeastern University Press, 2002), 184.

20. According to an interview with Lake. As far as the author knows, this fact has not been reported before.

21. "The Road to Ground Zero," The Sunday Times, January 6, 2002.

22. Abdullah Azzam, speaking in Oklahoma City in 1988 as cited by Steven Emerson in *American Jihad: The Terrorists Living Among Us*, (New York: Free Press, 2002), end paper. Though this quote comes more than ten years after bin Laden first heard Azzam speak, and in a forum some 10,000 miles from Saudi Arabia, it is remarkably similar in spirit and tone to the late 1970s speeches of Azzam. Azzam had a consistent theme and repeated it, by all accounts, throughout the 1970s and 1980s.

23. Dore Gold, *Hatred's Kingdom: How Saudi Arabia Supports the New Global Terrorism*, (Washington, D.C.: Regnery Publishing, 2003), 94.

24. As quoted by Jane Corbin in *The Base*, (London: Simon and Shuster, 2002), page 13. Strangely, Corbin does not cite Fisk by name.

25. Sometimes translated as the "office of services."

26. According to an informal estimate by a retired CIA official who worked in Afghanistan.

27. Interview with the author.

28. Milt Bearden's latest book is *The Main Enemy*. His novel on Afghanistan is called *The Black Tulip*.

29. Interview with CIA station chief. He spoke on the condition of anonymity. The e-mail in question was sent to the author in June, 2003.

30. Interview with author January 2002 in Rohrbacher's Capitol Hill office.

31. One variant of the CIA-funded-bin-Laden argument is that the CIA created the conditions that made bin Laden's rise possible by bankrolling the anti-Soviet resistance in Afghanistan. See, for example, "Charlie Wilson's War: The Extraordinary Story of the Largest Covert Operation in History" by George Crile (New York: Atlantic Monthly Press, 2003). This argument is also implausible. The chaos in Afghanistan was caused by the Soviets who invaded in 1979. And bin Laden's ideology-which turned him against the U.S.—was forged in the 1970s.

32. Indeed, some intelligence sources claim the car bomb was the work of Pakistani intelligence or a pro-Soviet Afghan warlord.

33. These stories are believed to be false by most experts. But they built the bin Laden legend.

34. Yossef Bodansky, *Bin Laden: The man who declared war on America*, (New York, Forum Books, 2001).

35. Turki al-Faisal was director from 1977 to 2001. He was let go shortly after the September 11 attacks, for reasons that one Defense Department official told the author are still "mysterious."

36. Yossef Bodansky, *Bin Laden: The man who declared war on America*, (New York, Forum Books, 2001).

37. See http://www.cfrterrorism.org/groups/binladen

38. Dore Gold, *Hatred's Kingdom: How Saudi Arabia Supports the New*

Global Terrorism, (Washington, D.C.: Regnery Publishing, 2003), 169.
39. Some 3,000 of the 14,000 fighters in Afghanistan were believed to be
Yemenis according to an estimate by Jane's Intelligence Review, a respected
London-based organization that tracks security issues. See April 1, 1995.
40. "Arab Veterans of Afghan War," by James Bruce, Jane's Intelligence
Review, April 1, 1995.
41. McCollum founded the task force in 1989.
42. This is the same Yossef Bodansky who wrote *Target America: Terrorism
in the U.S. Today*, (New York: Shapolsky Publishers Inc, 1993) and *Bin
Laden: The man who declared war on America*, (New York, Forum Books,
2001).
43. Author interview.

CHAPTER TWO

1. Simon Reeve, *The New Jackals: Ramzi Yousef, Osama bin Laden and the
Future of Terrorism* (Boston: Northeastern University Press, 2002).
2. "The Lesson: Incident at the Towers, 1993" by Tom Robbins, *New York
Daily News*, December 9, 1998.
3. "'Apostle of Evil' Judge Sentences Defiant Terrorist to Life in Solitary
Confinement," by Patricia Hurtado, *Newsday*, January 9, 1998.
4. Laurie Mylroie, *A Study of Revenge: Saddam Hussein's unfinished war
against America*, (AEI Press, Washington, D.C., 2000), 48–50.
5. The Lesson: Incident at the Towers, 1993" by Tom Robbins, *New York
Daily News*, December 9, 1998.
6. Simon Reeve, *The New Jackals: Ramzi Yousef, Osama bin Laden and the
Future of Terrorism* (Boston: Northeastern University Press, 2002), 36.
7. Ibid., 8.
8. He later told authorities that he thought he was helping Yousef deliver
boxes of soap. He has steadfastly insisted on his innocence. His mother, who
flew from Jordan and was the only relative of the accused to attend any of
the World Trade Center bombing trials, also insisted on his innocence and
said "he loves America." He was duly convicted and sentenced to 240 years
without possibility of parole.
9. Simon Reeve, *The New Jackals: Ramzi Yousef, Osama bin Laden and the
Future of Terrorism* (Boston: Northeastern University Press, 2002), 36.
10. Some news accounts say five or six months pregnant.
11. "Pictures of N.Y. Bombing Victims Stir Emotional Response from
Jury," by Jeanne King, Reuters News Service, *The Houston Chronicle*,
August 8, 1997.
12. The official death toll of the 1993 World Trade Center attack is six
dead. Oddly, that figure leaves out the loss of Smith's baby son. The death

of the boy is well-established in court documents and photos.

13. Simon Reeve, *The New Jackals: Ramzi Yousef, Osama bin Laden and the Future of Terrorism* (Boston: Northeastern University Press, 2002). This section is based on Simon Reeve's excellent book, as well as court documents and contemporaneous accounts.

14. "The World Trade Center Bombing: A Tragic Wake-Up Call," New York State Senate report, Committee on Investigations, Taxation and Government Operations, August 3, 1993, page 9. See the testimony of Port Authority Director Stanley Brezenoff.

15. "The Property Report: The Day New York Stood Still," by Fred R. Bleakley, *The Wall Street Journal*, December 17, 1997.

16. Ibid.

17. Ibid.

18. "WTC Bomber, 30, is Given Life, Plus Contentment to Live with Himself—Only," by Greg B. Smith, *The New York Daily News*, January 9, 1998.

19. Public Statement of Edward Smith, May 24, 1994. This also appears in the endpaper of Laurie Mylroie, *A Study of Revenge: Saddam Hussein's Unfinished War Against America*, (Washington, D.C: AEI Press, 2000).

20. Simon Reeve, *The New Jackals: Ramzi Yousef, Osama bin Laden and the Future of Terrorism* (Boston: Northeastern University Press, 2002), 19–21.

21. Laurie Mylroie makes a persuasive case that Iraq is tied to the 1993 World Trade Center attack. See Laurie Mylroie, *A Study of Revenge: Saddam Hussein's Unfinished War Against America*, (Washington, D.C: AEI Press, 2000). Mylroie, a Clinton campaign adviser, had access to Fox and many other government sources.

22. Simon Reeve, *The New Jackals: Ramzi Yousef, Osama bin Laden and the Future of Terrorism* (Boston: Northeastern University Press, 2002), 21

23. Lake, when the author asked him about the "salute issue," said he simply didn't remember. But he added it probably happened because so many people had written about it. The author is relying on an account published in George Stephanopoulos, *All Too Human: A Political Education*, (Boston: Little, Brown, 1999), 132-33.

24. "At least five died, 500 hurt as explosion rips and garage under world trade center; bomb suspected in midday blasted; thousands flee," by Malcolm Gladwell, *The Washington Post*, February 27, 1993.

25. Ronald Kessler, *The Bureau: The Secret History of the FBI*, (New York: St. Martins' Press, 2002), 278-283.

26. This is precisely the kind of malapropos that would have gotten former Vice President Dan Quayle or President George W. Bush a lot of scornful attention in the press. It passed unnoticed.

27. Official transcript as reproduced by the Associated Press. See

"President Clinton's Saturday radio address," February 27, 1993.

28. See, for example, "Clinton says American people back his economic plan," by Nancy Benac, Associated Press, February 27, 1993.

29. "Clinton says American people back his economic plan," by Nancy Benac, Associated Press, February 27, 1993.

30. "Crisis At the Twin Towers: The Overview; Inquiry is Pressed on Cause of Blast at Trade Center," by Ralph Blumenthal, *New York Times*, March 2, 1993.

31. "While Clinton fiddled," by Dick Morris, *Wall Street Journal*, February 5, 2002

32. "White House Feeling Tremors from Bombing," by John W. Mashek, *The Boston Globe*, March 2, 1993. This quote is also cited by Dick Morris in *Off With Their Heads: Traitors, Crooks and Obstructionists in American Politics, Media and Business*, (Regan Books: June 2003), 73.

33. Ibid., 72.

34. "Crisis At the Twin Towers: The Overview; Inquiry is Pressed on Cause of Blast at Trade Center," by Ralph Blumenthal, *New York Times*, March 2, 1993. This quote is also cited by Dick Morris in *Off With Their Heads*.

35. This wording appears in the unpublished draft of the chapter on terrorism. The author received the draft directly from Morris, before his book was published, via e-mail. The same thought is expressed in different words in Dick Morris, *Off With Their Heads: Traitors, Crooks and Obstructionists in American Politics, Media and Business*, (Regan Books: June 2003).

36. "A New Strain of Terrorism; Groups are Fast, Loose, Hard to Find," by Pierre Thomas, *The Washington Post*, August 3, 1993.

37. "Clinton did little substantive to fight terror, says former FBI agent," by Mark E. Rondeau, *The Advocate*, October 31,2001

38. "The Road to Ground Zero," *The Sunday Times*, January 6, 2002.

39. According to Laurie Mylroie, in an e-mail to the author.

40. "Sergeant's Life Reads More Like Fiction," by Joseph Neff and John Sullivan of the *Raleigh News and Observer* and *The Washington Times*, October 28, 2001. "The Road to Ground Zero," *The Sunday Times*, January 7, 2002.

41. Zawahiri had been bin Laden's personal doctor since the mid-1980s and is believed to have been present at the founding meeting of al Qaeda in 1988. For more on Zawahiri's visit and on the life of Ali Mohammed, see Mohammed's trial testimony following the 1998 embassy bombings.

42. "Bomber Says Cabbie Assisted Terrorists: Ihab M. Ali of Orlando Received Spy Training in Africa, A Court Witness Testified," by Pedro Ruz Gutierrez, *The Orlando Sentinel*, October 25, 2000.

43. "Sergeant's Life Reads More Like Fiction," by Joseph Neff and John Sullivan of the *Raleigh News and Observer* and *The Washington Times*,

October 28, 2001.

44. Testimony of Oliver "Buck" Revell, Committee on International Relations, U.S. House of Representatives, October 3, 2001.

45. Steven Emerson, *American Jihad: The terrorists among us*, (New York: Free Press, 2002), page 56

46. Laurie Mylroie, *A Study of Revenge: Saddam Hussein's Unfinished War Against America*, (Washington, D.C: AEI Press, 2000), 18.

47. This plot began as part of an FBI undercover sting operation.

48. Laurie Mylroie, *A Study of Revenge: Saddam Hussein's Unfinished War Against America*, (Washington, D.C: AEI Press, 2000), 12.

49. This fascinating detail appears only in *Al Qaeda: Brotherhood Of Terror*, by Paul L. Williams (New York: Alpha, 2002), 83.

50. Nightline Special Edition transcript, August 20, 1998.

51. One author maintains that Ramzi Yousef was a senior field operative for al Qaeda. See Adam Robinson, *Bin Laden: Behind the Mask of the Terrorist*, (New York: Arcade Publishing, 2001), 163. This book is widely criticized by Peter L. Bergen, author of *Holy War, Inc*. Laurie Mylroie, a well-regarded expert of the 1993 World Trade Center bombing, also doubts Robinson's claim in conversations with the author. One East African intelligence service considered the claim to be possible, but not likely. No American or British intelligence report, that the author has seen confirms this account.

CHAPTER THREE

1. Lawrence E. Casper, *Falcon Brigade: Combat and Command in Somalia and Haiti*, (Boulder: Lynn Rienner, 2001), 25. Casper was the commander of the Quick Reaction Force, which included elements of the Tenth Mountain Division from Fort Drum, New York, in Mogadishu in September 1993. Courage 53 was part of the forces he commanded. This is the best available account of the downing of Courage 53.

2. Ibid., 26.

3. Ibid., 25-26.

4. Ibid.

5. Scott Peterson, *Me Against My Brother: At War in Somalia, Sudan and Rwanda*, (London: Routledge, 2000), 140.

6. This was widely reported. See, for example, Col. David Hackworth, *Hazardous Duty: America's Most Decorated Soldier Reports From the Front and Tells it Like it is*, (New York: William Morrow and Company, 1997), 159.

7. "Firefight in Mogadishu: The Last Mission of Task Force Ranger," by Rick Atkinson, *The Washington Post*, January 30 and 31, 1994, Page A1.

8. Ibid.

9. CYA is military slang for "Cover Your Ass." This quote first appeared in "The Road to Ground Zero," *The Sunday Times*, January 6, 2002.

10. Khat is an addictive drug, somewhat similar in intensity to cigarettes. It can have a mild mind and mood-altering effect.

11. "Experiences of Executive Officer from Bravo Company, Third Battalion, Seventy-fifth Ranger Regiment and Task Force Ranger during the Battle of the Black Sea on 3-4 October 1993 in Mogadishu, Somalia," by Captain Lee A. Rysewyk, page 4. This monograph is available from the U.S. Army library at Fort Benning, Georgia.

12. Across the street is the residence of the Spanish Ambassador to Sudan. Apparently, the Clinton Administration never asked Spanish intelligence to survey bin Laden while he lived there from April 1991 to May 1996. Another opportunity squandered.

13. "Part one of a series of reports on bin Laden's life in Sudan," No byline given, *Al-Quds Al-Arabi*, a London-based Arabic language publication that tends to be sympathetic to bin Laden. (London: November 24, 2001) The gardener's name is Mahjub al-Aradi. (The author relied on a translation from the Foreign Broadcast Information Service, a U.S. government agency.)

14. This is not meant to exclude the possibility that bin Laden's organization received substantial sums from Iraq and, possibly, Iran. And, of course, bin Laden's terror network received funds from other sources, including Gulf State sheikhs, bogus charities and his own investments and other operations.

15. Intelligence source in Sudan.

16. Ibid.

17. "Part one of a series of reports on bin Laden's life in Sudan," No byline given, *Al-Quds Al-Arabi*, November 24, 2001. The author relied on a translation from the Foreign Broadcast Information Service, a U.S. government agency.

18. As serialized in *Al-Sharq Al-Awsat*, a London-based Arabic newspaper. The author relied on a translation from the Foreign Broadcast Information Service (FBIS), a U.S. government agency that translates newspapers and broadcasts from around the world for intelligence and other purposes.

19. This is fairly widely reported. See, for example, "Somalia Redux?" by Jonathan Stevenson, *The Wall Street Journal Europe*, January 4, 2002. Stevenson covered Somalia as independent journalist from 1992 to 1994.

20. According to the sworn statement of Jamal al-Fadl (Southern District Court of New York, February 6, 2001), Mohammed Atef's daughter is married to one of bin Laden's sons.

21. This assertion appears in numerous places. See, for example, Yonah Alexander and Michael S. Swetnam, *Usama bin Laden's al-Qaida: Profile of*

a Terrorist Network, (Ardsley, New York: Transnational Publishers, 2001), 7.
22. Atef is believed to have died on one such dangerous mission near
Kabul, Afghanistan, when an American spyplane, known as the Predator,
found him entering a house in November 2001. The remote-controlled
pilotless plane fired a single Hellfire missile that killed him.
23. Author interview with a Sudanese intelligence source. While the source
has provided new information, the general conclusion seems to have been
widely accepted by American intelligence for some time. The former head
of the FBI counterterrorism program, Oliver "Buck" Revell, listed Somalia
as one of bin Laden's first strikes against Americans in his congressional
testimony and other public remarks. Other knowledgeable observers accept
this view as well. See "Campaign keeps al Qaeda out of Somalia," by Rowan
Scarborough, *The Washington Times*, April 19, 2002, front page, in which
the reporter, who is known for his excellent sources inside the national
security structure, notes: "Bin Laden once put his operational headquarters
in the Sudan and sent his terrorists south into Somalia to train recruits."
24. One high-ranking U.S. Marine Corps officer, who had served in
Vietnam, told the author that the Vietcong had a similar technique. U.S.
forces never developed an effective counter-measure. If his recollection is
correct, then this is a serious failing of the U.S. military. Knowledge spreads
fairly quickly among groups of armed men in the developing world. But, not
apparently, at the Pentagon.
25. "Charges against 2d suspect detail trail of terrorists," by David
Johnston, *New York Times*, Aug. 29, 1998.
26. Testimony of James Francis Yacone, *United States of America v. Usama
bin Laden, et al*, U.S. District Court, Southern District of New York, S(7) 98
Cr. 1023, April 23, 2001, see pages 4459-4470. The most striking passage,
which is quoted in the chapter, appears on page 4459. Former Black Hawk
helicopter commander, Yacone later became an FBI Special Agent and was
an employee of the FBI at the time he testified.
27. Ibid., 4459.
28. Technically Arabic is one of the three official languages of Somalia.
Somali and English are the other two. Only 1.2% of the population claims
Arab ethnicity, according to UN estimates. Less than 1% actually speaks
Arabic; some clans like to claim Arab ethnicity as a point of pride. But that
claim doesn't necessarily indicate the language they speak. Aideed's soldiers
generally did not speak Arabic. So the interception of Arabic commands on
enemy radio is strongly indicative of a foreign presence, allied with Aideed.
29. "Responsibility for the terrorist atrocities in the United States, 11
September 2001," an official public document issued by Prime Minister
Tony Blair's office at 10 Downing Street on October 4, 2001. See paragraph
37.
30. This paragraph is based on a description in George Stephanopoulos, *All*

Too Human: A Political Education, (New York: Little, Brown and Company, 1999), 156.

31. Ibid., 156-57.

32. Ibid., 160.

33. Elizabeth Drew, *On the Edge: The Clinton Presidency*, (New York: Simon & Schuster, 1994), 319.

34. As cited by Lawrence E. Casper, *Falcon Brigade: Combat and Command in Somalia and Haiti*, (Boulder: Lynn Rienner, 2001), 10.

35. Actually, total U.S. troop strength was 3,000. Some 2,000 of the soldiers were non-combat support troops.

36. Boutros Boutros Ghali's last name is Boutros Ghali.

37. "Experiences of Executive Officer from Bravo Company, Third Battalion, Seventy-fifth Ranger Regiment and Task Force Ranger during the Battle of the Black Sea on 3-4 October 1993 in Mogadishu, Somalia," by Captain Lee A. Rysewyk. (unpublished)

38. Ibid.

39. Elizabeth Drew, *On the Edge: The Clinton Presidency*, (New York: Simon & Schuster, 1994), 319.

40. "Somalia Mission Control: Clinton Called the Shots in Failed Policy Targeting Aideed," by Patrick J. Sloyan, *Newsday*, Dec. 5, 1993.

41. Elizabeth Drew, *On the Edge: The Clinton Presidency*, (New York: Simon & Schuster, 1994), 320.

42. "Somalia Mission Control: Clinton Called the Shots in Failed Policy Targeting Aideed," by Patrick J. Sloyan, *Newsday*, December 5, 1993. Sloyan is quite clear on this point, citing a well-placed anonymous source: "It was between Lake and the president with some phone calls afterwards."

43. "Firefight in Mogadishu: The Last Mission of Task Force Ranger," by Rick Atkinson, *The Washington Post*, January 30 and 31, 1994.

44. Ibid.

45. Mark Bowden, *Black Hawk Down: A story of modern war*, (New York: Penguin Books, 1999), 79.

46. Daniel P. Bolger, *Death Ground: Today's Infantry in Battle*, (Presidio, Presidio Press 1999), 213.

47. "Night of One Thousand Casualties," by Rick Atkinson, *The Washington Post*, January 31, 1994.

48. Col. David Hackworth, *Hazardous Duty: America's Most Decorated Soldier Reports From the Front and Tells it Like it is*, (New York: William Morrow and Company, 1997), 77.

49. "Firefight in Mogadishu: The Last Mission of Task Force Ranger," by Rick Atkinson, *The Washington Post*, January 30 and 31, 1994, Page A1.

50. As cited in "Full of tears and grief; for elite commandos, operation ended in disaster," by Patrick J. Sloyan, *Newsday*, December 7, 1993.

51. "Experiences of Executive Officer from Bravo Company, 3d Battalion,

75th Ranger Regiment and Task Force Ranger during the Battle of the Black Sea on 3-4 October 1993 in Mogadishu, Somalia," by Captain Lee A. Rysewyk, page 14.

52. The specialist or military veteran will no doubt point out that there were a variety of M-16s used by the Rangers and by Delta Force, including M-16As. For simplicity's sake, the author refers to them all as M-16s. The ammunition for all models is interchangeable with all other M-16 models and in all cases there simply wasn't enough ammunition.

53. George Stephanopoulos, *All Too Human: A Political Education*, (New York: Little, Brown and Company, 1999), 211.

54. Ibid.

55. Elizabeth Drew, *On the Edge: The Clinton Presidency*, (New York: Simon & Schuster, 1994), 316.

56. George Stephanopoulos, *All Too Human: A Political Education*, (New York: Little, Brown and Company, 1999), 212.

57. Ibid., 213.

58. Ibid., 214.

59. Ibid. Lake told the author that he doesn't remember Clintons' exact words, but says that Stephanopoulos's account is probably right.

60. Ibid.

61. Col. David Hackworth, *Hazardous Duty: America's Most Decorated Soldier Reports From the Front and Tells it Like it is*, (New York: William Morrow and Company, 1997), 168.

62. Elizabeth Drew, *On the Edge: The Clinton Presidency*, (New York: Simon & Schuster, 1994), 317.

63. Jeffrey H. Birnbaum, *Madhouse: The Private Turmoil of Working for the President*, (New York: Times Books, 1996), 81.

64. Confirmed by Lake, in an interview with the author.

65. "Public Papers of the Presidents," 29 Weekly Comp. Pres. Doc. 2022. "Address to the Nation on Somalia," October 9, 1993.

66. Scott Peterson, *Me Against My Brother: At War in Somalia, Sudan and Rwanda*, (London: Routledge, 2000), 151. Peterson disputes Osama bin Laden's involvement in Somalia.

67. From an interview by ABC News' John Miller, conducted on May 28, 1998. The quote is not in the original edited show broadcast on "Nightline" on June 10, 1998 but the complete Miller transcript can be found on the PBS Frontline website.

CHAPTER FOUR

1. According to Laurie Mylroie, *A Study in Revenge: The First World Trade Center Attack and Saddam Hussein's War Against America*, (Washington,

D.C.: AEI Press, 1999), 49, Yousef often wore sunglasses at night.

2. Simon Reeve, *The New Jackals: Ramzi Yousef, Osama bin Laden and the Future of Terrorism* (Boston: Northeastern University Press, 2002), 96.

3. "Weaving a wide web of terror," by Charles P. Wallace, *The Los Angeles Times*, May 28, 1995. This is the most thorough account of Ramzi Yousef to be found in the popular media during President Clinton's first term.

4. He was eventually captured in Pakistan in 2003.

5. "Early Scheme to Turn Jets into Weapons," by Terry McDermott, *The Los Angeles Times*, June 24, 2002. This is a solid piece of reporting largely overlooked by the East Coast press.

6. Ibid.

7. "Bust and Boom," by Matthew Brzezinski, *The Washington Post Magazine*, December 30, 2001. A truly excellent piece of reporting.

8. "Weaving a wide web of terror," by Charles P. Wallace, *The Los Angeles Times*, May 28, 1995.

9. "Bust and Boom," by Matthew Brzezinski, *The Washington Post Magazine*, December 30, 2001.

10. Ibid.

11. Ibid.

12. "Early Scheme to Turn Jets into Weapons," by Terry McDermott, *The Los Angeles Times*, June 24, 2002.

13. Bust and Boom," by Matthew Brzezinski, *The Washington Post Magazine*, December 30, 2001.

14. Ibid.

15. Clarke left the National Security Council staff in 2003.

16. Escobar was later killed in a shoot out with the Colombian police in the first year of the Clinton Administration. See Mark Bowden's excellent little book, *Killing Pablo*.

17. According to a National Security Council press spokesman, whom the author talked to in January 2002.

18. Some accounts, including Laurie Mylroie's in *A Study in Revenge*, say "dirty white smoke." Simon Reeve says "acrid black clouds" in *The New Jackals*.

19. "Bust and Boom," by Matthew Brzezinski, *The Washington Post Magazine*, December 30, 2001.

20. Ibid.

21. Ibid.

22. Ibid.

23. "Weaving a wide web of terror," by Charles P. Wallace, *The Los Angeles Times*, May 28, 1995.

24. "Bust and Boom," by Matthew Brzezinski, The Washington Post Magazine, December 30, 2001.

25. Ibid.

26. Ibid.

27. Ibid.

28. Ibid.

29. Laurie Mylroie, *A Study in Revenge: The First World Trade Center Attack and Saddam Hussein's War Against America*, (Washington, D.C.: AEI Press, 1999), 200.

30. Ibid., 205.

31. Ibid., 29.

32. Ibid., 199

33. In fact, the Clinton administration was caught unprepared. When notified of the Bojinka plot, Lake told the author he couldn't get the head of the FAA on the phone on a Saturday. "We were flipping through the White Pages," he told the author. Eventually, the administration grounded all Africa-bound flights for 24 hours.

34. According to Richard A. Clarke in an interview with the author.

35. "The Road to Ground Zero," *The Sunday Times*, January 6, 2002. This account is also in Simon Reeve's *The New Jackals*, 105.

36. This account is reconstructed from an interview with Lake.

37. "Early Scheme to Turn Jets into Weapons," by Terry McDermott,*The Los Angeles Times*, June 24, 2002.

38. According to an interview with a Sudanese intelligence source in Khartoum, March 2002.

39. Author interview with Janet McElligott, a former lobbyist for the government of Sudan who maintains close ties with its intelligence and political services.

40. See Robert Baer, *See No Evil: The True Story of a Good Soldier in the CIA's War on Terrorism* (New York: Crown, 2002), 270. Baer does not specify Qatar in his book.

41. Bill Gertz, *Breakdown: How America's intelligence failures led to September 11*, (Washington D.C.: Regnery Publishing, 2002), 56.

42. According to Woolsey in an interview with the author, June 2003.

43. Hubbell later resigned from the department, pled guilty to two felony charges of defrauding his Arkansas law firm, and fought a series of legal efforts to compel him to testify before an independent council.

44. One source, who knows Clinton well, suggests that it was Woolsey's persistent visits to the White House that might have turned him against Woolsey.

45. Author interviews with Woolsey, December 2001 and June 2003.

46. This fact is widely reported. See, for example, "Memogate," by Richard Miniter, The *New Republic*, June 3, 2002, page 14.

47. The actual amount of the CIA's budget is classified. In the one year in which the total budget was made public, the figure was just under $30 billion.

48. It always is. Is Leonid Kuchma, the president of Ukraine, the next
Saddam Hussein? Five years from now, the answer may be clear and the
pundits may cluck their tongues and say the Bush Administration ignored
the "Kuchma threat" for too long. In reality, it takes a intelligence agencies a
long time to identify emerging threats. All we know now, from news reports
about Kuchma, is that he personally authorized sales to Iraq of components
used to make weapons of mass destruction, that he possess a large number
of Soviet-era missiles and nuclear devices, that he is tyrant who brutalizes
his own people and is strongly suspected of murdering journalists. But does
that make him a threat today? Essentially, in the early 1990s, under
President Clinton, U.S. intelligence had a similarly hazy picture of the
threat posed by bin Laden. It is the nature of the business.

49. *Sunday Times* (of London) interview with Lake, December 2001, in
Washington, D.C.

50. A 1995 U.S. State Department report notes in passing that Saudi
Arabia has stripped bin Laden of his citizenship the year before. Daniel
Benjamin and Steven Simon in their book, *The Age of Sacred Terror*, (New
York: Random House, 2002), 235, also unearth a 1995 court deposition in
which an FBI investigator briefly asks a suspect about "Osem Ben Laden."

51. Of course, it is possible that Lake's memory—like the memory of other
Clinton figures—is conveniently vague. He may be saving a nugget for a yet
unwritten memoir or trying to blunt criticism of himself and the president
he served. But the author considers that possibility unlikely.

52. Vinnell Corp. is now owned by Northrop Grumman.

53. Testimony of Mohammed Rasheed Daoud al-'Owhali.

54. Testimony of Jamal al-Fadl, 1998.

55. "Survivors recount Saudi blast," by Staff Sgt. Timothy Hoffman, *Air
Force News*, November 1995.

56. Ibid.

57. Bill Gertz, *Breakdown: How America's intelligence failures led to
September 11*, (Washington D.C.: Regnery Publishing, 2002), 7.

58. This is the date of the first *confirmed* bin Laden attack on Americans.
Bin Laden told Time magazine in 1998 that he had been at war with
America "for ten years." It is possible that there were earlier bin Laden
attacks.

CHAPTER FIVE

1. Ambassador Shinn told the author.

2. He is now Sudan's Ambassador to the United Nations.

3. Shinn served in that post from 1993 to June 1996.

4. The author does not reveal the names of active intelligence agents, as a rule. Despite several inquiries at the CIA, in which the officer was asked for by name, the author was unable speak to him. This is not surprising. However, it means that this account rests on the recollections of three men: Erwa, Carney, and Shinn, and not on the fourth man present.

5. "Saga of Secret Airlift; Ethiopian Jews: Exodus of a Tribe," by Charles T. Powers, *The Los Angeles Times*, July 7, 1985.

6. According to Erwa in an interview with the author, October 2002.

7. The author's account is the first account to provide dialogue and other key details. The meeting itself was first reported in *The Washington Post*. See "U.S. Was Foiled Multiple Times in Efforts To Capture Bin Laden or Have Him Killed; Sudan's Offer to Arrest Militant Fell Through After Saudis Said No," by Barton Gellman, October 3, 2001. Gellman's reporting is a must-read for any serious student of the Clinton-bin Laden history.

8. The following dialogue is reconstructed from the recollections of General Erwa, Ambassador Shinn and Ambassador Carney.

9. "Decision to Strike Facility in Sudan Based on Surmise Inferred from Evidence," by Tim Weiner and James Risen, *The New York Times*, September 21, 1998.

10. The CIA, like other federal agencies, almost invariably spells bin Laden's first name as "Usama."

11. "U.S. Was Foiled Multiple Times in Efforts To Capture Bin Laden or Have Him Killed; Sudan's Offer to Arrest Militant Fell Through After Saudis Said No," by Barton Gellman, *The Washington Post*, October 3, 2001.

12. According to a deputy director of the Mukhabarat, Sudan's external intelligence agency. Also see documents received from Sudanese intelligence that are reproduced in the Appendix.

13. Interview with author.

14. Ibid. Erwa isn't certain that these were his exact words, although he is certain that he said something very similar to this. This bit of dialogue is based on the recollection of Shinn.

15. While the first of these secret meetings is now publicly acknowledged, what exactly was discussed is controversial. In the months following the September 11 attacks, three senior Clinton Administration officials have essentially denied that Sudan ever offered to turn over bin Laden in May 1996. Clinton's last National Security Advisor, Sandy Berger, asserted that he knew nothing of Sudan's offer to turn bin Laden, in a phone interview with the author in January 2002. Berger's denial doesn't track with President Clinton's own acknowledgement of the Sudanese offer. In the weeks after the September 11 attacks, the president was dining in a Manhattan restaurant roughly one mile north of Ground Zero. He told several dinner companions that turning down Sudan's offer to seize bin Laden in May 1996 was "the biggest mistake of my presidency." Curiously, in denying the existence of the Sudanese offer, Berger used language remarkably similar to that later used by Clinton's director for counterterrorism, Daniel Benjamin, and senior director for counterterrorism, Steven Simon, who argue in their recent book *The Age of Sacred Terror*, that "no senior government official from the Clinton Administration is aware of any such offer, nor has any record of one surfaced." In any account, this is a remarkably hedged and careful denial. Of course, following the carnage of the September 11 attacks, Berger et al. have reasons to hedge. They fear damage to the Clinton legacy and to their own reputations. Berger made this quite clear to the author. Early on Sunday morning, January 6, 2002, Berger phoned the author. When calmly asked about the Sudanese offer and other secret offers to turn over bin Laden, Berger erupted: "You're accusing me of killing three thousand people!" By contrast, there is the calm testimony of a career diplomat, Ambassador Carney, who was present at the meeting with General Erwa—while Berger et al. were not. Carney, now retired, has no incentive to hedge and has nothing to gain. And, we also have the word of General Erwa, whose government now enjoys better relations with the United States. Today he speaks of the events of May 1996 with great reluctance precisely because he has no desire to undo the considerable diplomatic progress that his nation has enjoyed since September 11, 2001. Carney and Erwa have each, separately, provided remarkably similar accounts of a meeting in which both were present. On balance, the author finds the two diplomats more convincing.

16. According to Erwa's recollection.

17. Bill Gertz, *Breakdown: How America's intelligence failures led to September 11*, (Washington D.C.: Regnery Publishing, 2002), 10–11.

18. In a December, 2001 interview in the senator's hideaway office in the U.S. Capitol building.

19. "Patterns of Global Terrorism" (Washington: U.S. Department of State, 1996), 27.

20. According to a Sudanese intelligence source who works closely with Saudi intelligence.

21. Author interview in Khartoum, March 2002.

22. The author interviewed Gutbi al-Mahdi in his office at the Presidential Palace in Khartoum in March, 2002. Curiously, Mahdi—who is related to the Mahdi who slew British general Charles "Chinese" Gordon in Khartoum—has an office in what was once General Gordon's bedroom.

23. "Allied Against Terrorism," by Prince Turki al-Faisal, *The Washington Post*, September 17, 2002.

24. Although, importantly, she did not represent Sudan at the time it offered bin Laden to the Saudis. She was briefed by senior Sudanese officials, including President Bashir, more than a year later.

25. As McElligott told the author in an e-mail dated October 30, 2002.

26. "Allied Against Terrorism," by Prince Turki al-Faisal, *The Washington Post*, September 17, 2002.

27. Ibid.

28. See P.M. Holt and M.W. Daly, *A history of the Sudan: from the coming of Islam to the present day*, (London: Longman, 2000).

29. By 2000, power plants replaced private generators. The National Electric Co-op says it supplies steady power to 93% of Khartoum.

30. "U.S. Offers Data to Link Sudan to Plot," by Barbara Crossette, *The New York Times*, April 4, 1996.

31. Ethan Bronner, "'Holy War, Inc.': 21st-Century Jihad," *The New York Times Book Review*, November 18, 2001. Bronner was the Middle East correspondent for *The Boston Globe* from 1991 to 1997 and covered the 1995 conference in that capacity. He is now an editor at *The New York Times*.

32. Rohan Gunaratna, *Inside Al Qaeda: Global Network Of Terror*, (New York: Columbia University press, 2002),159.

33. Ibid., 158.

34. "U.S. Was Foiled Multiple Times in Efforts To Capture Bin Laden or Have Him Killed; Sudan's Offer to Arrest Militant Fell Through After Saudis Said No," by Barton Gellman, *The Washington Post*, October 3, 2001. Some of these details—which do not appear in Gellman's article—were based on the recollections of Ambassador Tim Carney and his wife, Vicky Butler, both of whom the author interviewed.

35. He is now Minister of Peace and Development.

36. "U.S. Was Foiled Multiple Times in Efforts To Capture Bin Laden or Have Him Killed; Sudan's Offer to Arrest Militant Fell Through After Saudis Said No," by Barton Gellman, *The Washington Post*, October 3, 2001.

37. "Thanks, But No Thanks," by Jennifer Gould, *The Village Voice*, October 31–November 6, 2001 (available at http://www.villagevoice.com/issues/0144/gould.php).

38. Robert D. Kaplan, "New Books Confront the Faceless Enemy of Terrorism," *The New York Times Book Review*, October 14, 2001

39. He is now the vice president of Sudan.

40. The detail about bin Laden leading prayers comes from Janet McElligott, a one-time lobbyist for the Sudanese with extensive continuing contacts with its top officials.

41. Evan Thomas, "'See No Evil': How the C.I.A. Went to the Dogs," *The New York Times Book Review*, February 3, 2002.

42. According Bruce Hoffman, a terrorism expert, in testimony entitled "Security threats to Americans Overseas," before the U.S. House of Representatives' subcommittee on National Security, Veterans Affairs, and International Relations, April 3, 2001.

43. Daniel Benjamin and Steven Simon, *The Age of Sacred Terror*, (New York: Random House, 2002) page 220.

44. The anti-intelligence mindset paints with too broad a brush. The FBI also monitored groups, such as the Weather Underground, who planted bombs in federal buildings and murdered policemen. The CIA, however ineptly, was resisting covert attempts of the USSR to dominate the Third World and worked to foil plots against Americans abroad. A more balanced approach to intelligence operations should lead to closer oversight, not wholesale rejection of intelligence efforts.

45. "U.S. Was Foiled Multiple Times in Efforts To Capture Bin Laden or Have Him Killed; Sudan's Offer to Arrest Militant Fell Through After Saudis Said No," by Barton Gellman, *The Washington Post*, October 3, 2001.

46. "Thanks, But No Thanks," by Jennifer Gould, *The Village Voice*, October 31–November 6, 2001 (available at http://www.villagevoice.com/issues/0144/gould.php).

47. "Part one of a series of reports on bin Laden's life in Sudan," No byline given, *Al-Quds Al-Arabi*, (London: November 24, 2001). The author relied on a translation from the Foreign Broadcast Information Service, a U.S. government agency.

48. According to Carney, this letter was received by him on May 20, not May 15 as *The Washington Post* and other newspapers have reported.

49. Erwa also said this to Jennifer Gould, a Village Voice writer. See "Thanks, But No Thanks," by Jennifer Gould, *The Village Voice*, October 31–November 6, 2001 (available at http://www.villagevoice.com/issues/0144/gould.php)

50. According to interviews conducted by the author.

51. Even in its capital city, Sudan does not have radar. Its air-traffic controllers rely on the radio and their wits. There are very few flights in and out of Khartoum on most days. Lufthansa, for example, only sends its planes to Sudan three times per week.

52. "Thanks, But No Thanks," by Jennifer Gould, *The Village Voice*, October 31–November 6, 2001 (available at http://www.villagevoice.com/issues/0144/gould.php)

53. Indeed, if bin Laden had stayed in Sudan, he may well have been ruined financially. Sudanese officials received hard currency bribes from bin Laden in exchange for work that bin Laden's companies were never paid for, even in the much debased Sudanese dinars.

54. "U.S. Was Foiled Multiple Times in Efforts To Capture Bin Laden or Have Him Killed; Sudan's Offer to Arrest Militant Fell Through After Saudis Said No," by Barton Gellman, *The Washington Post*, October 3, 2001.

CHAPTER SIX

1. This account is reconstructed from an interview with Mansoor Ijaz conducted by the author in Brussels, September 2002.
2. Using records compiled by the U.S. Federal Election Commission, the author looked at all contributions by anyone named Ijaz in the 1992, 1994, 1996, and 1998 campaign cycles.
3. "Democratic Fund-Raiser Pursues Agenda on Sudan," by David B. Ottaway, *The Washington Post*, April 29, 1997.
4. Clinton would later tell Ijaz that they had something in common: they were both Leos.
5. As part of his political awakening, Ijaz become involved with alternative Pakistani schools, hoping to save the next generation of Pakistanis from Islamic extremism.
6. "The Road to Ground Zero," *The Sunday Times*, January 6, 2002. The author was part of the reporting team that broke this story.
7. The events that follow are reconstructed from Ijaz's recollections, his letters, interviews conducted by the author in the Sudan in the spring of 2002, and from Sudanese government documents. Since Turabi has been under house arrest since 1996, the author was unable to confirm Ijaz's recollections with him. Turabi's spoken words, except where otherwise noted, are based on Ijaz's recollection and his contemporaneous notes, some of which he shared with the author.
8. The author was unable to locate Sanousi to confirm this account.
9. An interesting and dubious assessment of the annual conferences that included leaders of every major terrorist organization in the world as well as intelligence chiefs from across the Middle East. Bin Laden had attended each conference from 1991 to 1995, when the summits were finally stopped by relentless U.S. pressure.
10. Author interview with Carney in Washington, D.C., March 2002.
11. This meeting was detailed in Chapter Five.
12. This is documented in Chapter Five.
13. According to Ijaz.
14. "U.S. Diplomats Return to Sudan," by Thomas W. Lippman, The Washington Post, Sept. 24, 1997.
15. State Department Briefing, June 30, 1997. Briefer James Rubin said the previous week's annoucement to restaff the U.S. embassy in Sudan was "premature."

Ijaz Campaign Contributions

The earliest recorded federal campaign contributions by any variant spelling of Ijaz or Crescent, Ijaz's company, date from 1994. The records before 1998 are not online and had to be researched in person. Ijaz is sometimes listed as "Mansoor" Ijaz, sometimes as "Musawer," his legal first name, and sometimes as other variants, most likely typos. "Ijaz Group" contributions are also listed. Yasmine Ijaz was Mansoor Ijaz's first wife. Claus Buescher was a business partner of Ijaz at the time and his contributions, most likely encouraged by Ijaz, are also noted. Money raised at fundraisers organized by Ijaz or held at his home cannot be tracked by the FEC; participants write individual checks and are not required to list the event organizer's name. So it is ultimately impossible to verify whether Ijaz raised nearly a million dollars of other people's money for Clinton-Gore. But the records clearly show that he was major donor to Clinton and Democratic Party candidates from 1994 to 1998.

1994 Ijaz Contributions

Mansoor Ijaz:	Democratic Senatorial Campaign Committee	$28,000
	Senate Victory '94	$10,000
	Moynihan Committee	$2,000
Yasmine Ijaz:	Democratic National Committee	$20,000
	TOTAL:	$60,000

[Ijaz Group also contributed $80,000 to the DNC]

1996 Ijaz Contributions

Mansoor Ijaz:	Democratic National Committee	$32,500
	Torricelli for U.S. Senate	$2,000
	Alexander for President	$1,000
	Citizens for Harkin	$1,000
	Carol Moseley Braun for U.S. Senate	$500
	Evan Bayh Committee	$2,000
	Friends of Schumer	$1,000
	Democratic Congressional Campaign Committee	$1,000
	Massachusetts Democratic Party	$1,000
	Kennedy for Senate	$1,000
	Democratic Senatorial Campaign Committee	$15,000
	Kerry Committee	$2,000
	Clinton/Gore '96 Primary Committee	$1,000
	Clinton/Gore '96 General Election	$500
Yasmine Ijaz:	Democratic National Committee	$15,000
	Kennedy for Senate	$1,000
	Clinton/Gore '96 Primary Committee	$1,000
	TOTAL:	$79,500

[Ijaz Group contributions to the DNC: $12,500]
[In addition, Mohammed Ijaz contributed $3,400; Mohsin Ijaz contributed $220, and Hasim Ijaz contributed $1,500]

1996 Claus Buescher contributions

Buescher:	Evan Bayh Committee	$1,000

Kennedy for Senate	$2,000
Citizens for Harkin	$1,000
TOTAL:	$4,000

1998 Ijaz Contributions

Mansoor Ijaz:	Democratic Senatorial Campaign Committee	$15,000
	Friends of Harry Reid	$500
	98 Friends of Chris Dodd	$1,000
	South Dakota Democratic Party	$3,000
	Schumer '98	$2,000
	TOTAL:	$21,500

[Claus Buescher also contributed $1,000 to Schumer 1998]
[Sabiha Ijaz contributes $500]

TOTALS FROM 1992 TO 1998
Mansoor and Yasmine Ijaz

1994:	$60,000
1996:	$79,500
1998:	$21,500
TOTAL:	$161,000

Mansoor Ijaz, Yasmine Ijaz with the Ijaz Group

1994:	$60,000
[Ijaz Group 1994]:	$80,000
1996:	$79,500
[Ijaz Group 1996]:	$12,500
1998:	$21,500
TOTAL:	$253,500

Mansoor Ijaz, Yasmine Ijaz, the Ijaz Group and Claus Buescher

1994:	$60,000
[Ijaz Group 1994]:	$80,000
1996:	$79,500
[Ijaz Group 1996]:	$12,500
[Claus Buescher 1996]:	$4,000
1998:	$21,500
[Claus Buescher 1998]:	$1,000
TOTAL:	$258,500

CHAPTER SEVEN

1. The dialogue and details of this encounter are based on interviews with Janet McElligott conducted by the author in April, May, and September 2002. Ambassador Mohammed Ibrahim has confirmed McElligott's recollections.

2. Interview by the author, October 2002.

3. The Sudanese elite is quite fond of dining in hotels. This is simply because the best food available in Khartoum is located in that city's Western-owned hotels, especially the vintage 1960s Khartoum Hilton. Its buffets are legendary among Sudanese officials, but an American visitor might not be impressed.

4. The author was in Lokichoggio in February and March 1999 and this description is based on the author's recollections only.

5. This description is based on a February 1999 visit to Lokichoggio by the author. The operation looked much the same two years earlier, according to James Jacobson, president of Christian Freedom International, which ran aid operations out of there in 1997.

6. "A surreal transaction in Sudan wins freedom for 3 aid workers," by Tim Weiner, *The New York Times*, December 9, 1996.

7. Ibid.

8. The history of internal splits within the Sudanese People's Liberation Army is incredibly complicated and no Western academic or journalist had compiled an authorative history. Kerubino is now believed dead. He died like he lived, with a gun in his hand.

9. According to an interview with McElligott.

10. According to McElligott.

11. Ibid.

12. In the end, he became UN Ambassador and later Energy Secretary.

13. According to McElligott.

14. Ibid.

15. Ibid.

16. According to McElligott's recollection.

CHAPTER EIGHT

1. This is reconstructed based on a wire service report. See "CNN tape shows bin Laden announcing jihad against the West, vows Americans will die," by Robert H. Reid, Associated Press, August 20, 2002.

2. http://www.fas.org/irp/world/para/ladin.htm

3. "Saudi Arabia: world front groups support but do not claim bombings," *Al-Sharq Al-Awsat*, August 13, 1998, as translated from Arabic by FBIS, a U.S. agency.

4. "U.S. jury indicts bin Laden on terrorism charges," by Vernon Loeb, *The Washington Post*, August 25, 1998.

5. According to an article writtenby Ismail Khan for a Pakistani newspaper, *The Dawn*, May 1998.

6. Their videotape was later obtained by CNN and broadcast to the world in August, 2002.

7. "CNN tape shows bin Laden announcing jihad against the West, vows Americans will die," by Robert H. Reid, Associated Press, August 20, 2002.

8. "An ear-splitting visit to bin Laden's hideout," (no byline), The Daily Telegraph (U.K.), September 27, 2001.

9. Interview with the source in Paris, August 2002.

10. "Africa blast suspects to stand trial in U.S.," by Michael Grunwald, *The Washington Post*, August 28, 1998.

11. Tenet's remarks eventually became public. See "Where the CIA wages its New World War," by Vernon Loeb, *The Washington Post*, September 9, 1998.

12. "Where the CIA wages its new world war; counterterrorist center makes many arrests with aid of FBI, NSA," by Vernon Loeb, *The Washington Post*, September 9, 1998.

13. Ibid.

14. "Broad effort launched '98 attacks," by Barton Gellman, *The Washington Post*, December 19, 2001.

15. "Point Man on Terrorism Knows National Security Issues," by M.J. Zuckerman, *USA Today*, May 22, 1998.

16. "Militant leader was a U.S. target since the spring," by James Risen, *The New York Times*, September 6, 1998.

17. Ibid.

18. The author did not interview General Shelton.

19. "Clinton's war on terror," by Barton Gellman, *The Washington Post*, December 19, 2001.

20. "Blast suspect held in U.S. and is said to admit role," by David Johnston, *The New York Times*, August 28, 1998.

21. "Africa blast suspects to stand trial in U.S.," by Michael Grunwald, *The Washington Post*, August 28, 1998.

22. "Tourist hub also draws those with terrorist ties," by Paige St. John, Gannett News Service, September 22, 2001. The key passage: "A former U.S. Army sergeant and an associate of Ihab Ali, Mohamed trained al Qaeda's international recruits in surveillance and was part of an al Qaeda surveillance team that studied the American embassy in Kenya. Mohamed told FBI agents that bin Laden himself picked where to send the bomb-laden truck that rammed that embassy in 1998."

23. According to al-Owhali's testimony in a U.S. District Court in New York.

24. "On high alert; casting a global net; U.S. security forces survive terrorist test," by Neil King, Jr. and David S. Cloud, *The Wall Street Journal*, March 8, 2000.

25. This account is based on sworn trial testimony by Ambassador

Bushnell.

26. These events are reconstructed based on Ambassador Bushnell's sworn testimony in a U.S. District Court in New York and from news events.

27. "A failure of intelligence?" by Daniel Benjamin and Steve Simon, *New York Times Book Review*, December 20,2001

28. "Trial reveals a conspiracy of calls, but only tidbits about bin Laden," by Phil Hirschkorn, CNN.com, posted April 16, 2001.

29. "After the attack: the overview," by David Johnston, *The New York Times*, August 27, 1998.

30. Ibid.

31. Saudi Arabia, Pakistan, and Yemen.

32. "Getting Osama is easier said than done," by Syed Talat Hussain, *The Nation* (Islamabad), August 30, 1998. The author relied on a text from FBIS.

33. "After missiles U.S. tries talks to get Osama," by Syed Talat Hussain, *The Nation* (Islamabad), August 29, 1998.

34. According to McElligott. The reconstructed conversations are based entirely on her account.

35. The author was unable to reach Posto and several messages left for his then-superior David Williams were unreturned.

36. Williams did not respond to messages left by the author, through agent Kevin Faust. Bur he has made these charges publicly on an MSNBC website story.

37. "Pakistan: Osama's narrow escape, camps hit reported," by Kamran Khan, *The News* (Islamabad), August 22, 1998. The author relied on FBIS for this article.

38. Ibid.

39. According to McElligott, who said she was told by Ifzal Chauhan, a former boyfriend who was the brother-in-law of the then-deputy prime minister of Pakistan.

40. The author met the plant's sole guard, a sleepy black southerner whose only fear was that the demise of the plant might cost him his job.

41. According to McElligott.

42. Associated Press Newswires, September 19, 1998. Clarke was talking about chemical, biological and electronic attacks—not turning planes into flying bombs. But he showed that he and other senior Clinton Administration officials were worried about attacks on the mainland of the United States as early as 1998. To demonstrate America's vulnerability, he had government-paid hackers break into the Pentagon's most secure computer systems in 1998. Clarke's hackers —in three days' time, using off-the-shelf PCs–gained control of the nation's military command center systems, the very ones that would be used during an attack on the United States. Clarke had proved—and repeatedly warned—that a "digital Pearl

Harbor" could happen. "It's as bad as being attacked by bombs," he told the Dallas Morning News in 1999.

CHAPTER NINE

1. Black is now head of counterterrorism at the U.S. State Department.
2. "On High Alert: Casting a Global Net, U.S. Security Forces Survive Terrorist Threat," by Neil King, Jr., *The Wall Street Journal*, March 8, 2000.
3. "Jordan links terrorists put to bin Laden," by Stephen Kinzer, *The New York Times,* February 4, 2000.
4. Officials later learned that the attacks were slated for January 3, the end of Ramadan that year. Of course, the millennium actually began on January 1, 2001. But popular understanding and innumeracy put the turn of the millennium a year earlier.
5. "On High Alert: Casting a Global Net, U.S. Security Forces Survive Terrorist Threat," by Neil King, Jr., *The Wall Street Journal*, March 8, 2000.
6. "The Road to Ground Zero," *The Sunday Times* (of London), January 6, 2002.
7. "On High Alert: Casting a Global Net, U.S. Security Forces Survive Terrorist Threat," by Neil King, Jr., *The Wall Street Journal*, March 8, 2000.
8. Daniel Benjamin and Steven Simon, *The Age of Sacred Terror*, (New York: Random House, 2002), 311.
9. "On High Alert: Casting a Global Net, U.S. Security Forces Survive Terrorist Threat," by Neil King, Jr., *The Wall Street Journal*, March 8, 2000.
10. Covert transfers of suspected terrorists to Egypt, like many elements of the Clinton anti-bin Laden strategy, is currently used on a much larger, bolder scale by the Bush Administration in its war on terror. American, Egyptian and Sudanese intelligence officers have told the author that upwards of 500 al Qaeda prisoners have been sent to Egypt for questioning since October, 2001. (These prisoners originated in Sudan, Libya, Algeria and elsewhere.) This is in addition to those terrorists held in Bagram air base in Afghanistan and in various camps run by the U.S. military in Cuba.
11. "On High Alert: Casting a Global Net, U.S. Security Forces Survive Terrorist Threat," by Neil King, Jr., *The Wall Street Journal*, March 8, 2000.
12. "The Terror Countdown," by Massimo Calabresi, *Time* magazine, December 27, 1999.
13. Ibid.
14. According to Ressam's testimony at trial.
15. "The Terror Countdown," by Massimo Calabresi, *Time* magazine, December 27, 1999.
16. "On High Alert: Casting a Global Net, U.S. Security Forces Survive Terrorist Threat," by Neil King, Jr., *The Wall Street Journal*, March 8, 2000.

17. "The Road to Ground Zero," The Sunday Times, January 6, 2002.

18. "The Counterterrorist," by Lawrence Wright, *The New Yorker*, January 14, 2002.

19. There was no specific evidence that bin Laden wanted O'Neill dead.

20. "An obscure chief in U.S. war on terror," by Michael Dobbs, *The Washington Post*, April 2, 2000.

21. Ibid.

22. Ibid.

23. "The Night of Power" is reckoned according to a lunar calendar and is not locked to any specific date.

24. According to an interview with an Arab intelligence source with the author in Cairo, in March 2002.

25. "Failed plan to bomb a U.S. ship is reported," by Steven Lee Myers, *The New York Times*, November 10, 2000.

26. See Associated Press reports dated November 11, 2000 and CNN reports dated November 12, 2000.

CHAPTER 10

1. "Broad Effort Launched After '98 Attacks," by Barton Gellman. *The Washington Post*, December 19, 2001.

2. Ibid.

3. Amin is no longer the Northern Alliance representative in Washington, D.C.

4. According to interview with the author, February 2002.

5. According to an author interview with Amin.

6. Clarke interview with the author, July 2003

7. According to interview with the author, February 2002.

8. According to Haroun Amin, who was interviewed by the author in December 2002 and January 2003.

9. The author did not receive this information from Saleh, but from a reliable source with direct knowledge of the meetings.

10. According to Ottilie English, in an interview with the author.

11. After the October 2000 attack on the USS *Cole*, Clinton's counterterrorism czar Richard Clarke told the author that the CIA was told to tell the Alliance that the gloves were off—you can kill bin Laden now.

12. According to Haroun Amin, who was interviewed by the author in December 2002 and January 2003.

13. This dialogue is based on the recollection of Ms. English, who was interviewed by the author in December 2002 and May 2003.

14. "Broad Effort Launched After '98 Attacks," by Barton Gellman. *The Washington Post*, December 19, 2001.

15. According to Richard Clarke, in an interview with the author, July 2003.

16. "Broad Effort Launched After '98 Attacks," by Barton Gellman. *The Washington Post,* December 19, 2001.

17. Ibid.

18. Ibid.

19. The author did not interview Shelton. This account is based on the recollection of military officials and press reports, principally Barton Gellman's work in the *Washington Post.*

20. "Broad Effort Launched After '98 Attacks," by Barton Gellman. *The Washington Post*, December 19, 2001.

21. "The Road to Ground Zero," *The Sunday Times* (of London), January 20, 2002

22. Ibid.

23. According to Clarke, who described the meeting in an interview with the author, July 2003.

24. "The Road to Ground Zero," *The Sunday Times* (of London), January 6, 2002.

25. According to Clarke in an interview with the author.

26. "The Road to Ground Zero," The Sunday Times (of London), January 6, 2002.

27. Ibid.

28. Clarke, in an interview with the author, July 2003

29. Pakistani newspapers, including *The Dawn*, reported bin Laden's medical problems in 1999. A medical doctor who is believed by American officials to have treated bin Laden was interviewed by the CIA and military intelligence officers, in October 2002 in Afghanistan.

30. The author did not interview Podesta, but saw a series of e-mails between Podesta and Ijaz. The Ijaz-Podesta meeting was also confirmed by Clarke and Berger.

31. According to an interview with Berger, January 2002.

32. "Broad Effort Launched After '98 Attacks," by Barton Gellman. *The Washington Post*, December 19, 2001. Gellman reports on the details of Sharif's plan but not that it was developed at a July 5, 1999 meeting at the White House.

CHAPTER 11

1. "New FBI evidence links Saudi Militant to the *Cole* blast," by Daniel Klaidman, *Newsweek*, March 26, 2001.

2. Ibid.

3. That letter was later recovered, from Badawi's apartment, by Yemeni investigators. This development is fairly widely reported. See, for example, "Yemen said to be holding six suspects in *Cole* Attack," the *Virginian-Pilot* and the *Ledger-Star*, (no byline), (Norfolk, Virginia), April 22, 2002. In general, the local papers of the major Navy port cities and towns near Army bases often provide illuminating details overlooked by *The New York Times* or *The Washington Post*.

4. "Six suspects named; all fought together in Afghanistan," by Donna Bryson, The Associated Press, December 13, 2000.

5. "How a mighty power was humbled by a little skiff," by John F. Burns, *The New York Times*, October 28, 2000.

6. "Six suspects named; all fought together in Afghanistan," by Donna Bryson, The Associated Press, December 13, 2000.

7. See "Yemen Gateway" web site. See http://www.al-bab.com/yemen/cole8.htm, the section marked "The investigation."

8. "Laden's poetry of terror; new FBI evidence links Saudi militant to *Cole* blast," by Daniel Klaidman, *Newsweek*, March 26, 2001.

9. Badawi, though a "disposable," was linked to another senior bin Laden operative: Mohammed Omar al-Hirazi, a shadowy Saudi with a shoebox full of aliases. Hirazi telephoned Badawi from the United Arab Emirates and gave the final order to strike. Badawi said his only previous contact with Hirazi was during the Afghan jihad. Hirazi is also believed to have paid the expenses of the Aden cells, according to a Yemen weekly military newspaper. See, "Sources identify six *Cole* bombing suspects; all reportedly fought against the Soviets in Afghanistan war," by Donna Bryson, The Associated Press, in the *Virginian-Pilot* and the *Ledger-Star*, December 14, 2000; Associated Press Newswires, December 13, 2000; "Six suspects named; all fought in Afghanistan," by Donna Bryson, Associated Press Newswires, December 13, 2000; and "*Cole* suspects tied to Afghan conflict; one Yemeni got bombing instructions," (no byline) The Associated Press, *Houston Chronicle*, December 14, 2000.

10. Clarke told the author.

11. "Fateful voyage; calm before blast," by Robert Burns, The Associated Press, October 14, 2000.

12. "Desperate Hours; The blast claimed 17 lives and crippled a destroyer. The inside story of the heroic bid to save the USS *Cole*," by Evan Thomas and Sharon Squassoni, *Newsweek*, March 26, 2001.

13. "How a mighty power was humbled by a little skiff," by John F. Burns, *The New York Times*, October 28, 2000.

14. "*Cole* bombers identified as veterans of the Afghan war," by Karl Vick, *The Washington Post*, November 17, 2000.

15. "Yemen Gateway," an English-language portal devoted to Yemen and the USS *Cole* investigation at http://www.al-bab.com/yemen/cole8.htm.

16. "Desperate Hours, The blast claimed 17 lives and crippled a destroyer.

The inside story of the heroic bid to save the USS *Cole*" by Evan Thomas and Sharon Squassoni, *Newsweek*, March 26, 2001, page 36.

17. Ibid.

18. Ibid.

19. Ibid.

20. Ibid.

21. Ibid.

22. As cited in: "*Cole* crew memorialized but case not closed," by Shannon Watson, *Veterans of Foreign Wars Magazine*, October 10, 2001.

23. There were no direct flights to Yemen, so the took a full day, including a stopover in Europe.

24. This dialogue is supplied by a source who knew O'Neill. The author did not verify it by interviewing Bodine.

25. See *Al-Ayyam*, an Arabic language daily, October 17, 2000. The author is relying on a translated summary found on the "Yemen Gateway" web site. See http://www.al-bab.com/yemen/cole8.htm, the section marked "The investigation."

26. "Desperate Hours; The blast claimed 17 lives and crippled a destroyer. The inside story of the heroic bid to save the USS *Cole*," by Evan Thomas and Sharon Squassoni, *Newsweek*, March 26, 2001.

27. Many of the U.S.S. *Cole* bombers are still at large, as of June 2003.

28. This detail comes from Sheehan.

29. In a e-mail follow-up to one of the author's interviews with Clarke.

30. Clarke interview with the author.

31. In a e-mail follow-up to one of the author's interviews with Clarke

32. Ibid.

33. Ibid.

34. While the author repeatedly contacted CIA press spokesman Bill Harlow, in all fairness, Tenet was not given enough time to respond.

35. According to a e-mail that Albright's spokeswoman, Meridith Webster, sent the author.

36. In a e-mail follow-up to one of the author's interviews with Clarke

37. Sheehan confirmed this quote in an interview with the author.

38. "*Cole* crew memorialized but case not closed," by Shannon Watson, *Veterans of Foreign Wars Magazine*, October 10, 2001.

39. "Laden's poetry of terror; new FBI evidence links Saudi militant to *Cole* blast," by Daniel Klaidman, *Newsweek*, March 26, 2001.

40. This poem, in various translations, is widely available in the al Qaeda literature. One translation appeared in the March 2, 2001 edition of USA Today. This particular translation comes from a web site called "Yemen Gateway," an English-language portal devoted to Yemen and the USS *Cole* investigation at http://www.al-bab.com/yemen/cole8.htm.

41. "*Cole* crew memorialized but case not closed," by Shannon Watson,

Veterans of Foreign Wars Magazine, October 10, 2001.

42. "Attack on America; tracking terror; dark heart of terror," by Phil Hirschkorn, Rohan Gunaratna, Ed Blanche and Stefan Leader, The San Diego Union-Tribune, September 23, 2001. This opinion piece is a version of longer commentary article that appeared in Jane's Intelligence Review in August, 2001. The four authors are among the giants in the field of bin Laden analysts. Their close connections with intelligence services (as well as Jane's Intelligence Review) makes them a must-read, especially Gunaratna.

APPENDIX A

1. "Some Analysts Fear a bin Laden, Saddam Pairing," by John Walcott, *The Charlotte Observer,* February 14, 1999.

2. "Kings, Queens, and Despots," *Forbes* magazine, March 17, 2003.

3. "Saddam Link to terror group," by Philip Smucker and Adrian Blomfield, *The Daily Telegraph* (U.K.), April 17, 2003.

4. Ibid.

5. "Iraq Kurd said to admit bin Laden link," no byline, United Press International, September 25, 2002.

6. "Iraq Harboring al-Qaida Network, Powell says," by Warren P. Strobel, Knight Ridder News Service, February 6, 2003.

7. "September 11 and Iraq," Editorial, *The New York Sun*, March 12, 2003. Tenet testified on February 11, 2003.

8. "Saddam 'Forging Links with bin Laden,'" by Julian Borger, *Guardian Weekly*, February 14, 1999.

9. "Who Did It?" Jane's Foreign Report, September 19, 2001. He was allegedly shuttling between Baghdad and Ayman al-Zawahiri.

10. "The Terrorist Hunter Speaks: An amazing story of an Iraqi Jew at the heart of dismantling terrorism," by Kathryn Jean Lopez, *National Review Online*, June 26,2003.
http://www.nationalreview.com/interrogatory/interrogatory062603.asp

11. "What Makes Them Tick?" by David Van Biema, *Time* magazine, September 24, 2001.

12. "Study of Revenge: The First World Trade Center Attack and Saddam Hussein's War Against America," by Laurie Mylroie (Washington: AEI Press, 2001), p. 29. The caller was Mohammed Salameh.

13. "Jihad Against Jews and Crusaders," issued by the World Islamic Front. See statement on fas.org.

14. See "Iraq's New Way: The U.S. Bull," *The Guardian*, May 23, 1998.

15. "Trial Spotlights America's Top Terrorist Threat," by Phil Hirschkorn,

Counterterrorism Inc., Journal of Counterterrorism & Security International, 2001 Summer Vol. 7, No. 4

16. "Threats and Response: Powell's Address, Presenting 'Deeply Troubling'" Evidence on Iraq, *New York Times*, February 6, 2003.

17. Laurie Mylroie, *Study of Revenge: The First World Trade Center Attack and Saddam Hussein's War Against America*, (Washington: AEI Press, 2001), 50-62. Mylroie makes the case that Ramzi Yousef, the mastermind of the 1993 World Trade Center bombing, used a fake identity taken from a Kuwaiti man named Abdul Basit. Yousef's fingerprints are found in Basrit's official passport file in Kuwait. The passport Yousef presented Pakistani officials as "Basit" when requesting a new passport has several blank pages, including ones that would show an entry from Basit into Kuwait in 1989. Yousef is 6 feet tall, while the "Basit" passport he presented listed Basit as being 5 feet 8 inches. Mylroie believes that Iraqi intelligence seized Basit's passport, along with other Kuwaiti identification documents, after the Iraqi seizure of Kuwait in 1990.

18. "Israel Security Issued Urgent Warning to CIA of Large-Scale Terror Attacks," by David Wastell and Philip Jacobson, *The Sunday Telegraph*, September 16, 2001.

19. U.S. intelligence sources told *The Washington Times*' Bill Gertz. "Iraq Suspected of Springing Terrorist Attacks," by Bill Gertz, *The Washington Times*, September 21, 2001.

20. See "Czechs Assert Atta Met with Iraqi Spy," by Brayn Whitmore, *The Boston Globe*, May 8, 2002.

21. "Attacks Draw Mixed Response in Mideast," CNN.com, September 12, 2001.

22. "America Prepares: The Global Dimension," by John Donnelly and Anthony Shadid, *The Boston Globe*, September 27, 2001.

23. "U.S. Is Urged to Preempt Terrorists; Panel Proposes Unfettering CIA, Tracking Students," by Vernon Loeb, *The Washington Post*, June 4, 2000.

24. "Security Advisor Berger Discusses Bosnia, Israel Policy," by Tyler Marshall, *The Los Angeles Times*, December 9, 1996.

BIBLIOGRAPHY

Abukhali, Ad, *Bin Laden, Islam And America's New "War on Terrorism,"* New York: Seven Stories Press, 2002. A harshly critical account of the war on terror.

Alexander, Yonah and Michael S. Swetnam, *Usama bin Laden's al-Qaida: Profile of a Terrorist Network,* New York: Transnational Publishers, Inc., 2001. A good primer.

Alexander, Yonah, *Combating Terrorism,* Ann Arbor: University of Michigan Press, 2002.

Anonymous, *Through Our Enemies' Eyes*, Washington D.C.: Brassey's, Inc. 2002.

Armstrong, Karen, *Islam: A Short History,* New York: Random House, 2000. A good overview of the development of Islam. Tends toward a passive definition of jihad.

Baer, Robert, *See No Evil,* New York: Three Rivers Press, 2002. A good read and some good leads for aficionados.

Bamford, James, *Body of Secrets,* New York: Anchor Books, Random House, Inc., 2002.

Bearden, Milt, *The Black Tulip,* New York: Random House, 1998. This is a novel written by a former CIA officer responsible for working with the Afghan mujihideen and conveys a good sense of what the U.S. hoped to gain with its Faustian bargain with the anti-Soviet guerillas. Also worth reading by Bearden, *The Main Enemy*, a nonfiction account of spy vs. spy in the cold war (with James Risen).

Benjamin, Daniel and Steven Simon, *The Age of Sacred Terror*, New York: Random House, 2002. One of the very few inside accounts of the Clinton years.

The authors were directors on the National Security Council. Though unduly defensive in certain areas and, in one case, going too far to tar a critic, this is an important book. A fundamental building block for any serious understanding of Clinton and bin Laden.

Bergen, Peter L., *Holy War, Inc.*, New York: Simon and Schuster, 2002. An excellent early account of bin Laden.

Bodansky, Yossef, *Target America,* New York: Shapolsky Publishers, Inc., 1993. Unlike his later works, this was not a best-selling book. But any serious student of terrorism should read it; among other things, it describes terrorist sleeper cells in the United States and a surprisingly detailed account of the terrorist attack outside CIA headquarters in 1993.

Bodansky, Yossef, *The High Cost Of Peace,* Roseville, California: Prima Publishing, 2002. Primarily concerned with Israeli-Palestinian peace process, it contains interesting insights into the priorities of the Clinton Administration.

Bodansky, Yossef, *Bin Laden,* Roseville, California: Prima Publishing, 1999. Meeting in his hideaway office, a senator on the Intelligence Committee summed it up best: "great book, no footnotes." A treasure trove of information and analysis. Given the nature of his sources, it can be hard to verify some items. The ones that the author has been able to check through intelligence sources have all checked out. Essential reading.

Bowden, Mark, *Black Hawk Down,* New York: Penguin Books, 1999. The best account of the events in Mogadishu in October, 1993.

Carew, Tom, *Jihad!,* Edinburgh: MainStream Publishing, 2000

Carr, Caleb, *The Lessons of Terror,* New York: Random House, 2002. An interesting extended essay from a novelist.

Casey, Ethan, *09/11 8:48 am,* New York: BookSurge.com, 2001.

Cooley, John K., *Unholy Wars,* London: Pluto Press, 1999. A critical account of U.S. intelligence and bin Laden.

Corbin, Jane, *The Base,* London: Simon & Schuster UK Ltd, 2002. A well-written book by a well-informed reporter.

Drell, Sidney D, Abraham D. Sofaer and George D. Wilson (edited by), *The New Terror,* Stanford: Hoover Institution Press, 1999. A strong collection of essays.

Dresch, Paul, *A History of Modern Yemen,* Cambridge: Cambridge University Press, 2000. Good, recent books on Yemen are hard to find. This is one of the few and probably the best.

Emerson, Steven, *American Jihad,* New York: The Free Press, 2002. A excellent account of sleeper cells within America, the insidiousness of terror financing, and the blindness of the American establishment in the 1990s.

Esposito, John L., *Unholy War,* New York: Oxford University Press, 2002.

Gertz, Bill, *Breakdown,* Washington D.C.: Regnery Publishing Inc., 2002. By the dogged Washington Times investigative reporter, with excellent intelligence sources. The section about "Project Bojinka" in the Philippines is especially good.

Gunaratna, Rohan, *Inside Al Qaeda,* New York: Columbia University Press, 2002. Thorough and academic, but a must-read. Gunaratna is widely respected in the field, often consulted by intelligence services, and carefully parses his facts. One small example: we learn that bin Laden never got a degree in engineering, as was widely reported.

Hoffman, Bruce, *Inside Terrorism,* New York, Columbia University Press, 1998. Hoffman is a giant in this field. This book shows why.

Hoge, James F. Jr. and Gideon Rose, *How Did This Happen?,* New York: Council on Foreign Relations, Inc., 2001.

Holt, PM, and MW Daly, *A History of the Sudan,* Essex, U.K.: Pearson Education Limited, 2000. A good history of post-1956 Sudan. Important for understanding the various deep currents in Sudanese politics.

Jordan, Eric, *Operation Hebron,* London: International Media Group Ltd., 2000. A novel by a former CIA station chief. And fun. Like the Bearden novel, it is not a source for facts. But it helps one enter the mind of intelligence operative.

Kessler, Ronald, *The Bureau,* New York: St. Martin's Press, 2002. A good, critical history of the FBI.

Klein, Joe, *The Natural,* New York: Doubleday, 2002. A fresh look at Clinton.

Laqueur, Walter, *The New Terrorism,* New York: Oxford University Press, 1999. An unblinking look at the root causes of terror.

Lesser, Ian O., Bruce Hoffman, John Arquilla, David Ronfeldt, Michele Zanini, *Countering The New Terrorism,* Santa Monica: Rand, 1999.

Lewis, Bernard, *What Went Wrong?,* Oxford: Oxford University Press, 2002. A masterful essay about Islam and the west, from one of the premier scholars in the field.

Lewis, Bernard, *The Middle East,* New York: Touchstone, 1995. Probably the best single-volume history of the Middle East available to the layman.

Maley, William, editor, *Fundamentalism Reborn?,* New York: New York University Press, 2001.

Morris, Dick, *Off with Their Heads: Traitors, Crooks & Obstructionists in American Politics, Media & Business,* New York: Regan Books, 2003.

Mylroie, Laurie, *Study of Revenge,* Washington D.C.: The AEI Press, 2000. The book argues that Iraq was behind the 1993 World Trade Center bombing. Students of the Clinton-bin Laden duel will find a good account of the WTC investigation and a good sense of how the Clinton Administration did not want to probe too deeply. A solid work by a thorough investigator.

Moore, Robin, *The Hunt for bin Laden*, New York: Random House, 2003.

Nojumi, Neamatollah, *The Rise of the Taliban in Afghanistan,* New York: Palgrave, 2002.

Prados, John, editor, *America Confronts Terrorism*, Chicago: Ivan R. Dee, 2002.

Parfrey, Adam, editor, *Extreme Islam,* Los Angeles: Feral House, 2001.

Patterson, Bradley H. Jr., *The White House Staff*, Washington, D.C.: The Brookings Institution, 2000.

Rashid, Ahmed, *Jihad,* New Haven: Yale University Press, 2002.

Rashid, Ahmed, *Taliban,* London: Pan Books, 2001. Well-written with a reporter's eye for telling detail. The best book on the subject.

Reeve, Simon, *The New Jackals: Ramzi Yousef, Osama bin Laden and the Future of Terrorism*, Boston: Northeastern University Press, 1999. A very readable, reporter's account of the 1993 World Trade Center bombing investigation.

Reich, Walter, *Origins of Terrorism,* Washington, D.C.: Woodrow Wilson Center Press, 1998.

Robinson, Adam, *Bin Laden,* New York: Arcade Publishing, 2001. Hard to verify, especially with respect to bin Laden's teenage years. But interesting.

Silvers, Robert B. and Barbara Epstein, editors, *Striking Terror,* New York: The New York Review of Books, 2001.

Stephanopoulos, George, *All Too Human: A Political Education,* Boston: Little, Brown and Company, 1999. A remarkably honest and thorough book. A must-read.

Weaver, Mary Anne, *A Portrait of Egypt,* New York: Farrar, Straus and Giroux, 1999. Beautifully written and penetrating, by a writer who lived in Egypt during the pivotal late 1970s. Good background.

Williams, Paul, L., *Al Qaeda,* New York: Alpha, 2002.

Woodward, Bob, *Bush at War*, New York: Simon & Schuster, 2002.

INDEX

307

madrassas, 135
Maduni, Saif al-Adl al-, 51
Mahdi, Gutbi el-, 97, 108; Kenya
 embassy bombing and, 178–79;
 Sudan hostage crisis and, 157; U.
 S.-Sudanese relations and,
 138–39, 142, 144, 145
Maier, Karl, 64
Makawi, Mohammed Ibrahim, 51–52
Maktab Khadamat al-Mujihideen.
 See al Qaeda
Manila, Philippines, 73
Marine One, 26
Masry, Abu Hafs al. *See* Atef,
 Mohammed
Massoud, Ahmad Shah, 167, 196,
 197–98
Matthews, Thomas, 63
McCollum, Bill, 17–18
McElligott, Janet, 184–85; Kenya
 embassy bombing and, 179–80;
 Sudan hostage crisis and,
 154–58; U. S.-Sudanese relations
 and, 109, 151–52, 158–60
McLarty, Mack, 16, 53
Mercado, Wilfredo, 22, 23
Michigan, 196
Millennium After-Action Review,
 195
Millennium Plot: al Qaeda and,
 194–96; bin Laden and, 187, 193;
 Clinton Administration and,
 191–93; discovery of, 187–90;
 preparation for, 194–95; Taliban
 and, 191; targets of, 190
Mitty, Walter, 132
Mohammed, 6
Mohammed, Ali: al Qaeda and, 50;
 as double agent, 36–38; Kenya
 embassy bombing and, 171
Mohammed, Azan. *See* Yousef,
 Ramzi

Mohammed, Kassem, 3
Mohammed, Khalid Shaikh, 34,
 183, 236; attempts to capture,
 85–87; bin Laden's Philippine
 operations and, 72–75
Montgomery, Thomas, 44
Morocco, 10
Morris, Dick, 32
Moynihan, Daniel Patrick, 129
Msalam, Mohammed Ali, 171
mujihideen, 10, 12, 17–18
Murad, Abdul Hakim, 72, 74–75,
 79–80
Musharif, Prime Minister, 182
Muslim Brotherhood, 6
Mutawakil, Maulvi Abdul Wakil, 176
Muttawakil, Wakil Ahmend, 191
Myers, Dee Dee, 27
Mylorie, Laurie, 34, 236

Nairobi, Kenya, 115, 140
Nasir, Mustaf. *See* Mohammed,
 Khalid Shaikh
National Islamic Front, 102, 111
National Philippine Police, 80
National Review Online, 235
National Security Council, 59, 138;
 U. S.-Sudanese relations and, 116,
 126, 140, 148; war on terrorism
 and, 78
Navy Times, 219
NBC, 184
Netherlands, 191
New Port, 46
Newsweek, 216, 239
New York Fire Department, 24
New York Police Department, 37
New York Times, 118
Nidal, Abu, 76, 232
North, Oliver, 77
Northern Alliance: bin Laden and,
 167, 197–200; CIA and, 166–67;